The Jews of the Middle East
1860 – 1972

The Jews of the Middle East 1860-1972

Hayyim J. Cohen
INSTITUTE OF CONTEMPORARY JEWRY
THE HEBREW UNIVERSITY OF JERUSALEM

A HALSTED PRESS BOOK

JOHN WILEY & SONS, New York · Toronto
ISRAEL UNIVERSITIES PRESS, Jerusalem

ISRAEL UNIVERSITIES PRESS
is a publishing division of
KETER PUBLISHING HOUSE JERUSALEM LTD.
P.O.Box 7145, Jerusalem, Israel
IUP Cat. No. 2568

Published in the Western Hemisphere and Japan by
HALSTED PRESS, a division of
JOHN WILEY & SONS, INC., NEW YORK

Library of Congress Cataloging in Publication Data

Cohen, Hayim J. 1930–
The Jews of the Middle East, 1860–1972.

"A Halsted Press book."
Translation of *ha-Yehudim be-artsot ha-Mizrah ha-tikhon be-yamenu.*
Bibliography: p.
1. Jews in the Near East. I. Title.
DS135.L4C6413 301.45'19'24056 73–9236
ISBN 0–470–16424–7

Composed, printed and bound by Keter Press, Jerusalem
PRINTED IN ISRAEL

Contents

Preface

Today, when practically all the Jews of Asia and Africa have been gathered together in the State of Israel, it is especially important to be acquainted with their history in the lands of their dispersion, both to supplement our knowledge about the people of Israel in the Diaspora and to be able to facilitate the absorption of immigrants from Eastern lands. Several books and research papers have been written about the Eastern Jews from the beginning of their exile from Palestine until the Middle Ages, but no serious work has appeared on the history of these Jews in the last hundred years. True, there are many articles on the contemporary history of the Oriental Jews, but the greater part of these are based on the impressions of journalists and travellers. There is also a limited number of books, mainly devoted to the distressing political situation of these people and their sufferings in the Diaspora. But no book has attempted to examine the way of life of the Eastern Jews: their numbers and their wanderings, their economic circumstances, the state of their education, their attitude to the Jewish religion and the status of the Jewish woman. Material on these subjects is deficient and is mainly to be found scattered among many hundreds of newspapers, periodicals, books and archives, but it is not entirely lacking. During the past eight years much work to collect this material has been done by the Institute of Contemporary Jewry of the Hebrew University. The Institute has also collected many scores of testimonies provided by immigrants from the various Eastern lands, which supplement our information in areas in which the written material is insufficient. After classification and examination of the material gathered to date, it seems worthwhile to publish a book on the subject—both to furnish information for those who are interested and to supply material for the researcher seeking to increase his knowledge on the Jews of the East, and in particular, specific problems in their history.

Because of the wide scope of the work, we shall deal here only with the Jews of the Middle East. From their history a general picture may be obtained of the situation of other Jewish communities in Asia and Africa during a very important period of their lives, a period in which they were transformed from a mediaeval society into a modern one. Some chapters in their history, such as Zionism and Aliya, which have been insufficiently studied, are yet to be written.

We should like to thank, first and foremost, the scores of immigrants from the Middle Eastern countries who were good enough to relate their histories and to tell about the communities in which they lived. Thanks are due also to Prof. Moshe Davis, Head of the Institute of Contemporary Jewry, and to my friends Prof. Moshe Maoz and Prof. Yehuda Bauer of the Hebrew University, who read the Hebrew manuscript of this book and suggested some important changes.

I am indebted also to Mr. and Mrs. Z. and L. Alizi for translating the Hebrew manuscript into English and especially to the Keter Publishing House press for their fine work in producing the book.

Finally, I would like to express my gratitude to the Memorial Foundation for Jewish Culture, New York, which made possible the preparation of this volume through a generous grant.

H.J.C.

Introduction

HISTORICAL BACKGROUND (UP TO 1870)

Up to the 16th Century

Jewish communities were to be found in each of the Middle Eastern countries from the time of the destruction of the Second Temple, and in some of them even before that. In each one of them, Jewish communities continued, and still continue, to exist, with the exception of the Ḥijāz (today part of Saudi Arabia), where they were destroyed or whence they were expelled by Muhammad at the beginning of the 7th century C.E., with only remnants remaining in the south, in Najrān, on the northern border of the Yemen. These remnants, too, emigrated to Israel in 1950. Since then, practically no Jewish communities have remained in the Yemen, in Southern Yemen (Aden), Iraq, Syria, the Lebanon and Egypt, and the number of Jews in Turkey and Iran was decreased.

The events which overtook the Jews from the destruction of the Second Temple differ from one country to another. Those who went into exile in states which were under Christian rule (Syria, Turkey, Egypt) often knew suffering and persecution, while those who wandered to pagan states generally enjoyed complete freedom, although they, too, suffered at certain periods. In the Yemen, on the other hand, the Jews benefited, in the 6th century, from the reign of a royal dynasty which converted to Judaism. The economic and cultural situation of the Jews, too, varied from one country to the other, and from region to region, in accordance with the economic and political conditions prevailing in their place of exile. When all the states of the region, except Turkey, came under the domination of Islam in the 7th century, the political status of the Jews underwent a change. The Jewish tribes living in the Ḥijāz were driven out or destroyed, while the Jews residing in the other countries overrun by the Muslims were entitled to the protection of the new conquerors, and, like the Christians in those areas, were also granted freedom of religious worship. However, throughout the entire Muslim world, neither the Jews nor the Christians were considered equals, but were viewed as strangers who were permitted to live under Muslim rule against payment of a poll-tax *(jizya)*. The amount of the tax varied from period to period, and often from one region to another, but from the beginning of Islam rich non-Muslim men were compelled to pay a certain annual sum. Those whose economic situation was considered moderate paid half the amount paid by the rich, while the poor paid a quarter. For the most part, the tax was collected from the entire community in a lump sum, in each place of settlement separately, one of the Jews being held responsible for its collection. This tax remained in force in the Yemen up to the present time, in Iran until 1925, and in Egypt, Turkey, Iraq, Syria and the Lebanon until the 19th century, when it was called *bedèl-i-'askar* (in exchange for military service); this, too, was abolished in 1909. The payment of this tax was the main condition under which Jews (and Christians) were permitted to live in a Muslim country.

A second provision applying to the Jews in the lands of Islam was their agreement to live under humiliating conditions. More than once were royal orders promulgated obliging Jews and Christians to wear patches on their clothes, or forbidding them to ride on horses, or to build high houses, and so on. However, these humiliations were not strictly implemented in the Sunni countries of Islam (Turkey, Egypt, Iraq, Syria and the Lebanon). Whenever a fanatically religious ruler came to power, he would renew the orders; hence we may gather that the Jewish and Christian minorities had ceased to observe strictly the orders issued previously. Moreover, it is known that in the capitals of the Muslim world—Granada, Baghdad, and Cairo—the Jews served, in various periods, in distinguished positions at the courts of the Caliphs, as their doctors and bankers. For the most part, they also enjoyed internal autonomy in all matters connected with religion: they were free to observe their religious duties, they opened synagogues and *yeshivas,* especially in Babylon, Damascus and Aleppo.[1] Although, from the legal standpoint, the Jews did not have equal rights, the rulers displayed an attitude of respect to their leaders. The *Nesieim* (heads of Jewish community) in Baghdad and the *Negidim* (title of head of Jewish community) in Egypt earned the appreciation and respect of the Muslim population as well, although there were periods when Jews were abased and even oppressed also in the Sunni lands, as in the period of the rule of al-Ḥākim in Egypt (996–1021).

In the 13th century a change for the worse occurred for Jews in most of the Muslim countries, and especially in Iran, Iraq and Syria, as a result of the incursions of the Mongols, who destroyed every town they reached; in 1260 they had reached the north of Palestine. On their way, they slaughtered the local inhabitants—Muslims, Jews and Christians—without distinction, until they left these lands heaps of ruins. This is the period of decline and decay in the Middle Eastern countries, also for the Jews there, and this had its effect on their economic and cultural circumstances, as well as decreasing their numbers. The Jews in these countries did not recover (except in Aleppo, Syria, which gained new blood with the arrival of the exiles from Spain in the 16th century) until the end of the 18th century in Iraq and the beginning of the 20th in Iran.

The Jews of Egypt, too, were badly hit in the 13th century, especially during the rule of the Burjī Mamlūks, and their number greatly declined. Only in the 16th century, with the settlement in Egypt of thousands of Jews from among the Spanish exiles, did a change for the better occur.

On the other hand, the Jews in Turkey, who were under the rule of the Byzantine regime, rejoiced at the Turkish conquest, which began in the 14th century and ended with the Turks taking control of Istanbul in 1453. Under the Turkish Muslims the status of the Jews improved and when the exiles from Spain came to Turkey at the end of the 15th century, they not only attained an increase in number, but also experienced a cultural and religious revival. In this period, at the beginning of the 16th century, Egypt, Iraq, Syria and the Lebanon were conquered by the Turks and thus the majority of the Jews in the Middle East came under the tolerant Sunni-Turkish rule.

The Jews in the Yemen and Iran remained under Muslim-Shī'ite rule, which abased them exceedingly and often even forced conversion on them, as occurred in the Yemen, for example, where the Rambam was compelled to send to the Jews his "Yemen Epistle" of 1172 to encourage them to remain firm. It may be said, therefore, that the gap which existed between the political, economic and cultural position of the Jews of Iran and the Yemen and that of the Jews of the other Eastern countries widened from the 16th century. The difference was great between the Jews of the Shī'ite lands (Iran and the Yemen) and those of the Sunni lands (Egypt, Turkey, Syria, the Lebanon and Iraq).

From the 16th Century to 1870

1. THE SHĪ'ITE COUNTRIES

In the two Shī'ite countries, the Yemen and Iran, the status of the non-Muslims was more difficult than in all the other Muslim lands during the entire period in question. They were not only deprived of rights, but were also defenceless and considered unclean. According to Muslim religious law, which was the law of both states, a murderer is not put to death, if his victim is not a Muslim. His only punishment is the obligation to pay blood-money to the victim's family, and he must do this only if two Muslim witnesses can be produced to give evidence against him. For the law states that the evidence of a Jew or a Christian against a Muslim is not valid. That was the rule also in respect to other offences against Jews. Needless to say, the offender generally went unpunished for not often was a Muslim prepared to give evidence against a fellow believer for the benefit of a Jew, in a case of robbery for example. A Jew was forbidden to build a high house, to ride a horse or high animal, so that he should not be raised up higher than a Muslim. And in both states, the Jews were still obliged to pay the poll-tax.

In the *Yemen*, the Jews suffered during the entire period under discussion. In the years 1627–1629 many were imprisoned and tortured because they refused to convert to Islam, and much Jewish property was plundered. Several years after that, during the rule of al-Mahdī Ismā'īl (1644–1676), the persecutions against the Jews were intensified and new instructions were issued for their humiliation. In 1673 they were forbidden to wear turbans, being obliged to go bareheaded; only in the course of time were they permitted to cover their heads with a cloth. This decree—known by the Yemenite Jews as the *Aṭarot* (crowns) decree—remained in force until the conquest of San'a by the Turks in 1872. In 1676, Ismā'īl's successor, the Imam Ahmad ibn Hasan (ruled 1671–1681), ordered the destruction of synagogues in the Yemen and the prohibition of public prayers. Two years later, in 1678, followed one of the most difficult decrees in the history of Yemenite Jewry: exile. The ruler, out of his fanaticism for the Muslim religion, wished to purge the Arabian peninsula of Jews and therefore compelled the Jews of his country to become Muslims or leave the state. Needless to say, the masses preferred the second possibility and they left San'a, the capital. After a year and a half, the Jews remaining in the Yemen—those from Ṣa'da in the north to Jabla in the south—followed suit. They left the cities and villages, their destination the shores of the Red Sea. The only exceptions were those in areas where the governors did not heed the instructions of the Imam in the capital, as was the case in eastern Yemen. The exiles travelled on foot, and sometimes on animals, reaching the city of Mauza', near the port of Mocha, a salty region with a difficult climate and very few inhabitants. Here, the governor enabled the Jews to remain—to be more exact, he gave this possibility to those thousands who, despite the hardships of the way, had the good luck to arrive alive, for large numbers had died of hunger, thirst and illness, or from sheer fatigue. In Mauza', many more died as a result of the difficult climate.

In 1781, a short time before the death of the Imam Ahmad ibn Hasan, the Jews were permitted to return.[2] There is a version that says that the reason for the cancellation of the exile decree was the pressure exerted on the Imam by the governors and the inhabitants to bring back the Jews. For after their departure there were no longer any craftsmen in the cities and villages of the Yemen—the Jews had been the only ones in the entire state. As far as is known, this is the only instance in the Middle East during the past few hundreds of years where the Jews were obliged to go into exile.

The Mauza' exile ended, and those who remained alive returned to their cities and villages. The Jews of San'a were not permitted to go back to the houses they had lived in, but were allocated an area outside the city, near the city wall, where they set up their own quarter and surrounded it with a wall. In this new quarter, the

Jews of San'a lived about 270 years, until their mass emigration to Israel. Those who returned to other cities, such as Ḥajja, al-Mūd, Wada', al-Ḍāhir, suffered forced conversion and murder at the end of the 17th century.

Since the beginning of the 18th century, no cases are known of forced conversion, but the Jews endured frequent years of famine starting from 1717 and especially in 1724. That year, about 800 Jews in San'a alone accepted Islam so as to get food promised by the Imam, but many more died of hunger. At that time, however, there came to power in the Yemen the Imam al-Abbas ibn Hasan ibn Qāsim, known as al-Mahdī, who, during the 48 years of his reign (1727–1775), acted kindly towards the Jews and the population as a whole. He even retained a Jew, Shalom Iraqī Cohen, as Minister of Currency and as his adviser at the Royal Court for about 30 years. This man made use of his position and his wealth for the benefit of Jews and Muslims alike by contributing funds for the hungry. During this time, the Jews knew peace, although Shalom Cohen himself was imprisoned by the Imam in the years 1760–1762. It is not known exactly of what he was accused.

At the beginning of the 19th century, years of suffering and famine were again the lot of the Jews in the Yemen. In 1805, hunger caused many deaths among them. A year later the San'a Jews were given the task of removing the animal carcasses from the city's streets and cleaning the latrines. This decree, which was complied with by some Jews against payment from the community's treasury, remained in force up to our time. In 1808, when the Bakīl tribes laid siege to San'a, many died of hunger, especially among the Jews, since they had not been accustomed to keep supplies of produce in their homes. Ten years later, the tribes broke into the Jewish quarter, the Arab guards having been bribed to open its gates, and many Jews were killed; others fled and their houses were destroyed. The famine years added more dead, 1836 being the most difficult year of all. Internal wars, too, meant trouble for the Jews. During 20 years (1840–1860), rulers of San'a changed 13 times, with the resultant suffering of many inhabitants, especially Jews—the defeated took their revenge on them and in their joy the victors went wild and rioted against them. Many of the city's Jews left for the neighbouring villages, where they received shelter against payment: the rest were plundered by the rioters.[3] They applied to Paris, in 1863, and to London without avail, nor did the intervention of the Anglo-Jewish Association at the British Foreign Office yield any results.[4]

However, we must not generalize. In the city of al-Madīd, for example, Jews dwelt in safety: there were wealthy men among them whose houses were sometimes even higher than those of the Muslims, a thing which was forbidden in the Yemen. These Jews were then under the protection of a tribe which feared that they would seek the protection of an enemy tribe. During the early 1860's the former even went to war against another Arab tribe because one of its members had robbed a Jew.[5] As in other Arab countries, so, too, in the Yemen, the situation of the Jews living in the small towns and villages was better than that of those in the large cities, because of the daily contacts between the inhabitants.[6]

The situation of the Jews in the Yemen from 1872, when a new period opened up for them, until their mass emigration to Israel, is discussed in the following chapters.

In the light of the political situation which was not always the same in all parts of the Yemen, in view of the economic conditions and the Jews' dispersal over many hundreds of settlements, and because of lack of means of communication between north and south Yemen, quite outstanding dissimilarities were created over the generations among the Yemenite Jews, especially between those who lived in the north and those in the south. Some people also consider the Jews of the centre as a separate group. The differences were manifested in character, in physiognomy, and even in customs and accent, in cultural level and in living style. Shmuel Yavnieli, who was in the Yemen in 1911, and Israel Yesha'yāhū, of the city of Shar'ab, describe the Jews in the north (Ṣa'da, Ḥaydān al-Shām and environs) as tall, with well-developed bodies, black hair, long faces and large protruding eyes, black and very bright. Until a few years ago, they used to repair weapons, a fact which contributed to their pride and courage. On the other hand, the Jews of the south (such as Shar'ab, Udīn, Ḥubaysh and environs) are described as short, with reddish-brown hair, their skin a greyish colour, their faces wide, with protruding foreheads. Yavnieli found in Ḥubaysh, Ḥabīl, 'Amrān, Ḥabbān and the environs of Bayḍa a small number of Jews who were completely fair-skinned, blond with blue eyes. The Jews of the south were considered mystics, hence their deep interest in the Kabbala. Israel Yesha'yāhū discerns a third group—the Jews in Central Yemen (as in San'a and Dhamār), who, according to him, differed from the other Jews of the Yemen, at least in that most of them engaged in commerce and artistic crafts. They adapted themselves quickly to new conditions, and were more influenced by the West, especially as a result of living under Ottoman rule.[7] These and other variances gave rise to diversified Jewish communities in the Yemen,[8] which remained so until our time. Following their immigration into Israel, however, these differences became blurred.

As to the Jews of *Aden,* their history is less known, but the evidence available indicates that their lot was no better, they, too, having been humiliated by the Muslims[9] until Aden was conquered by the British in 1839. Even after that year and until the middle of the 19th century they often suffered from persecution and humiliation. The few Jews in Ḥaḍramaūt and its environs (an area which was known as the Protectorate of Aden) lived under more comfortable conditions among the Arabs—against payment of taxes to the local governor, of course.

In *Iran,* the Shī'ite faith became that of the state with the rise of the Ṣafawī dynasty (1502–1736). From then on, the political situation of the Jews in Iran worsened, resembling that in the Yemen, but with one difference. While in the Yemen the Imam was both the religious and the lay authority, in Iran the Shah (king) did not have religious authority; the laws humiliating and oppressing the non-Muslims were issued by the religionists, and the Jews had the right to complain to the king against oppression. Not all the kings who reigned in this period, however, were strong enough to help the Jews, and even when they were able to curb the religious functionaries, this was the case mainly in their capital city and the rest of the Jews in the state did not, for the most part, enjoy any protection whatsoever. At times the king himself was so weak that he was prepared to reinforce the stand of the religious leaders, so as not to give them an excuse to incite the population against him. The reign of Shah Abbas the First (1586–1628) is a case in point. In his time a collection of laws known by his name, Jāmi'-i-Abbas (Abbas collection), was promulgated, which included, *inter alia,* instructions degrading the Jews; similar laws were issued afterwards by the religionists, although not in the name of the king. However, even when the kings and governors were liberal, they were unable to change the State Law, at least not the courts. Until 1906, the courts in Iran judged according to Muslim religious law, as in the Yemen, in contrast to the practice in the Ottoman Empire, where state courts passed judgement according to lay laws. Muslim religious law granted privileges to Muslims over non-Muslims—for example, the evidence of Muslims was always accepted against that of non-Muslims. We have already referred to the Muslim religious law stipulating that a Muslim or a Jew who kills a Muslim is sentenced to death, but if the victim is a non-Muslim, the murderer has only to pay blood-money. In Iran the ministers of religion introduced a further practice, namely, that a Jew who converted to Islam was entitled to the entire inheritance of all his Jewish relatives. Apart from these discriminatory measures, the Jews were humiliated particularly by the Shī'ite religious belief that a non-Muslim is impure, a belief not held by Sunni Islam: the Shī'ite Muslim faith had taken it from the Zardushtra religion, which had previously been the faith of Iran.[10]

When Iran was conquered by the Muslims (in the year 640) and accepted Islam, it introduced to the new religion some of its former beliefs. From Iran the idea of non-Muslim impurity moved to all the other Shī'ites in the eastern world, such as those in southern Iraq. The religious functionaries in Iran extended it to include many more restrictions—for example, a Jew was forbidden to leave his house on a rainy day, lest he sprinkle rainwater on a Muslim while walking out; a Jew was forbidden to touch a fruit before purchasing it; and Jewish women were sometimes obliged to go out either with their faces revealed or covered with a white scarf, so as to distinguish them from Muslim women who cover their faces with a black scarf. These commands, and others, turned the Jews in Iran into objects of humiliation, and also laid them open to plunder at the hands of every hostile Muslim, as they were seldom entitled to any protection. In this way, the Jews in Iran, like those of the Yemen, were reduced to ruin. In their great degradation and poverty, and from lack of language contact with world Jewry, many of them even forgot their religious duties—unlike the Yemenite Jews, who retained their contact with the Jews of the world and with Judaism.

The persecution of the Iranian Jews was intended, from this period on, not only to humiliate them, but even to compel them to change their religion, and indeed many converted to Islam in the 16th and 17th centuries. A Jewish poet who lived at that time, Bābī Luṭuf, described these persecutions in his poems in the Persian language. Later, in the days of Nādir Shah's rule (1736–1747), came a period of such relative calm that, in the cities of Shīrāz and Kāshān, the study of the Torah flourished and both cities were called 'little Jerusalem'. From Shīrāz, too, rabbis went out to the other cities of the state.[11] Not long afterwards, however, the persecutions were renewed, and at the end of the 18th and the beginning of the 19th century, as a result of various false charges, Jews were butchered, or expelled from the cities of northern Iran in the vicinity of the Caspian Sea, such as Tabrīz, and Marāgha.[12] In 1839 the Jews of Meshed in north-west Iran were forced to convert after some dozens of them had been slaughtered.* In this area, instances are also known of blood libels by Muslims, as in Tabrīz in 1826,[13] a rare phenomenon among the Muslims. Oppression and humiliations continued until the beginning of the 20th century, although in the 'seventies of the 19th they decreased, thanks to the intervention of representatives of a number of states, mainly France and Britain, on behalf of the Jews. It should be pointed out that the situation of the Christians in Iran was no better, and at times even worse,[14] although they occasionally benefited from the protection of foreign consulates.

2. COUNTRIES OF THE OTTOMAN EMPIRE

During the period of Turkish domination over most of the Middle Eastern countries, from 1517–1518 to 1839, the Jews in Turkey, Syria, the Lebanon and Iraq were, like all the non-Muslims, second-class residents, their right to live in the state depending on payment of the poll-tax *(jizya)*. Theoretically, they had no more rights than did the Jews of the Shī'ite lands, but in fact there was a great difference. True, the Jews of the Ottoman Empire, too, like the Christians there, were sometimes required to wear special dress and to pay higher taxes than the rate imposed on Muslims, in addition to enduring other legal discriminations until 1839.[15] In general, however, neither the rulers nor the religious functionaries oppressed them. The Sultans saw to it that the local governors who were sometimes tyrannical protected them: this included protection from occasional provocations and from robbery and injuries inflicted from time to time by the Janissaries (army units in the

* See below, pages 165–166.

service of the Turkish regime) on Jews and non-Jews alike.[16] They were also protected by the rulers against blood libels, which were frequent in this period (until the 'sixties of the 19th century) especially in Turkey,[17] and to a certain extent also in other cities of the Middle East in which new groups of Armenian and Greek Christians were settled. The Turkish rulers prevented grave injury being done to the Jews as a result of these blood libels, and in general they did not claim Jewish victims.[18] The Ottoman rulers readily accepted the settlement of the Spanish exiles (1492) all over the Empire, and enabled the Jews freely to observe their religious duties, and hardly restricted them as to the means of earning their livelihood. Moreover, although the Jews did not have equal rights with the Muslims, some of them acquired important posts in the courts of the Sultans and district governors as physicians (such as Moshe Hamon and Josef Hamon in the 16th century), as bankers and advisors to the Sultans (such as Josef Nasi) and as civil servants, in the foreign service as well (e.g., Gabriel Benbenisti at the beginning of the 19th century).[19] In Syria, too, members of the Farḥi family served as Ministers of Finance to the district governors of Damascus, Aleppo and Acre at the beginning of the 19th century. Abraham Castro was responsible for the issue of currency in Egypt in the 16th century, and Jews were to be found in banking positions and as advisors to district governors also in Baghdad and Basra from the end of the 18th century.[20]

The situation of the Jews economically, culturally, socially and politically, was not the same everywhere. In the cities located on the international trade routes, as was the case with Damascus, Aleppo and Mosul, they lived under good conditions. In cities where the Spanish exiles settled, such as Istanbul, Izmir and Adrianople in Turkey, and Aleppo in Syria, yeshivas were founded in which famous rabbis were educated, some of whom wrote important works. The Spanish exiles and their descendants brought new blood into the local Jewry, which had greatly declined numerically as well during the hundreds of years of suffering, wars, plagues and famine. Many of the Spanish exiles had settled in Turkey, where they absorbed the small local community already there. A much smaller number had settled in Aleppo and Damascus, where they became absorbed by the larger local communities; only a few Spanish exiles came to Iraq.

Until the 17th century the Jewish community in *Turkey* was perhaps the wealthiest in the Middle East, but since then its economic situation deteriorated. From the religious-cultural viewpoint, however, it continued to be the leading eastern community, especially owing to the large number of Spanish exiles there. The Turkish Jews were the first in the East to found Hebrew printing houses—in Istanbul in 1494 and in Adrianople in 1554. Another characteristic of the Turkish Jews was their retention of the Ladino language, both spoken and written; with few exceptions they did not even learn to write in the language of the native inhabitants. For that reason, a Turkish-Jewish dialect was never created in Turkey.

In the year 1839, the Sultan Abd-al-Majīd issued the *Khaṭṭ-i-Sherīf* (a distinguished decree) of Gülkhāné, in which were promised, for the first time, equal rights and security to the lives and property of all the minorities in all parts of the Ottoman Empire. From then on, the Sultan made official the appointment of Chief Rabbi, who was chosen by the community. Jews, though only a few, were appointed to Government posts and to the courts, and several were made representatives to district and municipal councils; a short time later modern schools were opened for Jews, who also began to be accepted in Government schools. Hence, the 'thirties of the 19th century can be viewed as the beginning of a period of change in the lives of the Jewish communities of Turkey.

In *Egypt,* a brighter future seemed to be in store for the Jews, when Napoleon Bonaparte conquered the country in 1798. A short time after the French occupation, on September 7, 1798, Napoleon issued a decree recognizing all inhabitants, including the Jews, as having equal rights, and so the small Jewish community of 6,000–7,000 souls[21] was the first in the Middle East to attain this. The French employed many Jews and Copts in their service as translators and tax-collectors; they also permitted them and the other Christians to sell wine, a factor which led to rioting in October of 1798 against the non-Muslim minorities in Cairo. The Egyptian historian Abd al-Raḥmān al-Jabartī, who lived in that period, relates that the crowd wished to slaughter the Christians and the Jews because some of them worked for the French, and had become insufferable because they began to ride on horses and to bear arms. Thanks to their escape to the Cairo fortress, they were saved from massacre.[22] Apart from this episode, the year 1798 witnessed the first change for the better in the lives of the Egyptian Jews. Unfortunately, French rule did not last long, terminating in 1801. In its trail, the Jews suffered at the hands of the Muslims, who oppressed and blackmailed them because they saw in them collaborators with the French.[23] They again had to pay poll-tax, as did all the inhabitants of the Ottoman Empire in those days.

In 1805, Muhammad Ali, an officer from Albania, seized the reins of government in Egypt and in the 44 years of his rule tried to develop the Egyptian economy. For that purpose, he was assisted by foreign experts from Europe, as well as by local Jews and Copts, several of whom became important industrialists and bankers. In his time, Egypt began to receive immigrants from Europe, among them Jews as well, mainly from Greece and Eastern Europe; on the whole, however, the Jewish community remained small until the middle of the century, their number standing at 5,000–6,000. Except for rich individuals,[24] most were still poor and illiterate. It is true that in 1840 schools were opened for the Jews (two in Cairo for boys and girls and one in Alexandria for boys), but these were closed down after two years.

Although Muhammad Ali did not remove the *jizya* tax, he improved indirectly the situation of the minorities. He established civil courts and reduced the jurisdiction of the religious ones. Thus, it was made possible for Jews, as for others, to be judged before civil courts, where their testimony against Muslims was accepted. Muhammad Ali also established municipal councils, in which Jewish members were nominated, although these councils had little authority.

The modern period in the history of the Egyptian Jews began only in the 'sixties of the last century.

The Jewish community in *Iraq* remained weak numerically, as well as economically and culturally, from the time of the Mongol incursions in the middle of the 13th century, especially in the central and southern regions. The community did not benefit from the Spanish exiles, very few having come to Iraq. The Jews of Kurdistan and northern Iraq, who had suffered less in the days of the Mongols, were in better circumstances. From among them came the family of the Chief Rabbis of Baghdad from the beginning of the 17th century until the year 1742—the family Barāzānī. On the death that year, of plague, of the last of the rabbis of this family, the Jewish community in Baghdad was so short of learned rabbis that it was compelled to apply to Aleppo, whence came Rabbi Ẓedaqa Ḥuẓiyn, who served as Chief Rabbi of Baghdad until 1773.[25] In the meantime, the Jewish community in Kurdistan, too, began to weaken, suffering from the frequent uprisings of the Kurdish tribes against Ottoman rule. One result may be seen from the fact that from the 17th century on there were practically no yeshivas in Kurdistan; although there were in Zākho, 'Amādiya and Sandūr at the beginning of the 18th century[26] they disappeared shortly thereafter. Up to the middle of the 19th century only one rich Jewish community existed in northern Iraq, that of Mosul, owing, no doubt, to the fact that part of the international transit trade from Europe to the Far East passed through this city.

In contrast to the decline in the economic and cultural situation of the Kurdistan Jews, the Jewish communities in Baghdad and Basra began to recover at the end of the 18th century. The missionary, Joseph Wolff, who visited Baghdad in 1824, tells of 1,500 Jewish families living in Baghdad;[27] David d'Beth Hillel (1827) speaks of about 6,000 families,[28] but apparently he was referring to souls; and the traveller J. R. Wellsted (1831) reports on 7,000 Jews in Baghdad.[29] Then came recovery, and according to Benjamin ben Joseph (1848), 3,000 families were residing in the city;[30] according to Yeḥiel Fischel Kastelman (1860), there were 20,000 souls.[31] Economically, too, the Jews' situation improved, with several of them holding important positions in the commercial life of the city, and others serving as bankers to the district governor.[32] Gradually foreign trade began to pass into Jewish hands.[33] Their numerical increase and economic recovery were accompanied by spiritual and religious revival. In this period, a number of Baghdad rabbis became famous,[34] and in 1832 a large Talmud Torah institution was opened in the city, there having been, up to then, only *"ḥeders"*. Although the level of this Talmud Torah was certainly not high, from among its pupils came the students of the first yeshiva, which was founded in Baghdad in 1840, after hundreds of years during which there had been no yeshivas in Iraq. At its head was Rabbi Abdalla Somekh, and by 1848 about 60 young men were studying there.[35] A great many Jews, however, still remained in straitened circumstances, earning a livelihood from peddling and crafts.

In Basra, too, the Jews increased in number, and in 1826 David d'Beth Hillel found about 300 Jewish families there, among them merchants and several who served in important posts with the district governor.[36] In contrast to Baghdad, however, progress ceased before it could develop further. In 1831, the city was struck by plague, which caused thousands of deaths; travellers who visited the city immediately thereafter described it as desolate, and its Jewish population consisted of a few score families.[37]

Thus, in the middle of the 19th century, there were only two large Jewish communities in Iraq—in Baghdad and in Mosul, and two small communities (in Basra and Ḥilla) in all of southern Iraq, with the remaining Jews dispersed among the cities of Kurdistan. The other communities which had existed in the south at the time of Benjamin of Tudela's visit in the 12th century[38] had been destroyed in the 13th century and thereafter. Most of the few communities left were small in number, destitute and with a low level of education. A really substantial change for the better for the Iraqi Jews began only in the 'sixties of the 19th century.[39]

Somewhat different was the situation of the Jews in *Syria.* Their economic and cultural development in Damascus differed from that in Aleppo. At the beginning of the 16th century, the number of Jews in Aleppo began to increase, and from the middle of that century the number of Damascus Jews also rose, thanks to the settlement there of Spanish exiles and their descendants. Thanks to them too, many yeshivas were opened in these two cities, and at the beginning of the 17th century Jews even emigrated from Palestine to Damascus to study Torah with Rabbi Ḥayyim Vital, who settled there and spread the study of the works of the *Ari* (Rabbi Luria). Aleppo and to a certain extent Damascus as well were important centres of trade between Europe and the Far East, and the Jews were among the outstanding merchants there. Their security situation, too, was satisfactory, and they lived in peace with their neighbours. It is true that a number of incidents of robbery and murder occurred, but these were carried out by gangs of thieves who used to attack city dwellers, irrespective of whether they were Jews or non-Jews.[40]

In the 18th and 19th centuries there began a slow, but persistent, deterioration in the political and cultural position of the Syrian Jews. At that time Greek Christians began to settle in the state, several of whom succeeded in seizing the Jews' place in trade, while others spread blood libels against them; the most famous case was that which occurred in Damascus in 1840. These blood libels did not, however, bring disaster to the Jews. Up to the beginning of the 19th century, they were to be found occupying important positions in the economic and political life of Syria—for example the Farḥī family, which had influence in Damascus, Aleppo and Acre, and the Angel and Stambūlī families, Turkish-born but living in Damascus. But they did not advance culturally: the Spanish Jews, being few in number, began to assimilate with the local Jewish population. They almost ceased to speak Ladino, and adopted the dress, customs and Arabic language of the local population. The Spanish exiles' schools, cemeteries and burial societies, too, which had been separate, were amalgamated with those of the local Jews in the 18th century.[41] The Syrian Jews' assimilation was also evident from their names, especially in the city of Damascus. Names common among the Arabs such as Bakrī, Majīd, Khaḍir, 'Ārif, Nakhla and 'Abdū, and, among the women, Badriya and Bahiya were used by Jews there.[42] There are practically no Jews in the other countries of the East called by Arab names such as these.

In the 19th century, the economic position of the Jews in Aleppo and Damascus also began to decline, principally because then the British and French decreased their transit trade through Aleppo.[43]

With regard to the Jews in the *Lebanon,* their number was small during this entire period, and they were scattered over a number of places: Beirut, Sidon, Tripoli and Dīr el-Qamar. The Jewish settlement in Dīr el-Qamar was liquidated in 1847 as a result of the Druze rebellion in the area.[44] In the remaining cities there were only a few tens of families.[45] Only in the middle of the 19th century did the Jewish community in the Lebanon begin to develop economically and numerically.

To sum up, it may be said that in the 'fifties and 'sixties of the 19th century there were some hundreds of thousands of Jews in the Middle East, dispersed over many hundreds of cities and villages, a few Jewish families living in many of the villages, and large communities of over 20,000 in three cities, Istanbul, Izmir and Baghdad. There were considerable differences in spoken language, customs, economic and cultural circumstances, between Jews in one state and another, and even between those within each state. Up to the middle of the 19th century, the majority of the Eastern Jews were destitute and uneducated; from that time important changes began to take place in all countries of the region, with the exception of the Yemen. In the last 100 years, the economic, political and social situation of the Jews in the Middle East improved, although not to the same extent in all countries, the changes depending on the development in each country where a Jewish community existed. In all of them, except the Yemen, these changes were accompanied by a process of urbanization, with the Jews concentrating in one or two main cities of each country.

It is the aim of this book to explain the demographic, political, economic, educational and cultural changes occurring in the last 100 years.

Chapter One
POLITICAL CHANGES

On November 3, 1839, the Sultan Abd-al-Majīd issued the Khaṭṭ-i-Sherīf of the Gülkhānė assuring equal rights to all subjects of the Ottoman Empire irrespective of religion; on February 18, 1856, the same Sultan issued the Khaṭṭi-i-Hümāyun in which he repeated his former promises.[1] These orders gave the impetus to vast political changes which were to take place in the life of the Jews in the Ottoman Empire. Henceforth, Jews ceased, legally, to be protected subjects without rights. In the year 1855, the poll-tax *(jizya)* was also abolished. Until then, payment of this tax had entitled them to the protection of the authorities; from that date on, they gained this protection by virtue of their being citizens. True, the tax actually remained in force, now being called *bedèl-i-'askar* (in exchange for military service): since Jews were not recruited into the army they were obliged to pay collective service fees. The change, however, was that whoever did wish to do military service could do so from then on—for the first time in the history of the Jews in the Ottoman Empire. And, indeed, a number of cases are known of Jews serving, mainly, although not exclusively, as officers in the medical corps.[2] Gradually, Jewish children were accepted in state schools, Jews were represented in district and municipal councils, and, when the first Turkish parliament was opened in 1876, Jews from the large communities of the Empire were appointed to it.

As far as the law was concerned, there was almost complete equality, although in practice the situation varied from district to district throughout the Empire, depending on the inclinations of the district governors and the extent of Istanbul's influence on them. The Muslim populace's attitude towards the Jews was also not the same in all parts of the Empire. We shall deal with these dissimilarities when we discuss each country separately. But let it be stated here that from 1839 up to the First World War the political situation of the Jews, on the whole, had been improving in Turkey, Iraq, Syria and the Lebanon, and to a slight degree also in the Yemen, where Ottoman rule was symbolic. In Egypt, too, conditions were more satisfactory, thanks to Muhammad Ali, who ruled that country from 1805 to 1848, and his successors, as well as to the British occupation of the country in 1882.

Following the First World War, the Ottoman Empire disintegrated, Turkey alone remaining under the rule of the Turks. Iraq came under a British Mandate (1920–

1932), Syria and the Lebanon under a French Mandate (1921–1945) and Egypt became independent, under the terms of an agreement with Britain (1922–1936), and independent, without British protection, in 1936. As long as the Arab countries were under European protection the political situation of the Jews remained satisfactory. The moment they received their independence, the Arab governments of Syria and Iraq began to take an active part in the Palestine problem, and they soon set out to impose restrictions on the Jews—in practice, not by the enactment of laws. Egypt was the last Arab state in the region to appear on the scene of Arab political activity. In 1945, it joined the Arab League, and immediately thereafter the Jews began to be harried. Following the partition of Palestine the persecution was intensified. Jews began to flee the Middle Eastern countries. In some cases they were permitted to emigrate, or were even expelled. In Egypt, Iraq, Syria, the Yemen and Aden not more than 5,000 Jews remained in 1972, against about 275,000 in 1947. In Turkey, Iran and the Lebanon the number of Jews also decreased, although not on the same scale—to 99,000 as against 185,000 in 1947. In these three states Jews were not oppressed, and only those desiring to do so emigrated.

During many centuries the Muslim populace humiliated the Jews. When they were under the influence of religious agitators they would go so far as to rob and massacre them. Muslims usually responded willingly against a religious minority, and even against a Muslim tribe or countrymen of their own religion when spurred on by religious or other agitators.

Since the 1920's however, and especially since the 1940's, anti-Jewish propaganda became more influential. Muslim nationals began to regard Jews as a national-Zionist minority and not as a weak religious minority. As Zionists, Jews were considered traitors to Arab ideals. The Arabs, although of different races, never tolerated national minorities among themselves. During this century Christian Armenians and Assyrians as well as Muslim Kurds were massacred. Arab leaders, although they often claim to distinguish between Jews and Zionists, hardly ever do so and the Arab masses are usually unable to distinguish between a Jew and a Zionist. Every Jew is considered a Zionist, or a potential Zionist, and for this reason there is no room for Jews in Arab countries.

The Christians in the Arab countries usually behaved honestly towards the Jews. The cases of blood libels against Jews were mostly inspired by Christians who had only recently settled in Muslim countries, such as the Armenians and the Greeks. Veteran Christians such as the Copts almost never issued such libels. It was the new Christian immigrants who settled in the cities and had to compete with the other city-dwellers, the Jews, that were most hostile towards the Jewish populace.

Jews in the Middle East were usually not active in politics, for several reasons. Most parties were extremely fanatic, or even anti-Jewish, anti-British, and anti-French. Jews did not want to belong to these parties since they considered the foreign rulers to be their protectors. Other parties were founded by some politicians but these parties did not last long. Hence, Jews in Iran, Iraq, Syria and Egypt were attracted to Zionist and Communist parties but since these parties were underground, only the youth dared to belong to them.

It is almost certain that another reason for Jewish inactivity in politics was their reluctance to belong to a group or an organization. Philanthropic Jewish organizations were always directed by a few well-to-do Jews. Communal Jewish organizations in Syria, Lebanon, Iran and Yemen were always weak. Even the good Jewish organizations in Iraq and Egypt had only a few active members.

Turkey

Under the decree of equal rights granted the Jews of the Ottoman Empire, Turkish Jews received appointments as judges and university lecturers, and as civil servants in the Foreign Ministry, the Police, the Ministry of Education, the Treasury and the Post Office. They also were appointed to district and municipal councils,[3] even in such small towns as Bāsh Qal'a[4] and Diyarbakir.[5]

Their right to observe the dictates of their religion was also recognized by the authorities, who even assisted the rabbis in imposing on Jews the duty to observe them, and their religious requirements were met.[6] Government and other banks were sometimes closed on Jewish holidays on the request of the Jews,[7] and in 1864, for instance, the Turkish authorities made a grant for the purchase of Passover *maẓẓot* and wine for the poor,[8] notwithstanding the fact that wine is forbidden to Muslims and Turkey was at that time a religious Muslim state.

The Turkish authorities also protected the Jews living in countries under their aegis. In 1872, following the outbreak of anti-Semitic demonstrations in Rumania, the Grand Vizier (Prime Minister of Turkey) urged the governments of Wallachia and Moldavia to protect the Jews there, and in the agreement concluded between Turkey and the Serbian governments in February 1887, the Serbs were required to grant equal rights to Jews living within their borders.[9] Turkey also gave shelter to thousands of Jews fleeing from the pogroms in Eastern Europe and permitted them to settle wherever they pleased in its territories.[10]

1839–1908

In this period little harm was done to the Jews by the Turkish authorities,[11] who, on the whole, regarded them favourably, more so than the Greeks, whom they considered a hostile, nationalist minority.[12] It would seem therefore that it was not only to fulfil an obligation that on Passover 1892 the Turkish Jews celebrated the 400th anniversary of the settlement of the Spanish exiles in Turkey, and it was not only to give lip service that they offered up a thanksgiving prayer for Turkey, and published hymns of praise for Turkey in the local Jewish press.[13]

Relations with the Muslim population during that period were also peaceful, although, of course, limited. In any event, there were no attacks worthy of note, except in the Kurdistan districts, where Jews suffered at the hands of the Muslim Kurds up to the beginning of the 20th century, to the extent that many Jews of that region left Turkey for Palestine or for Syria. The Istanbul Government orders to the district governors there to prevent such harassment[14] were not always implemented.

On the other hand, the Turkish Jews were caused much suffering by Christians, who spread blood libels against them. Although a number of blood libels were apparently initiated by Muslims, for the most part the Christians were to blame for them. There were many cases, particularly in Izmir,[15] where a large number of Greek Christians lived, but also in Istanbul,[16] Adrianople (1872), Urla, near Izmir (1874),[17] Churlo (Çurlo), near Istanbul (1884),[18] Manisa (1893),[19] Rodosto-Tekirdag on the Bosphorus shore (1892),[20] Bursa (1899)[21] and other places. Professor Abraham Galanté recorded 48 such cases, 11 of them in Izmir and seven in Istanbul.[22] In general, the authorities protected the Jews—in this period as in the past—against these libels and issued orders during the years 1840–1866 on how to handle cases of this kind.[23]

1908–1923

When the Young Turks seized power in July 1908, the Turkish Jews sent greetings to the revolutionaries expressing their loyalty and offered prayers for the life of the new Sultan, Muhammad Rashād the Fifth.[24] This expression of joy did not intend to reflect an end to oppression against Jews of the previous regime, but more the fact that the Jews, like the rest of the population, had suffered from the despotic rule of Abd-al-Ḥamīd, who was deposed by the Young Turks. And indeed, Jews were among the members of this underground movement. These Jews were from all over Turkey, and in particular from the city of Salonica (today in Greece), such as Abraham Galanté, Emmanuel Carasso, Albert Fua, Nissim-Rousso, Nissim Mazliah and Albert Férid Asséo.[25]

Political life was renewed, for the parliament which had been elected in December 1876 had been dismissed within a short time by Abd-al-Ḥamīd. In the new House, the Turkish Jews had two deputies (from Izmir and Istanbul) besides the two representing the Jews from Salonica and Baghdad. In August 1909, the military service law was promulgated obligating the non-Muslims to enlist in the army and abolishing the *bedèl-i-'askar* tax, the last symbol of minority inequality. Henceforth, Jews and Christians were required to do military service, like the Muslims, except for religious functionaries, sick people, sole breadwinners, and similar categories of persons. According to the Law, those who paid the service tax (*bedèl*)[26] could be released from service, as was the case with Muslims, but the tax from this time was individual and not collective.

During this period, the Jews continued to be employed as civil servants, but it appears, from the list of names presented by Professor Galanté, that their number in important posts was small, as compared with the period of Abd-al-Ḥamīd, notwithstanding the fact that Professor Galanté, who was an adherent of the Young Turks, was particularly interested in mentioning more Jews as serving in this period than in the previous period. It is reasonable to assume that the Young Turks limited the number of Jews in civil service.

There was subsequently an attempt to Turkify the minorities, to the disappointment of the Jews. But the downfall of the Young Turks after the First World War and the occupation of most of the Turkish cities by the Greeks from 1918 to 1922 was worse for the Jews. One reason for this was that the Greek Christians in the coastal cities felt themselves free to maltreat them. Professor Abraham Galanté, who wrote a great deal about the Jews' hardships in the period of Greek rule, speaks at length about their loyalty to the Turks, their opposition to the study of Greek, their declarations concerning their desire for Turkish rule instead of Greek and Bulgarian (the Bulgars ruled in Adrianople from 1912) and their rejection of an American Mandate over Istanbul.[27] This preference for Turkish rule was no doubt due to their fear of continued Greek rule and not because they felt themselves Turks. Despite the hundreds of years during which the Spanish exiles dwelt in Turkey, only a few of them, up to the establishment of the Turkish Republic (1923), could read and write Turkish,* although many of them were able to speak it; the mother-tongue of the Jews in Turkey remained Ladino for more than 400 years.[28] The Jews were also separate from the general population wherever they settled, concentrating in their own quarters in Istanbul, Adrianople, Izmir and Bursa.[29] They studied for the most part in Christian or Jewish schools, rather than in Turkish ones. Nor did they play any significant part in the political life of the state.

In the light of the fact that the Jews felt themselves strangers and were not acclimatized in Turkey, it is difficult to explain the calm life they enjoyed in that country, unless it was due to the Turks' tolerance of people of another faith and of strangers so long as they did not constitute a hostile and anti-Turkish factor, or were not suspected of anti-Turkish inclinations, as were the Greeks and the Armenians.

*See p. 134.

1923–1971

As a result of the Graeco-Turkish War, the Turks won their independence, which was recognized by the Powers in the Peace Treaty of July 24, 1923 concluded at Lausanne. A number of articles in this Treaty relating to non-Muslim minorities established that "the Turkish Government undertakes to assure full and complete protection of life and liberty to all inhabitants of Turkey, without distinction of birth, nationality, language, race or religion. All inhabitants of Turkey shall be entitled to free exercise, whether in public or private, of any creed, religion, or belief, the observance of which shall not be incompatible with public order and good morals. Non-Muslim minorities will enjoy full freedom of movement and emigration, subject to measures applied, on the whole or part of the territory, to all Turkish nationals, and which may be taken by the Turkish Government for national defence, or for the maintenance of public order." (*Art.* 38)

"Turkish nationals belonging to non-Muslim minorities will enjoy the same civil and political rights as the Muslims. All the inhabitants of Turkey, without distinction of religion, shall be equal before the law. Differences of religion, creed or confession shall not prejudice any Turkish national in matters relating to the enjoyment of civil or political rights, for instance, admission to public employments, functions and honours, or the exercise of professions and industries. No restrictions shall be imposed on the free use by any Turkish national of any language in private intercourse, in commerce, religion, in the press, or in publications of any kind, or at public meetings. Notwithstanding the existence of the official language, adequate facilities shall be given to Turkish nationals of non-Turkish speech for the oral use of their own language before the Courts." (*Art.* 39)

"Turkish nationals belonging to non-Muslim minorities shall enjoy the same treatment and security in law and in fact as other Turkish nationals. In particular, they shall have an equal right to establish, manage and control, at their own expense, any charitable, religious and social institutions, any schools and other establishments for instruction and education, with the right to use their own language and to exercise their own religion freely therein." (*Art.* 40)[30]

These articles of the Treaty of Lausanne, despite all their importance, did not improve the situation of the Jews in Turkey, as compared with what it had been up to the First World War, except, perhaps, that they could also study in classes above the fourth grade of elementary school in their language, contrary to the Ministry of Education's order of 1867 obliging them to study in Turkish starting with the fifth grade. On the other hand, these articles changed the status of the Jews into a protected minority and, to a certain extent, they also led the Turkish nationalists to consider them a traitorous minority interested in foreign interference in the internal affairs of their country. Because of this fear, young Jewish intellectuals organized propaganda calling on Jews to waive the rights. The Turkish Government, too, pressed the Jews to forego these rights and the Turkish press described the Jews as traitors. There were also those who demanded the expulsion of the Jews from their country.[31] Thus it came about that the Jews relinquished their rights in a written statement on February 16, 1926, expressing their desire to live as Turks.[32] The Greeks and Armenians, too, were compelled to follow the Jews. This renunciation was not recognized by the League of Nations within whose framework the Treaty of Lausanne had been signed, for the minorities in Turkey were not a party to the Treaty.

Thus, they again became equal citizens as regards Turkish law, as they had been before the signing of the Treaty. Their legal equality was now expressed, *inter alia,* in the abolition of their two fixed seats in the pre-war Turkish parliament. Henceforth, whenever a Jew was elected to the National Assembly, he obtained his seat not as a Jew, but as a Turk. There were years in which not even one Jewish deputy was elected. Despite legal equality, there is no doubt that the political status of the Jews in this period worsened, especially during Ataturk's rule (1923–1938) and even up to 1944. At these times, there was conspicuous discrimination against them on the part of the authorities,[33] which was evident in various spheres.

The law forbidding religious instruction in schools applied also to the Jews, so that they could not teach religion and the Hebrew language in the Jewish educational institutions. Thus there grew up a generation of Jews, few of whom could read Hebrew and the majority of whom did not recognize the religion of their fathers. Religious marriages were forbidden in the state, although Jews were permitted to hold a religious ceremony after the civil marriage. Jewish, Muslim and Christian religious leaders were forbidden to grow beards or to wear robes. Synagogues were confiscated, as were mosques, and turned into museums. Discrimination against the Jews was very evident from the fact that the authorities did not give financial support to the Jewish schools, notwithstanding requests for assistance, and despite the fact that these schools were subject, like all state schools, to the Ministry of Education curriculum.

Although Jews were recruited into the army, like all Turkish citizens, they were not trained with arms, but were given assignments in services, as clerks, as labourers digging trenches and similar jobs, and, in contrast to the previous period in the days of the Republic, they never attained the rank of officer. It is not clear to what extent this discrimination was exercised by virtue of the law; at all events, in 1937 it was reported that the Turkish authorities were about to permit the minorities to serve in the army with rights equal to those of the other citizens. Even if this promise was fulfilled, practically nothing changed until 1945. In that year, for the first time, two Jews were accepted into the military academy and since then Jews have been serving in the army like all Turkish nationals for a period of 18 months.[34]

Since the end of the 'twenties, practically no Jews have remained in the civil service, those who had been employed there having been dismissed together with the foreign officials. Jews who worked for the railroads, which were owned by foreign companies, also began to be dismissed, although after the Second World War, there was a slight change, and the Jews were employed again, mainly in the lowest grades.[35] Today, too, the number of Jews employed in the civil service is small, although one of the reasons for this may be the lack of interest in such work on the part of the Jews. In the 'thirties a number of Jewish professors and lecturers, most of them of German and Austrian origin, were on the staff of Istanbul University. Since their departure, a Jew is very seldom appointed to such a post. It is difficult to determine, however, whether there is discrimination in this field, since the intellectuals among the Turkish Jews tend to emigrate.

During the 'thirties and 'forties, the authorities made efforts to transfer commerce from the foreigners and the minorities to Muslim Turks. This they did by giving preference to Muslims in granting import and export licences. In order to hasten this process, a Varlık Vergisi (property tax) law was introduced, which ruined many Jews, among others.*

Worse trouble was the lot of the Jews in European Turkey—Thrace (Trakya). In July 1934 Muslim crowds stormed Jewish homes and plundered their property. Within a few days, 3,000 out of the 13,000 Jews of Trakya and Chanakal'a (Çanakkale) fled to Istanbul and Asian Turkey. Another report estimated that the majority of the Jews of the Trakya area left, especially from Adrianople, fleeing from the rioters. Since the disturbances occurred in many places at one time, it is difficult to assume that this was only an isolated incident. The accepted explanation is that the authorities were interested in clearing the border area of strangers and members of the minorities, and, since the district governor did not succeed in persuading them to leave, the disturbances broke out. This version may be correct, despite the fact that Kemal Ataturk, President of Turkey, ordered the cessation of the rioting and the return of the plundered property to its owners. Whether initiated by the local authorities or by others, this anti-Jewish outburst was the gravest known by the Turkish Jews in the past hundred years. It was also accompanied by the publication of inciting material.[36] From then on, inciters against the Jews appeared from time to time. On the eve of the Second World War, a demand was heard that Jews be prevented from entering Turkey, but the authorities stressed that there be no distinction between Jews and non-Jews.[37] In 1948 and thereafter, several Turkish newspapers published anti-Jewish news and articles, part of them influenced by Arab propaganda, and perhaps also financed by the Arab States. There were also papers which attacked the Turkish Government for permitting Turkish

* See pp. 97–98.

Jews to travel to Palestine. In 1955, during the demonstrations against the union of Cyprus and Greece (Enosis), strangers were molested and shops plundered, among them those of Jews, especially in Istanbul; this caused alarm among the Turkish Jews and stepped up emigration to Israel. In 1959, there appeared in Turkey an anti-Jewish book entitled *Turkey, Here is Your Enemy* by Juad Rifat Atilhan.[38] In the Turkish parliamentary election campaign of 1969, the right-wing parties and especially the newspaper *Bügün* published anti-Jewish articles. Jews were accused of smuggling and injuring the country's economy. The Turkish government ordered the closing down of the paper and its editor only escaped detention by leaving Turkey.

All these are only symptoms of the deteriorating plight of the Turkish Jews, undoubtedly due to increased chauvinism in this state. But, on the whole, during this entire period, and particularly since 1945, Jews experienced favourable political conditions in comparison with the circumstances of Jews in the Arab countries, for no virulent anti-Semitic movement emerged in Turkey and the Turks were not particularly interested in the Palestine problem. Even during the period of the Second World War, when many Germans were active in Turkey, then a neutral country, no Nazi propaganda was permitted. The Turani movement, which spread the idea of the superiority of the Turkish race, including propaganda against Jews since they were not Turanis, was prohibited and a number of its active members—army officers, students and journalists—were banished in 1944.[39] The Turkish Government also concerned itself with the fate of Turkish Jewish families in Paris, where they suffered during the War from the Nuremberg laws complied with by the Vichy Government; a number of these Jews were rescued and transferred to Istanbul at the beginning of 1943. Even Jews of non-Turkish origin were treated humanely by the Turkish authorities. In 1933, they invited scores of German Jewish professors and lecturers to Turkey, appointing them to the Istanbul University and refusing to hand them over to the German Legation in Ankara when the latter requested this in 1942. During the War, the Turkish authorities also allowed Jewish Agency representatives to be active in Turkey on behalf of European Jewry and permitted the passage of Jews from Europe through Turkey if they were in possession of entry visas to Palestine.[40]

The Jews, on their part, made efforts, during the period of the present Republic to become acclimatized in the state, particularly in all matters pertaining to the study of the Turkish language. Indeed, the youth studied the state language at school, but for the older generation a special effort was required. In 1928 the President of the Béné Bérith Organization in Turkey, Henri Soriano, appealed to the Jews to study and to spread the Turkish language. In 1931 Jewish societies were founded in Izmir and Milas for this purpose, and in 1934 a similar organization was established in Istanbul on the initiative of Henri Soriano, Marcel Franco and Moshe Cohen (Tekinalp). Furthermore, Jewish intellectuals published leaflets in which they called on their co-religionists to study the Turkish language (Abraham Galanté's *Citizen, speak Turkish,* Istanbul 1925) and appealed for the Turkification of all the state's inhabitants (Moshe Cohen-Tekinalp, *Türkleşmèk* (Turkification), Istanbul, 1928). These two Jews, as well as Albert Shmuel, called Birtal, considered themselves Turks of the Mosaic religion.

On the other hand, there is no evidence that the Jews joined the political parties in large numbers, except for the opposition party. In August 1930, Kemal Ataturk permitted one single party to constitute an opposition to his own party—the *Serbest Cumhuriyet Fırkası* (Liberal Republican Party). A sister of the President, Maqbula, was among the first to join it, but when it was dissolved in November of the same year and many of its members were arrested, there was a high proportion of Jews among those detained.[41]

Finally, during all these years the Turkish authorities have not allowed the Jews to take part in any Zionist activity, just as they have not permitted Turks to maintain contacts with organizations having their centres abroad; they do not, however, prohibit the maintenance of contacts between the Turkish Jews and the State of Israel and its representatives. In August 1953, they permitted, for the first time, two Turkish Jews to participate in the World Zionist Congress convening in Geneva, but they forbade the Jews to establish a communal organization embracing all the Jews of Turkey, and sometimes also intervened in the elections to the Istanbul Community Council.

Since 1945, under American influence, more and more freedom has been granted the minorities. Synagogues which had been confiscated by the authorities, as in Chanakal'a (Çanakkale) and Chorlu (Çorlu), were returned to the Jews.[42] They were allowed to teach Hebrew and religion in Jewish schools, and since the mass emigration from Turkey to Israel in 1948–1950, the Jews remaining in Turkey feel very secure (most of them are in Istanbul). As a minority of 0.3% in the entire state and 2%–3% in Istanbul, there is no danger to their existence. It is obvious, of course, that should there be political agitation in the country, this situation could change.

Iraq

The orders and laws promulgated between 1839 and 1914 pertaining to the Jews of Turkey applied also to Iraq, so that there too there was an improvement in the legal status of the Jews: they became citizens with equal rights and ceased to pay *jizya* (poll-tax); instead they paid a collective tax exempting them from military service. In 1909 this was also abolished and the Jews were required, like the other citizens of the Empire, to serve in the army. The Chief Rabbinate regulations applied also to Baghdad, whose Chief Rabbi received his appointment from the Sultan in Istanbul. In practice, too, the Jews' position improved. In 1876, when the first parliament was convened, the Baghdad Jews were represented by one deputy and when parliamentary life was resumed in 1908, they received representation for the second time. Jews were also appointed to Government courts and district and municipal councils, and a few also to the civil service, but many young people who were prepared to enter officers' schools in Baghdad were unable to do so. In 1912, the Chief Rabbi of Baghdad felt himself constrained to protest in Istanbul against the small number accepted.[43]

As a result of the positive attitude displayed by the Turkish governors who ruled in Baghdad the Jews felt more secure, so much so that a few began to leave the Jewish quarters in Baghdad, moving to mixed neighbourhoods,[44] and from Baghdad to cities and villages where no Jews had lived before.* Before 1914, only one governor had been hostile to the Jews. This was Musṭafa 'Āṣim, who governed in 1889. That year a plague broke out in Baghdad and, to avoid its spreading, he forbade the Jews to leave the city. During that same plague, Rabbi Abdalla Somekh died and out of their great esteem for him, the Jews decided to bury him near the grave of Joshua' the High Priest who, according to tradition, is buried outside Baghdad. In his anger, Governor 'Āṣim dismissed the four Jewish judges from office and arrested a number of notables. Following British intervention the governor was removed from office at the end of 1889.[45]

In the district of Kurdistan also, the local governors failed to establish a stable regime and at times they extorted from the people as much taxes as they could, apart from the taxes and gifts which the Jews were required to offer, as were all the small Kurdish tribes, to the big tribes under whose protection they lived. There were also cases of attacks on the Jews in Kirkuk (May 1895), Keu Sanjaq (1889 and 1896), and in other places.[46]

During this period, and up to 1914, there was a single case of an attack on Jews in Baghdad. After the Young Turks seized power in July 1908, the Baghdad Jews revealed their joy openly, which provoked a revolt by a Muslim group opposing the revolution. On October 15, 1908, they fell upon the Jews in the city, an attack which lasted several hours, until some Muslim notables intervened to stop it.[47]

A more difficult period faced the Jews with the outbreak of the First World War, which lasted up to the British occupation of Baghdad in 1917, and of Kirkuk, Mosul and Arbīl in 1918. During the war years, many Jews were recruited into the army and dispatched to the front. From others money was extorted, at times under torture, to finance the requirements of the army garrisoned nearby. Shirkers who

* See pp. 73–74.

were caught were hanged. Hundreds of the mobilized Jews did not return from the front.[48]

Small wonder that Jews and non-Jews alike in Baghdad and the north fled to southern Iraq. The day of the British entry into Baghdad in March 1917 was celebrated annually thereafter by the Jews with prayers and thanksgiving.[49]

Apparently it was not only their hardships during the War that impelled the Jews of Baghdad and the north to rejoice at the British occupation, but they hoped it would enable them to enjoy economic prosperity and good political conditions similar to those under which their Iraqi brethren in India and in Basra were living.

THE PERIOD OF BRITISH OCCUPATION AND THE BRITISH MANDATE

During the British occupation—which lasted until 1921—the Jews enjoyed full equality of rights, complete freedom and a feeling of security, so that most of the Iraqi Jews apparently felt themselves British citizens, or as if they were living on British soil. Many of them also became rich, some acquired jobs in the British Administration, particularly in Baghdad and Basra. They would have liked British rule to continue and it did not occur to them that Britain would hand over Iraq to an Arab regime. When, in January 1919, Muslim nationalists petitioned the British authorities to appoint a Muslim king in Iraq, the Jews (followed by the Christians) reacted by submitting an opposing petition urging the continuation of British rule. Only after much persuasion on the part of the British and a declaration by the Shī'ite Muslim Shaykhs ensuring the lives, honour and property of all the minorities, did twenty Jewish dignitaries in Baghdad put their signatures to an agreement on the establishment of Arab rule.[50] In October 1920, a provisional Arab government was set up and in August 1921, Fayṣal, son of Husayn of the Ḥijāz, was crowned king of Iraq under British mandate.

During the entire mandatory period, the Iraqi Jews enjoyed complete equality with the Muslims. Minority rights were ensured by the Iraq Constitution of 1924, and the Jews were given representation in the Iraqi parliament which was opened that year, by five members, and later (in the years 1925–1946) by four deputies and one senator. Jews continued to be accepted into the civil service as officials and judges. In the years 1920–1925, with a brief interruption, a Jew held the office of Minister of Finance of Iraq. The Jews continued to enjoy the right which they had had in the past to observe the dictates of their religion, to open their own schools and to be accepted without restriction in Government educational institutions of all kinds, including institutions of higher learning. From March 1921 to July 1922, a Zionist society was active in Iraq, with Government permission. In July 1922, the society's permit was not renewed, although it was allowed by the authorities to function until 1929. This was perhaps the only way in which the Jews were discriminated against before Iraq achieved independence. On the other hand, the authorities forcibly broke up the first anti-Zionist demonstration, which took place in Baghdad in February 1928, during the visit of Alfred Mond (Lord Melchett), the British Zionist. They even closed down a newspaper and expelled students of the law and teachers' training faculties who incited the people and participated in the demonstration.[51]

Following the outbreak of disturbances in Palestine in August 1929, the authorities began taking an active part in the struggle against Zionism in Iraq. Soon after, Zionist activity was forbidden, and Palestinian and Jewish newspapers were not admitted into the State. Instructors from Palestine teaching in Iraq were expelled from the country. But until 1934, no harm was done to Jews as Jews. There were no cases of discrimination against them on the part of the Government and no injury done them by the Muslim populace, although some newspapers published articles against Zionism, and sometimes against the Iraqi Jews. There were also cases of stones being thrown at a Jew, of a Jew being insulted and beaten up, but these were not organized attacks and they did not assume serious dimensions.

This was not only a period of progress in the economic, educational and social circumstances of the Jews: it was also the beginning of a process of their Iraqization, which was evidenced, especially, in the emergence of the first Jewish poets and writers writing in the Arab language as Iraqis.* Contributing to this process was undoubtedly the Arab education they received in state, and even in Jewish schools, as well as the feeling that the end of British rule was approaching and it was therefore desirable to prove their loyalty to the Arab regime, so as not to be suspected of being disloyal. This process of Iraqization developed throughout the 'twenties and it was only in 1934 that some of the Jewish youth began to doubt that they could ever live as Iraqis with equal rights. By June 1941, when riots against the Jews broke out, the number of those despairing of this possibility had grown.

INDEPENDENT IRAQ

After Iraq received its independence in October 1932, and particularly after the death of King Fayṣal the First in September 1933, the regime weakened. Fayṣal's son, Ghāzī, succeeded him as king: he was young, chauvinistic and weak. He was unable, and perhaps unwilling, to prevent the rise of nationalistic forces and he permitted such groups to conduct political activities. The leaders of these organizations were Arab refugees from Syria and Palestine who had found asylum in Iraq. At

* For Jewish poets and writers, see p. 125.

that time, too, the German envoy, Dr. F. Grobba, began to undertake pro-German activities. In several Government offices, ministers, directors-general and senior officials were appointed who were imbued with Nazi propaganda. The weakness of King Ghāzī's rule was also evident from the fact that, until he was killed in April 1939, five military revolts occurred in Iraq during which Prime Ministers were removed and replaced on the army's instructions.[52]

Against the background of the foregoing events, the changes in store for the Jews may be anticipated. True, from the legal standpoint, nothing changed. No law against the Jews was promulgated. Four deputies (1925–1946), and later (1946–1951) six deputies and one senator continued to represent the Jews in the parliament. But the attitude of the government and the Arab masses deteriorated.

The first sign of discrimination against Jews (and not only Zionists) was the dismissal in September 1934, immediately on the appointment of a new Minister, of dozens of civil servants from the Ministry of Economics and Transport. Non-Jews were also dismissed by him for organizational reasons, but they were re-engaged after a short interval; following a protest, by the Jews, a small number was also re-engaged from among the dismissed Jews.[53] In 1935, the Ministry of Education instructed the state secondary schools and those of higher education to accept only a limited number of Jews. These directives, which were not published, remained in force until the mass emigration, but it was always possible for some Jews to bypass them by several means, usually through contact with the school directors or with other personalities in the state. Jews wishing to emigrate to Palestine, or even to visit there, had to overcome many obstacles placed in their path by the Government, and again, not by virtue of law. Hebrew instruction in Jewish schools was also prohibited—it was permitted only to teach the reading of the Bible, without translation and interpretation of it.

In 1936, immediately after the outbreak of the disturbances in Palestine, incitements began against Jews, with some incidents of physical injury. On September 13, 1936, the Committee for the Defence of Palestine in Baghdad, headed by a deputy of the Iraqi parliament, Sa'īd Thābit, circulated manifestos against the Jews. After three days, on the eve of the Jewish New Year 5697 (16.9.1936), two Jews were murdered, and the following day, which was proclaimed "Palestine Day", gatherings were held in mosques, followed by demonstrations. One Jew was killed and another wounded that day. On the Day of Atonement (September 27) a home-made bomb was thrown into a synagogue in Baghdad; by chance, it did not explode. Some local newspapers called on the Jews to publish a declaration stating that they had no interest in Palestine, and out of fear a declaration to this effect was published, signed by the President of the Community Committee, Rabbi Sason Kadoori. But it was of no avail. Assaults and stone-throwing continued, and on several occasions bombs were hurled into the Jewish club, until the Jews felt compelled to close their businesses during the days of October 7–9. This had a bad effect on the commercial life of the capital. Only after the Government published an announcement threatening punishment to those causing incitement did the Jews return to their work, although for some time afterwards they shut themselves into their homes at night. The attacks went on, and some days later two more Jews were murdered.[54]

After the first military revolt of Bakir Ṣidqī on October 29, 1936, attacks on Jews ceased. This respite was due to Ṣidqī's opposition to all disturbances and his desire to make reforms within the country, being less interested in external affairs. In July 1937, however, the growing opposition to his regime succeeded in staging a demonstration in Baghdad, during which two Jews were killed. The murder of Bakir Ṣidqī on August 8 and the fall of his government aggravated the plight of the Jews. The new government revealed more sympathy for the Palestine Arabs. Between December 1937 and January 1938 and during August–October 1938, there were numerous attacks on Jews. In August 1938, 33 dignitaries of the Jewish community in Baghdad, in their fear, sent a telegram to the British Colonial Office and to the League of Nations expressing opposition to Zionism, but this did not put an end to the attacks. In October, the Government began to take a stronger hand against the inciters. From then until 1941 there are records of only isolated incidents.[55]

Outside of Baghdad, except for the murder of a Jew in Basra in 1936, incidents are unknown, whether in 1929 or in the years 1936–1940. The reason for this may be that there were no Palestinians and Syrians outside the capital to incite the populace—their leaders were all in Baghdad. The German Legation's activity, too, was restricted to Baghdad. The Arab masses did not hate the Jews, so that in the absence of inciters from outside, the Jews were able to live in peace, although not entirely without fear.

This also accounts for the fact that no *Farhūd* (pogrom) against the Jews occurred outside Baghdad in 1941. In May of that year, it is true, there was a case of looting in Basra, but there were no victims. This happened when the city governor fled from Basra; during the two ensuing days, until one of the Muslim notables had the situation under his control, the masses plundered Jewish shops. In the months of April–May 1941 demonstrations were staged in the cities of Mosul, Kirkuk, Arbīl, and 'Amāra, threats were heard against Jews, and there were cases of slight injuries. In Baghdad, however, the Jews suffered during riots in 1941, the likes of which had not occurred during the previous hundred years.

"FARHŪD" (POGROM) IN BAGHDAD[56]

After the Iraqi Regent, Abd-al-Ilāh, fled the capital on April 1, 1941, Rashīd 'Ālī al-Kaylānī seized the reins of government, and on the 18th of the month formed a cabinet among whose members was Yūnus al-Sab'āwī, a man known for his hostility to the Jews. From then until the flight of Rashīd 'Ālī, Hāj Amīn al-Husaynī, the Mufti of Jerusalem, and many of their followers to Iran, at the end of May 1941, the Jews endured provocations, beatings and arrests, particularly from members of the youth squads, who were entrusted with guarding the city. The Baghdad Jews, who anxiously anticipated what was in store for them, tried to appease the rulers by raising their financial contributions to the Iraqi army and the Red Crescent, the first-aid organization. To their great surprise, however, Rashīd 'Ālī and his followers fled at dawn on Thursday, May 29, as the British started to advance, reaching the gates of the capital that day. The same day a "Committee for Internal Security" was set up.

Yūnus al-Sab'āwī, who was the only member of Rashīd 'Ālī's government not to run away, summoned the President of the Jewish community, Sason Kadoori, on Friday, May 30, and ordered him to notify the Jews that they were not to leave their homes for the next three days (May 31–June 2) which included Saturday and the Feast of Shavu'ot (Pentecost). Presumably, al-Sab'āwī, who had been prevented by Rashīd 'Ālī from carrying out a massacre of the Jews, was anxious to exploit this opportunity to riot against the Jews, using the youth who had been organized and armed by him beforehand. Fortunately for the Jews, al-Sab'āwī was arrested by the "Committee for Internal Security" and expelled to Iran that same day. Immediately thereafter the Committee published three announcements, giving notice of the disbandment of the youth groups, their obligation to turn in the arms in their possession, and threatening the population with punishment for any disorder.

From that hour, the Jews in Baghdad had a feeling that the danger was over. Rashīd 'Ālī and his people were no longer in the city. The Jews were about to celebrate joyfully the Sabbath and two days of the Feast. Their joy intensified when they learned on the Sabbath that the Iraqi Regent and the members of the previous anti-German regime were to return on Sunday. That Sunday, June 1, was a triple holiday for the Jews: it was the Feast of Pentecost, it was a day to celebrate their deliverance from the pro-Nazi regime, and a day to celebrate the return of their protectors. Their happiness was not concealed. Many left their homes to visit friends and relatives, others went on walks. Jewish dignitaries, like the members of other communities, went out to greet the Regent and his entourage at the airport. On their return from the reception on foot, as they were crossing the bridge connecting al-Karkh (where the airport was) with al-Ruṣāfa (where the city was situated), they were attacked by soldiers. One Jew was murdered, and more than sixteen wounded, in the presence of the civil and military police. Shortly thereafter another Jew was killed, this time in the main street of Baghdad, Ghāzī Street. Another nine Jews were murdered in various parts of the city. A report, written by an Investigating

Committee appointed by the Government on July 8, 1941 stated that all these attacks were carried out by the army with the assistance of some civilians, without the police arresting anyone or protecting the Jews.

Apparently, the Jewish masses were unaware of the murders committed before noon and continued on their rounds of family visits. At six o'clock that evening a brutal massacre took place. Jews travelling by bus were forcibly pulled out, slaughtered on the spot and run over by the buses. During the evening and night hours, until after midnight, soldiers, policemen and members of the youth squads stormed the Jewish quarters—they murdered, raped, wounded, plundered and set houses on fire.

The next morning "at six o'clock, some soldiers began to loot and pillage, and to break down doors", states the Investigating Committee's report. Soldiers killed, robbed and removed looted property in military vehicles. Moreover, on this day the rioters were joined by a mob numbering many thousands, some of whom had come from the slums of the al-Karkh section of Baghdad, having heard about the looting going on and wishing to get their share of it.

Only after the chairman of the Committee for Internal Security realized the imminent danger to the city presented by the mob, which he reckoned was liable to inflict damage on non-Jewish property as well, did he decide to ask the Regent's permission to shoot at the mob. The Regent, Abd-al-Ilāh, as indicated, was in the city during the entire time the pogrom was going on. At five o'clock that evening, a curfew was imposed on the city and units of Kurdish soldiers shot into the crowds; within less than an hour the rioters fled, leaving part of the loot in the streets. Scores of rioters were killed by the Kurdish soldiers' fire. Quiet subsequently prevailed, though some sporadic cases of attacks on Jews occurred on Tuesday and Wednesday.

Of the various estimates made, the most reasonable is that 170–180 Jews were killed in the riots and several hundred wounded, and Jewish property worth £1 million or more was looted. Most of the killed and wounded fell during the first day and that night, and the greater part of the looting took place on the second day. On the first day the rioters were armed and imbued with anti-Jewish propaganda. They came to murder, first of all, then to rob. On the second day the number of victims was relatively small, despite the fact that the number of rioters was very much larger that day, for the majority of them were unarmed civilians whose only purpose was to loot. These crowds, although residing in Baghdad, had not been indoctrinated with deadly hatred of Jews. Looting seemed to them something that was permitted, even if the robbed were Muslims. The Government Investigating Committee's report leaves no room for doubt that the chief rioters were members of the army and the police. The report even clearly lays the blame on three of the four members of the Commiteee for Internal Security, the Director-General of the

Police, the Governor of Baghdad and the Commander of the First Division. Only the president of the Committee, Arshad al-'Umarī, is not mentioned among the guilty. But there is no doubt that he, as well as the Regent, knew what was happening during those two days. It is the irony of fate that the single case in the last hundred years of riots against the Jews of Iraq occurred just when the pro-Nazi regime had vanished from that country, and Abd al-Ilāh, Nurī Sa'īd and Jamīl al Madfa'ī were in the capital and large British forces stood at the gates of the city, none of them lifting a finger. Apparently the pro-British leaders were certain that the army and police, and the youth for years incited with pro-German ideas, would avenge Rashīd 'Ālī's failure. It was convenient that the Jews be the scapegoat.

On the morrow of the massacre, the Jewish Community in Baghdad now had to rehabilitate the injured. For this purpose they set up one committee to collect funds for the immediate rehabilitation of the sufferers and another to care for the orphans. The first committee concluded its task speedily, for at that time there was economic prosperity in Iraq, and it was not difficult to collect some tens of thousands of pounds sterling among the Iraqi Jews. The committee dealing with the orphans saw to their livelihood and their studies until the girls married and the boys completed secondary school. It completed its task in June 1951, when the last orphan left for Israel.[57]

Despite the efforts to calm them, the Baghdad Jews were stunned. Although they were not without fear in the period preceding the massacre, they did not expect such a calamity. Many tried, and succeeded, to obtain exit permits to India, others—to Palestine. There were also many who entered Palestine without certificates and without documents. Some of the youth, on the other hand, thought it necessary to establish a defence force which would resist a possible further outbreak. And such a possibility existed, in view of the continuing advance of the German forces in North Africa. The Muslim youth did not conceal their joy, for instance, on the day Tobruk fell (June 21, 1942). During many months, proclamations were circulated in Baghdad in which Jews were called upon to leave the country, and slogans flourished stating clearly that the Jews were to await the coming of "the Great Feast", when a greater massacre than that which occurred on the Feast of Pentecost would be carried out. Thus, there came into existence in Iraq the underground organizations *Shabāb al-Inqādh* (rescue youth), "Unity and Progress", "Community of Free Jews", and in April 1942, the *Hagana* organization. The latter was established by emissaries from Palestine who had arrived in Baghdad. All these organizations were small and weak, except for the *Hagana,* which was the only one remaining in Iraq until the mass emigration to Israel.

The great majority of Iraqi Jews, however, continued their work without realizing what was in store for them. Some developed the theory that there was no fear of renewed riots, since those of June 1941 had occurred when Iraq was without a government, and as long as the regime of Abd-al-Ilāh and Nūrī Sa'īd existed, they felt no harm would befall the Jews. Whether there were many or few who believed this, apparently the fact that there was no place for them to go and that nothing further happened after June 1941, as well as the fact that economic prosperity was being enjoyed in Iraq, by the Jews as well, led them to feel secure. Another reason was that the authorities stopped discriminating against Jews in the first year or two after the massacre. Thus the Jewish educational and health institutions continued to develop, Jewish life gradually returned to normal, and there were even those who were not afraid to build themselves villas in mixed neighbourhoods.

THE LAST FIVE YEARS OF THE EXILE IN IRAQ: 1945–1950

After several years of relative peace and quiet, the Palestine problem arose and anxiety now began to gnaw at the hearts of the Iraqi Jews. When it became known in Iraq that on November 2, 1945 riots against Jews had taken place in Cairo,* Arab nationalists called for a mass gathering on November 5, which forebode the worst. The gathering did not take place, however, because the Minister of the Interior prohibited it. Tension steadily increased, and on May 5, 1946, students organized demonstrations to take place in the streets of Baghdad on May 10, the day on which the conclusions of the Anglo-American Committee of Enquiry into Palestine were to be published. The Jews again began to hear threats as to what was in store for them. That year the *mujtahid,* the highest ranking minister of the Shī'ite sect in Iraq, joined the campaign against the Jews. At the beginning of 1946, he published a *fatwa* (religious law ruling) against the sale of land to Jews in all Arab countries. Propaganda against the Jews was intensified in 1947, becoming particularly dangerous when the Special Committee on Palestine was to publish its decision on the subject of the partition of Palestine. The Jews anxiously awaited the morrow. Fortunately for them, at this very time the political parties directed public attention to Iraq's domestic problems. The country's economic situation had begun to deteriorate, the trade deficit was steadily rising, and Iraq's sterling balance from the Second World War declined. The drought in 1947/48 also added to the mounting food prices, and long queues formed for bread. The communists, who were active in the underground, took advantage of the situation to organize frequent demonstrations against the regime. However, when the United Nations resolution was published on November 29, 1947, public attention was diverted to the Palestine problem. Demonstrations were staged in Iraq and protests voiced against the resolution. Iraq sent volunteers to Qāwuqjī's army in Palestine and fund-raising cam-

* See p. 49.

paigns were organized for "the rescue of Palestine" from the Jews; even Jews were made to contribute to them, and the president of the Community, Rabbi Sason Kadoori, was compelled to issue a declaration regarding Arab rights in Palestine.[58]

After a few weeks public attention was again diverted from the Palestine problem. At the beginning of January 1948, a statement was published to the effect that the discussions between Iraq and Britain regarding the signing of a new treaty were proceeding successfully. The opposition parties, who had set up an inter-party front, immediately organized a struggle against this treaty, including demonstrations. The parties saw to it that shops and businesses of Jews and others were not harmed, so that the masses' attention would not be diverted from the main subject—the Treaty of Portsmouth. On the publication of the Treaty on January 16, there were more demonstrations which became stormy; on January 21 the Government resigned and the Treaty was abrogated. Demonstrations of mourning were held for those killed in preceding ones, and demonstrations of joy were organized to celebrate the annulment of the Treaty.

After some weeks, this subject, too, ceased to occupy public opinion and the Palestine problem again appeared on the pages of the Iraqi press. On the death of Abd-al-Qādir al-Husaynī in 1948, in the vicinity of Jerusalem, the demonstrations were resumed in Iraq, this time accompanied by the cry: "Death to the Jews!" School pupils organized sit-down and hunger strikes to bring pressure on the Government to send an Iraqi army to the assistance of the Palestine Arabs. On April 27, 1948, a Jewish synagogue in Baghdad was attacked and its ritual articles desecrated. But in those same days the communists staged demonstrations in which they called for bread and work, and used such slogans as "Long live our Jewish brethren and death to Zionism, the enemy of the Jews!"[59]

Tension continued. The Jews, terrified of the Arab youngsters' threats, could do nothing except to place the *Hagana* organization on the alert from Friday evening, May 14. This organization had expanded since its establishment in Iraq in 1942, but it was not very strong in Baghdad and it was not clear for how long it could defend the Jews. Fortunately, it was not necessary to put it to the test, for the evening of the day on which the State of Israel was proclaimed, the Iraqi Government imposed martial law in the country, and prohibited gatherings and bearing of arms. After May 15, the state of alert in the *Hagana* ranks was cancelled.

During this period, Jews in the other Iraqi cities also lived under tension, except for those in the Kurdistan region, since the Kurds were sympathetic towards the Jews.[60] But in this region, too, in the cities of Arbīl, Kirkuk and Mosul, anti-Zionist demonstrations were staged.

A few days after the establishment of the State of Israel the Jews were given to understand that there was no danger of riots, but that there would be difficult days ahead of them. Jews began to be arrested and brought before military courts on various charges, such as receiving regards from a friend or relative in Palestine. The police conducted searches in Jewish homes for a letter, a picture of Palestine, or a Hebrew book. Many Jews, therefore, burned every letter or book in their possession, and even tore off the Magen David from their prayer shawls. Nevertheless, members of a family were sometimes arrested even if they did not carry Zionist symbols, the reason given being for purposes of "clarification" or something similar. Things became even more serious when, on June 28, 1948, Ṣādiq al-Baṣṣām, who was known even in the 'thirties for hatred of the Jews, became Minister of Defence. A few days later, in July 1948, the word "Zionism" was entered into Article 51 of the criminal law. This article established that communists were a group endangering the security of the state, and set the maximum penalty for membership in that group as death. Henceforth, anyone accused of Zionism could also expect prolonged imprisonment or even death. It was not difficult to make such an accusation, for under martial law two witnesses were sufficient to find a Jew guilty of Zionism, and there was no appeal against a judgment of the military court. By virtue of this article, hundreds of Jews were placed on trial in the months of June–September 1948. Most of them were fined, others were sentenced to various terms of imprisonment and one was sentenced to death. The person in question, Shafīq 'Adas, a Jew born in Syria who had lived in Iraq for many years and had acquired great riches, was publicly hanged. His contacts with the heads of the State did not succeed in saving him, for the Minister of Defence was not prepared to yield in this matter. After this hanging, however, the Minister was forced to resign (September 27, 1948), the number of military courts in Iraq was reduced from four to one, and fewer Jews were brought before this court thereafter.[61] Many Jews were expelled to far-off cities without standing trial—a punishment often meted out in the past as well.

In September 1949, a new wave of searches and arrests commenced. At that time a young Jew, who until 1946 had been a member of *Hehalutz* (an underground movement for spreading Zionist teachings), and later joined the communist party, was imprisoned. Since he was a communist at the time of his arrest, he sought to buy his freedom by revealing the address of one of his former comrades in *Hehalutz*. With this address in hand the police began searching for other members of the underground *Hehalutz* and *Hagana* organizations. Many were arrested and tortured. Others, especially commanders in these two organizations, were smuggled into Iran. The Jewish community was terrified, and, apparently influenced by the underground organizations, a group of Jewish mothers staged a demonstration against the President of the Community, Rabbi Sason Kadoori, calling on him to take action to have their arrested sons released. The Rabbi was compelled to resign from his post in November 1949. But the community remained tense until December 1949 when martial law was abolished throughout Iraq.

Throughout the period from 1945 to 1948, and particularly in the year 1948, the Jews were badly hit economically as well. In particular, the number of import and export licenses granted them was reduced, Jewish banks were forbidden to engage in currency transfers, and other restrictions were imposed on them.

All these oppressive measures undermined the Jews' trust in the Government and they were prepared to leave Iraq at any price. From the time of the abolition of martial law at the end of 1949 until March 1950, thousands of Jews were smuggled across the border to Iran. Most of them found an Arab smuggler for themselves; a few were smuggled across with the help of the Zionist underground movement. When, in March 1950, a Government law was published permitting Jews so desiring to leave the State, if they relinquished their citizenship, large numbers registered, and within a year—from June 1950 to June 1951—about 110,000 Jews emigrated legally to Israel. Besides these, some 13,000 Iraqi Jews left for Israel by illegal routes, small groups escaping almost every day. The masses of the Iraqi Jews left despite the fact that they were not permitted to take with them more than 50 pounds sterling per adult and 20 pounds sterling per child. Some of them succeeded in selling their property, but because of the great number doing so and the ruling of the religious law *(fatwa)* of Shaykh Muhammad al-Khāliṣī prohibiting the purchase of Jewish property, the prices they received were trifling. Others abandoned their possessions in Iraq and emigrated penniless. In March 1951 the Government froze the property of those who left or were about to leave the country. The total value of the property frozen was 150–200 million dollars.

In attempting to explain the mass departure of the Jews from Iraq, we note that it cannot be ascribed to legal measures taken against them. The only law enacted applying to Jews specifically was that of March 1950 permitting them to leave the country, and the only anti-Jewish law was that for freezing their property. But many directives to Government departments discriminated against Jews in many ways and although they succeeded in circumventing these measures by various means, they regarded the period of martial law (May 1948–December 1949) as foretelling the end of their lives in this State. Even the 1941 riots, which lasted two days and led to very many more lives being lost than were lost during the two years, 1948–1949, did not agitate them very much and did not move them to leave Iraq on the same scale, for they knew that the 1941 riots were the work of people incited by foreign elements and they believed that the Government was not against them. Now they realized that the Government was a hostile factor. Moreover, only a few were granted permission to enter Palestine in 1941. Now there was a Jewish State ready to receive them; now they had some place to go.

This was the end of the Iraqi exile: out of the approximately 130,000 Jews who were living there in 1949, only 6,000 remained in 1952.

If it is possible to explain the reasons for the mass departure of the Jews from

Iraq, it is difficult to find an adequate answer to the question as to what impelled the Iraqi authorities to reverse their position and permit the Jews to leave the country, despite the fact that they knew full well that they were going to Israel. Was it because of their desire to acquire the Jews' property, since Iraq was undergoing a financial crisis, or was pressure exerted on the Baghdad Government by the Western Powers? There is one other possibility: the desire of the Iraqi authorities to rid themselves of communist elements among the Jews and of the Jewish merchants and clerks, and to free their places for Muslims. In any event, it is evident that the Iraqi authorities did not anticipate a mass exit.

THE SMALL REMNANT

Following the mass departure from Iraq, the underground *Hagana* and *Hehalutz* organizations liquidated their branches, but before they succeeded in doing so, weapons were found in the possession of one *Hagana* member who was arrested together with some other members of the organization. He and one of his colleagues were condemned to death and the sentence was carried out publicly in January 1952. Thus, the Zionist underground in Iraq ended its activities in the most tragic manner.

The situation of the 6,000 Jews remaining in Iraq returned to normalcy. Their property was returned to them, they were permitted to conduct their businesses and their communal and educational institutions, and those so desiring were even permitted to apply for Iraqi passports and leave the country at any time. Many took advantage of this, leaving to visit Iran and Europe, some even returning to Iraq. When the monarchy in Iraq was abolished and Abd-al-Karīm Qassem came to power (1958–1963), their lot even improved. Qassem liberated Jewish prisoners who had been accused of communism and Zionism and expelled them from Iraq.

When Abd-al-Salām 'Ārif seized power, after killing Qassem, the situation of the Jews worsened: they were forbidden to leave the country, and later they were hampered in running their economic enterprises. Immediately after the June 1967 War in the Middle East (when only 3,000 Jews were left in the country) scores of Jewish merchants were imprisoned on the pretext of smuggling money out of the State. On March 4, 1968 an anti-Jewish law was promulgated providing that the transfer or the sale of a Jew's property should not be entered in the land register; and further providing that any amount due to a Jew from salary or commerce must be deposited in a bank account from which he may take out only a hundred dinars (equivalent of $280) a month. At the end of that year, scores of Jews were imprisoned, accused of spying for Israel. Nine of them were sentenced to death and hanged publicly on January 27, 1969, to the shouts of the jubilant crowds. Two more Jews were hanged in

August 1969, and many more were tortured to death in Iraqi jails.[61a] The Iraqi Jews endured then more difficult times than ever before, as the regime attampted to divert public attention from its failures in domestic affairs and its war against Israel. Only in mid-1971, as the result of pressure by foreign governments, did the Iraqi government stop persecuting its Jewish population. Since then, Jews have been allowed to leave Iraq, although without money or property. Many Jews have seized this opportunity and left the country. It was estimated that in mid-1972 only some 400-odd Jews were left in Iraq. Ten of them were detained in September 1972. It is assumed that they were killed in Iraqi prisons.

RELATIONS WITH THE LOCAL POPULATION

From the foregoing, it may be inferred that except for the *farhūd* in Baghdad in June 1941, which had been due to foreign elements, the Jews suffered no serious harm from the Muslim populace since the 'sixties of the 19th century. This fact, and the fact that they lived in Iraq for hundreds of years as local residents and not as foreign nationals (as was the case with the majority of the Egyptian Jews), and spoke Arabic (and not Ladino or French) should have created, *prima facie*, good relations between them and the rest of the population. We shall attempt to examine the whole complex of relations between the Jews and the other Iraqis. For lack of research on this subject according to areas of settlement, social strata, economic status and education, the following facts must necessarily be of a general nature.

A. LANGUAGE, DRESS, NAMES AND DWELLING PLACES

The Iraqi Jews spoke Arabic at home and in the street, and Kurdish in the Kurdistan areas. Rich and poor, learned people and illiterates did not use any foreign languages even at home, unlike those Jews in Egypt, the Lebanon, Algeria, Morocco and Tunisia, where they considered it a matter of pride to speak French, even if they knew Arabic. However, the Arabic spoken by the Iraqi Jews differed from that spoken by the Muslims, both in vocabulary (the Jews used many Hebrew, Persian, Turkish, French and English words), and in syntax and pronunciation, and it was easily possible to distinguish between the two dialects. The Jews, all of whom understood the Muslim dialect and used it in talking to Muslims, were not always proficient in it. In the provincial towns, where the Jewish communities were small and there was constant daily contact with Muslims, the Jews on the whole could speak the Muslim dialect correctly and exactly, and it was not easy to distinguish whether the speaker was a Jew. On the other hand, in Baghdad, where there was a large Jewish community, of whom many, especially the women, did not often have any contact with an Arab school or grocery, the Jews did not speak the Muslim dialect with its correct accent, and sometimes addressed themselves to a Muslim in the Jewish dialect, which occasionally led to ridicule on the part of the Muslim listener. The men who had studied in a state secondary school or whose business required daily contact with Muslims had complete command of the Muslim dialect, but they constituted only a part of the Baghdad Jews. Thus, despite the fact that the Jews in Iraq spoke the local tongue, their language was different and the dissimilarity between the two dialects lessened only slightly in the last generation.

The same could be said regarding attire. In the Ottoman period it was easy to distinguish between a Jew and a Muslim by the headdress worn; this has not always been possible in recent times. In the Ottoman period, most of the Jews in the Iraqi cities were accustomed to wear a turban (fez or tarbush) on their heads, while few Muslims wore this kind of headdress. After the British occupation, some of the Jews took to wearing the tropical hat, but the Arabs did not do so. During the rule of King Fayṣal, the majority of the Jews went over to the Sīdāra or Fayṣaliya, which was also worn by the intellectual and rich Arabs. Of late, the majority of young Arabs and Jews have gone bareheaded.

During the Turkish period, there was a slight difference in the way Jews and Muslims dressed. The Jewish and Muslim poor men in the city wore a robe called *dishdāsha* or *thawb* by the Muslims, and the rich notables wore a sort of gown—*zibūn*. After the British occupation, however, and perhaps a short time before that, more and more Jews took to wearing European suits, while the Arabs turned only gradually to such clothes. Thus, it was possible for a British tourist visiting Iraq in the early 'twenties to point out that the Baghdad Jew, in his outward appearance, was more European than any other Iraqi.[62] In recent years the difference in attire disappeared entirely in the large cities, with most of the young people, Muslims and Jews, wearing suits.

In the last generation of Jews in Iraq, the dissimilarities in names also began to disappear. Fewer Jews were called by Biblical names, and more by Arabic and European: Fayṣal, Ghāzī, Richard, Maurice, so that it was sometimes impossible to identify Jews by their names.

Understandably, Jews lived in their own quarters in all the Iraqi cities and towns, including Kurdistan, but after the First World War, Jews began to leave the Jewish neighbourhoods in Baghdad, Basra, Arbīl, Kirkuk and Ḥilla. But on the whole those who left for the new parts of the cities were also soon concentrated in a section of their own or in a street of their own with perhaps a small number of non-Jews living there. Only in a few places—in 'Ashār in Basra, and in the city of 'Amāra—did all the Jews live in non-Jewish quarters.

From the foregoing, therefore, it may be seen that during the last hundred years

Jews, especially those in Baghdad, could be recognized by their speech, attire, names and living quarters although these marks of identification have been less conspicuous in our times.

B. DAILY LIFE

The Jewish child in Iraq apparently grew up with feelings of fear of the Muslim. A Jewish mother would frighten her son with "the Muslim is coming!", and when the boy took his first steps in the street unaccompanied by an adult, he soon understood the meaning of this threat. In almost all parts of Iraq, in the time of the Turkish as in that of Arab rule, Jewish children were insulted, slapped, and beaten by Muslim boys. Sometimes their books were snatched from them, or their hats, or other articles in their pockets. Any effort to defend themselves meant further trouble, and so the young Jew grew up in fear.

Adult Muslims, however, did not act in this way. A Shī'ite, Sunni or Kurdi Muslim notable, merchant, shaykh or wealthy man considered it his duty to protect a Jew he knew. Only the Muslim masses were easily incited against Jews, although they did not hate them. Although they were seldom harmed and they knew that a distinguished Muslim would protect them in case of need, the Jews lived in fear of the masses. In earlier periods when a Jew was attacked it was generally for the purpose of robbing him, the Arab tormenting him and stealing his goods in exactly the same way as he would to one of his own faith if he thought himself stronger and able to do so. In more recent years, however, assaults on Jews were mainly due to chauvinistic motives, especially in Baghdad. Arab propaganda, both anti-Zionist and Nazi, was rife there since the 1930's. The newspapers, the refugees from Palestine and Syria as well as the foreign missions were all in Baghdad, and there were also large numbers of secondary school pupils there. The latter were frequently the first to be incited. In the other Iraqi cities, on the other hand, not only were there none of these elements and no means to spread propaganda, but the Muslim notables in the provincial towns felt themselves responsible for the Jews. They knew them, they traded with them in the market, sometimes their sons studied in the same state school and sometimes they lived on the same street. This is why riots never occurred in the provinces of Iraq, not even in 1941.

From 1941, however, the attitude of the inhabitants towards the Jews changed for the worse, due to the widespread propaganda against Jewish Palestine and Israel, often identified with the Jewish people as a whole.

Such, in general, were the relations between Jews and Muslims. Some details on the relations between Jews and the other minorities in the State, namely, the Shī'ites, Kurds and Christians must be added.

The Shī'ites were not a minority; they constituted more than half of the non-Kurdish population in the State, and they were a decisive majority in the south. Nevertheless, they were a minority, for the reins of power were held by the Sunnis. It may be that because they were not the ruling sect, the relations between them and the Jews were normal as compared with the relations between the Shī'ites in Iran and the Yemen and the Jews there. In Iran and the Yemen the Shī'ite Muslims were in power, and their religious leaders used the Shī'ite belief that a non-Muslim is impure as an instrument for humiliating them. In Iraq, on the other hand, since they were not the ruling power, their religious leaders were unable to maltreat or humiliate Jews. In Shī'ite cities like 'Amāra and Sāmrā, however, certain cafes and bath-houses did carry signs "For Muslims only" *(Khāṣ lil-Muslimin)* or "Entry forbidden to Jews". The Shī'ite Muslims would not eat in a Jew's home, unless the food or drink had been prepared by a Shī'ite. But a Jew was not prohibited from leaving his house on a rainy day. The Jews did not even feel injured by the Shī'ites considering them impure, but viewed it as an integral part of the Shī'ite creed,

Since the 'thirties, with the increase in the number of educated people among the Shī'ites, the idea of impurity also gradually lost its effect; the enlightened Shī'ites became estranged from the tradition and even felt themselves free to drink alcoholic beverages, to eat in Jewish homes, and so on.

The Kurds were the second largest minority in Iraq, but they were a nationalist minority, not a religious one, most of them being Sunni Muslims. In northern Iraq they constituted the decisive majority of the local inhabitants. During the Ottoman period, the Kurds enjoyed a sort of autonomy which permitted them, in practice, to rule in their own district. The authorities were not always able to protect the weak among them, including the small Kurdish tribes and the Jews. These tribes were constrained to receive the protection of a large tribe by paying tax in the form of gifts and free manual labour for the head of that tribe. The protecting tribe considered it its duty to defend the tribesmen under its aegis, to demand satisfaction for an insult to any of its members, and to avenge the blood of anyone. The Kurdish Jews also lived within this framework of relations. The protection which the Jews obtained may be considered serfdom or slavery, but this was the form of society in Kurdistan.

In the last few decades, the weak could expect assistance from the authorities, especially since the Kurds lost some of their autonomy under British and Iraqi rule. Certainly, from time to time, Kurdish Jews suffered injury from Muslim Kurds, but much less so than in the Arab parts of Iraq, for the Kurds had not been affected by Nazi and Arab propaganda, and did not regard the Palestine problem as one concerning them. At the same time, no deep friendship was formed between Jews and Kurds, and Jews never participated in the Kurdish revolts.

As to the attitude of the Christians towards the Jews it is noteworthy that no cases are known of blood libels,[63] not even in the city of Mosul, where most of the Christians were concentrated. The chief reason for this may be that the majority of the Christians in Iraq had lived there for many centuries, while in Turkey, Syria, the Lebanon, northern Iran and Egypt, blood libels were spread by Armenian and Greek Christians when they first began to settle in those countries—they used the libels as a means to seize Jewish positions.

C. *PUBLIC AND PARTY ACTIVITY*

During the Ottoman period, the Iraqi Jews did not take part in any non-Jewish public affairs, except in a few isolated cases. Only a few individual Jewish civil servants in the days of the Young Turks joined the "Unity and Progress" party. It is doubtful whether any Iraqis belonged to this party before its rise to power.

From the 'twenties until 1951, there were no political parties in Iraq which Jews could join. Most of the parties were ephemeral, being founded by members of the Government a short time before the elections for the Iraqi Chamber of Deputies. The few parties which existed for longer periods were made up of extreme nationalists, among them the *al-Istiqlāl*. From the 'thirties on, two left-wing parties emerged—an underground communist party and a socialist opposition one—both of them, especially the communist, including a few Jews. During the Second World War, particularly from 1942, the Iraqi Communist Party began to gain strength, attracting to its ranks many Jews, Assyrians and Armenians, who viewed it as representing the USSR, the rising power which was successfully opposing Nazi Germany. Intellectual young Jews, among them the sons of wealthy families, also joined it. It is doubtful whether the socioeconomic ideology of the party attracted them, or whether, in fact, those who joined had more than a very general knowledge of its ideology, and whether they had read any serious communist literature. But they believed that a change in the regime in Iraq would bring an end to their suffering from discrimination and persecution. An important factor attracting them to membership was that the communist party did not restrain Jews from rising to its leadership ranks. Two of them, indeed, did so: Yehudah Abraham Ẓaddīq and Sason Shlomo Dallāl. The latter was arrested in January 1947 together with the then secretary of the party, known as "Fahad", and both were sentenced to one year's imprisonment. During their confinement, Yehudah Ẓaddīq and Yūsuf Mālik, a Christian, conducted the party's affairs, but they soon quarrelled over the leadership, until they, too, were arrested. Conduct of the party's affairs was then transferred to Sason Dallāl, who, in the meantime, had been released. Zaddīq and Fahad were sentenced to death and both were hanged in February 1949. In June of that year, Sason Dallāl was also hanged. Although we are not in possession of figures on the total number of Communist Party members, and of its Jewish members in particular, we may assume that the latter were not few. In 1948, the communists gained the sympathy of the Jews who did not belong to any group or party, because despite the fact that the Communist Party was illegal, it openly defended the Jews at the time when the State of Israel was established—it was the only party to do so—and even demonstrated against the war in Israel.

A relatively smaller number of Jews joined other left-wing parties which were permitted to operate in Iraq in 1946. Nor were Jews active in the few public societies existing in Iraq, including Jewish communal organizations. Only the youth and the young men were prepared to endanger themselves by membership in illegal movements. In addition to the considerable number of Jews in the Communist Party, hundreds joined the ranks of the Zionist underground movement.

* * *

From this general survey of the complex relations between the Jews, the authorities and the Iraqi people, we may summarize as follows:

1. As far as the law was concerned, from the 'sixties of the 19th century the Jews had equal rights with the other Iraqis. Although there were acts of discrimination against them on the part of the authorities, no legal authority for such discriminatory measures existed and sometimes those responsible were Government officials who did not always act on instructions from above. Only when the Jews began to be considered as a national, and not a religious minority, in 1948, did they suffer open persecution by the authorities. For in Iraq, religious minorities—Christians, Ṣābians, Yazīdīs—were not harmed, while nationalist or religious nationalist minorities, such as the Muslim Kurds and the Christian Assyrians, were treated harshly by the Government and the local people.

2. Relations with the Muslims never reached the stage of real friendship, because of reservations on both sides. The Muslim notables tolerated the Jews as a minority who had the right to observe the commands of their religion, and they considered it their duty to defend "those under their protection". But the younger generation, excited by nationalist feeling, was easily incited against them.

3. The Iraqi Jews did not feel they belonged in the country—not even in this century. During a brief period in the 'twenties, some of the younger ones among them endeavoured to become more integrated into the life of the State and to become thoroughly Iraqi, but this attempt failed when foreign anti-Jewish propaganda penetrated Iraq. Thus, feeling themselves unwanted, it was easy for them to cut themselves off from the country, and when a country was found which was prepared to accept them, they left for Israel in their masses.

4. The Jews of Iraq tried to adapt themselves, as did most of the Jewish communities in the world, to the realities in which they lived. When they were required to cease Zionist activity at the end of the 'twenties, they did so without opposition. When state schools were closed to them, they established special elementary and secondary schools of their own. When Government posts were blocked for them, they became clerks and took up posts in the academic professions in which there was a shortage of workers in Iraq. One of the means open to them was bribery—a customary practice in Middle Eastern countries; sometimes a Jew was able to attain his goal by merely flattering a Muslim. All this enabled Jews to achieve greater success than other Iraqis economically, culturally and educationally.

Syria and the Lebanon

Like the Jews of Iraq and Turkey, those of Syria and the Lebanon were given equal rights by the *Khaṭṭ-i-Sherīf* of the Gülkhāné in 1839. Later, the poll-tax was abolished and in 1909 they were required to do military service. Jews began to be appointed as civil servants and to be represented in district and municipal councils.[64] During the entire period, from 1839 to the First World War, no cases are known of discrimination against them on the part of the authorities, except for the following incident: in 1910 an order was issued forbidding non-Ottoman Jews in Syria and Palestine to register non-movable property, so as to prevent Zionist "expansion". This order prevented even the local Jews in Sidon from having houses and lands they had acquired in that city entered in the land registry office.[65]

The Turkish authorities in Syria and the Lebanon defended Jews from attacks occasionally perpetrated against them, especially by the Christians, several of whom continued to spread blood libels. The famous blood libel case of 1840 in Damascus followed the Christians' attempt to seize important positions in the East by creating an enemy common to them and the Muslims. To that end they were supported by representatives of France in the East, who aspired to strengthen France's position in the area. The Muslims in the city evidently did not hate the Jews, so that the libel did not assume serious dimensions and the number of victims was very small.[66] Further cases of blood libel occurred in Syria and the Lebanon. They all ended without injury to the Jews or damage to their property, thanks to the action taken by the authorities.

Like the Iraqi Jews, those of Syria and the Lebanon, with a few exceptions, could not read or write Turkish before the First World War. The Jews in Aleppo spoke Arabic, but preferred to teach their children foreign languages, while the Damascus

Jews were more Arabized than their brethren in Aleppo,* as far as their names, customs and behaviour were concerned.[67] The Damascus Jews were the only ones in the Arab countries to establish, in 1909, after the Young Turks' revolution, a club—the Revival *(al-Nahḍa)* Society—for the study and dissemination of the Arabic language.[68]

THE JEWS IN THE LEBANON, 1919–1972

When the French occupied the Lebanon and the mandate was established, no change occurred in the legal status of the Jews, nor did the authorities discriminate against them. Even the prohibition against registering non-movable property in the names of Jews in Sidon was abolished by the French authorities in 1925.[69] The Jews were so satisfied with the French authorities that among them there were those who considered themselves French. This led some of the youth to enlist in the French Army as far back as in the 'twenties, as well as in the Second World War, notwithstanding the fact that military service was not compulsory. Several were promoted and decorated.[70]

After the Lebanon received its independence in 1946, Jews were not discriminated against, nor were they during 1947–1948. The authorities saw to it that they were not harmed during the anti-Zionist demonstrations staged at the time. Police forces were posted in the Jewish quarter in Beirut day and night when required. The Lebanese authorities, in contrast to the Iraqi, Egyptian and Syrian, did not arrest Jews, with a few exceptions, and did not confiscate their property, but even gave shelter to Jewish refugees from Syria and a few from Iraq. They also continued to employ Jews in the civil service, at least until 1957, despite the opposition's demand to dismiss them.[71] Even in 1958, when civil war broke out, and despite the opposition's incitement against the Jews, the authorities assigned soldiers to prevent any harm being done to them.[72] In June 1967, during the war in the Middle East, the Lebanese authorities again stationed guards in the Jewish quarters. Until 1972 the Lebanese government allowed Jews to leave the country with their money and with their property.

There are only a few cases recorded of attacks against Jews in the 'thirties, but a more serious incident occurred in 1945, when twelve Jews were killed in the Muslim town of Tripoli. In January 1948, a Jew was murdered in Beirut, and in January 1950 an *Alliance Israélite Universelle* school was demolished by a bomb, the institution's directress being buried under the ruins. Most of these incidents were instigated and carried out by Muslim organizations, which even extorted money from Jews as contributions to the Palestine Arabs.[73] There were also cases, at least up to

* There were many differences between the Jews of Damascus and those of Aleppo. See below, pages 99, 137–139, 176.

1938, of Christians spreading anti-Jewish propaganda of the blood libel kind, but no harm was caused.

Apart from these few incidents, the authorities and people in the Lebanon displayed no hostility to the Jews. The Lebanon even allowed Syrian Jewish refugees to settle in Beirut. The Lebanon was thus the only Arab State in which the number of Jews increased after 1948. From 1958, however, their number began to decrease. In 1968, when tension between Israel and the Lebanon was intensified, following the Lebanese Government's support of saboteurs penetrating Israel from its borders, many more Jews left.*

THE JEWS IN SYRIA, 1918–1945

During the brief British occupation of Syria, which lasted a year and a half (October 1918–March 1920), and during the short period of the Arab Kingdom in Syria, no cases are known of attacks on Jews or discrimination against them. Nor were any such incidents reported during the long period of the French mandate, which lasted 25 years (1920–1945). The only anti-Jewish act was that of not granting permission for Zionist activity. The Aleppo, Damascus and Qāmishlī Jews were given representation in the municipal and district councils.[74] When a parliament was set up in Aleppo (1923), the Jews demanded and received representation in it,[75] and when the first all-Syria parliament was convened in December 1936, it included one Jewish deputy. This representation was suspended by the New Syrian constitution of 1949, when only a few Jews remained in Syria.

In contrast, relations between the Jews and the rest of the population were generally tense, particularly after 1935. Until that year the Damascus Jews suffered only once, at the time of the Druze revolt against French rule, in October 1925. The Druze attacked the Jewish quarter; a number of Jews were killed, scores wounded, houses and shops were looted and set on fire. Some Jews were also kidnapped by the rebels, who demanded a large sum of money from the community as ransom. As a result, hundreds of Jews fled from Damascus to the Lebanon, and many of those who remained lost their source of livelihood.[76] With this exception, up to 1935 there had been only isolated incidents of Jews being murdered, and these were for non-political reasons. Blood libels, most of them spread by Christians, continued in Syria, at least until 1931.

In 1935, trouble began for the Jews of Damascus—they were accused of being Zionists. In 1938, when the Palestine issue was causing great agitation in Syria, attacks upon Jews became more frequent and more serious. That year a number

* For estimates of the number of the Jews in the Lebanon see pp. 79–80.

of Jews were stabbed, several to death, by young Muslims[77] and proclamations were circulated calling for the imposition of a boycott against the Syrian Jews.[78] In January 1944, and again in May 1945, the Jewish quarter in Damascus was raided, and in June 1945 the director of the *Alliance* school in the city was murdered.[79]

1945–1972

On obtaining their independence, the Syrians became even more intensively involved in the Palestine problem, and anti-Zionist demonstrations became more frequent and violent. More pamphlets calling for an economic boycott of the Jews in Syria were circulated.[80] In December 1947, the anti-Jewish attacks reached a climax in Aleppo, when the masses went wild in the Jewish quarter and burnt down the majority of the synagogues, among them an ancient one, with their books and furnishings. They also broke into 60 shops and 150 houses and set them ablaze. When quiet returned, the President of Syria explained to a Jewish delegation that incidents of this sort occur even in advanced countries; he promised to study the matter, while expressing the hope that there would be no recurrence of such violence. The Minister of Finance did not accede to a request for financial assistance to restore at least one synagogue in which the Jews could pray.[81]

In February 1948, bombs were placed in the Jewish quarter of Damascus, and in August 1949, in the same neighbourhood, scores of people were killed and wounded by bombs; the Damascus authorities demanded that the Jewish community committee make a declaration to the effect that the incident was "ordinary" and that the Jews had received full assistance from the authorities.

From the time Syria received its independence in 1945, the authorities placed difficulties in the path of Jews applying for passports to travel to Palestine; eventually, they were refused passports for any destination. When the Jews began to smuggle themselves over the border to Palestine in large numbers, instructions were given to shoot at anyone crossing the frontier without permission.[82] When members of a family were not found at home during a search, those who were present were arrested on the charge of rendering assistance to those fleeing. Several who had been sentenced on this charge were given periods of imprisonment.[83] In 1946 the Damascus authorities prohibited the entry into Syria of the Jewish newspaper appearing in Beirut,[84] and in 1948 a number of Jews working in the civil service were dismissed.[85]

It is not surprising that thousands of Jews escaped to the Lebanon or Palestine, especially after 1945. Several of those fleeing were caught and sentenced to various terms of imprisonment, others were murdered by their smugglers, but the flight went on, and many succeeded in reaching Palestine. Indeed, in 1945–1946 Christians, too, left Syria and emigrated to the Lebanon,[86] but this was because they were suspected of sympathy for the French Government, and now that Syria had received its independence, they feared that the Syrian nationalists would take revenge on them.

After the establishment of the State of Israel, the situation of the Jews did not improve, and in July 1949 thirteen Jews were murdered in Damascus and the synagogue there was damaged[87]. Since 1947 Jews were not allowed to leave Syria, except for short periods: in 1954 by Hāshim al-Atāsī, and in 1958 after the proclaiming of the United Arab Republic. While other religions were not mentioned on identification certificates, Jewish identification certificates were stamped with the word 'Mūsawī" (of Moses, a Jew). Jews were not allowed to leave their cities and many were detained on charges that they tried to leave Syria illegally. Some of these detainees were cruelly tortured. The property of those few Jews who managed to leave Syria illegally was confiscated, and their remaining relatives suffered at the hands of the the Syrian police. Jews are not accepted in the Syrian Civil Service and most of them live on donations sent to them from abroad. Worst of all their persecutors are the Palestinian refugees who dwell in the Jewish quarter of Damascus, where they maltreat their Jewish neighbours.

At the beginning of 1971 a Jewish man and woman who succeeded in leaving Damascus testified in Paris before the International Conference for the Deliverance of the Jews of the Middle East. In their testimony they claimed that Jews were being subjected to torture, imprisonment, unemployment, and poverty. Secret Police officially supervised all Jewish gatherings, including synagogue services. The identity of the witnesses was withheld for fear that their relatives would suffer.[87a]

Notwithstanding the interference of many governments and international organizations, nothing has been changed in the status of the Jews in Syria. According to the latest news, hundreds of them demonstrated in September 1972 in the streets of Damascus, complaining about the harsh treatment they suffer. This demonstration signifies their desperation; they had nothing to lose.

Egypt

The 'sixties of the 19th century saw the beginning of a new period in the life of Egyptian Jews. Egypt was then deeply in debt and Anglo-French control had been imposed on the State's funds (1876). By virtue of the Capitulations, foreign nationals enjoyed economic and legal advantages. They were exempted from taxation and received the protection of their consuls; they could not be summoned before the State courts but were able instead to appear before consular courts, and, in a legal claim between a foreign and a local national—before a mixed court. The economic development initiated by Khedive Ismā'īl (1863–1879) was a contributing factor in bringing many foreigners to Egypt, among them many Jews. The number of Jews grew from about 6,000 at the beginning of the period in question to 25,000 as counted in the population census of 1897, of whom 12,507 were foreign nationals, and to 59,581 in the 1917 census, when the majority (34,601, or 58.1%) were of foreign nationality. Except for the brief period of the British occupation and the 'Urābī revolt in 1882, which prompted many Jews to flee from Egypt to Malta, they enjoyed favourable political conditions.[88] The foreign nationals among them even had advantages over the local citizens. After the First World War, although the immigration of Jews to Egypt continued, many others left; most of those who emigrated to Egypt were Palestinians who had come to Egypt during the First World War. Jews who remained in Egypt continued to enjoy equality, and the foreign nationals among them continued to enjoy economic privileges until the Capitulations were abolished by the Montreux Convention of 1937, and legal privileges beyond those available to the local inhabitants up to 1949, when the consular courts were dissolved.

During this period, most of the Jews in Egypt, including the local ones, felt themselves to be strangers there; some did not even learn to read and write Arabic, and the majority attended foreign schools. They had a feeling of superiority over the local Muslims and had almost no interest in Egypt's struggle for independence. A few did participate in party activity and the national movement in Egypt, among them the journalist-satirist Jacob Sanu', who cooperated with those opposing the rule of Khedive Ismā'īl. The latter even expelled Sanu' from Egypt for doing so, but Sanu' continued to fight against him by publishing from his exile in Paris. Sanu' later supported 'Urābī's revolt against the British.[89] In the early days of the *Miṣr-al-Fatāt* (Young Egypt) movement in 1879, a number of Jewish intellectuals were among its members,[90] and from 1919 the lawyer, Leon Castro, cooperated with the *Wafd*.

When Britain granted independence to Egypt in 1922, no change occurred in the political situation of the Jews. From 1924 to 1952 they were even represented in the Egyptian Chamber of Deputies and Senate, and a Jew was appointed Minister of Finance. Scores of Jewish officials worked in the civil service. They also had representation in the Alexandria municipality, and even in that of al-Manṣūra, where there were few Jews.

Until the 'thirties, there were no signs in Egypt of hatred of Jews, except on the part of the Christians, who, until 1930, spread blood libels against them, especially in the years 1880–1905.[91]

From 1938 on, incitements against the Jews occurred, against a nationalist background. At that time, an organization headed by Ali 'Allūba Pasha began to be active in Egypt; it agitated, *inter alia*, for the imposition of a boycott against the

Jews in Egypt, accusing them of raising money for the Zionists in Palestine. In July 1939, bombs were discovered near three synagogues in Cairo, wrapped in warnings to Jews against supporting Palestinian Jewry.[92] But these incidents were not considered serious by the Jews, who paid no special attention to them.

1945–1949

In 1945, hatred of the Jews became more serious, and on November 2 of that year organized anti-Jewish riots took place in Cairo, the first in Egypt since the middle of the 19th century. These disturbances, which served as a signal to the Arab nationalists in the other Arab countries to riot against the Jews there, were started by members of the *Miṣr-al-Fatāt* (Young Egypt), a chauvinistic movement headed by Ahmad Husayn, who began to operate in the 'thirties and whose symbol was the green shirt. Several weeks earlier members of this group had threatened to attack the Jews if they did not dissociate themselves from Zionism. On November 2, they broke into the Jewish quarter in Cairo and set fire to a synagogue, with its twenty-seven Torah-scrolls; a hospital, an old people's home and other Jewish institutions were destroyed. Jewish shops in the city were also damaged.[93] Muslim and Christian shops, too, were damaged during these riots, but that was due to the fact that they were not identified as such. These riots caused many Jews to leave Egypt, and later on, in 1947, Jews were afraid to participate in any Zionist activity, lest this excite the Muslims, particularly since the Palestine issue was now being given increasing prominence in the Egyptian press. The authorities, too, began to demonstrate their opposition to Zionism. Five days before the partition of Palestine, on November 24, 1947, the Egyptian representative in the United Nations General Assembly, Haykal Pasha, declared that "the Arab Governments will do all in their power to defend the Jewish citizens in their countries, but we all know that an excited crowd is sometimes stronger than the police. Unintentionally, you are about to spark an anti-Semitic fire in the Middle East which will be more difficult to extinguish than it was in Germany."[94] Obviously the Egyptian spokesman was voicing a threat to the effect that the Jews in Egypt might become the scapegoat, if Palestine were to be partitioned. Apparently he meant what he said. Indeed, a move directed against the Jews had already been made in July of that year, when the "Company Law" was promulgated, entering into force on November 4, 1947. The law was ostensibly directed against foreigners, but the main victims were the Jews. It stated that most company directors should be Egyptian nationals,* while at that time about 20 per cent of the Jews were foreign nationals, about two-thirds stateless and only 15 per cent Egyptian nationals.

* On this law, see further, p. 88.

Here it should be explained that the Egyptian Nationality Law of 1929 provided that every resident's application for Egyptian citizenship would be granted unless it were proven that he held another nationality. With a few exceptions, the Jews in Egypt, including those born there, did not apply for Egyptian citizenship, as they did not attach much importance to it. Later on, when the law was amended to provide that only a person who could prove that his grandfather was born in Egypt, or that his family had resided in Egypt on a permanent basis since 1848, was entitled to citizenship, the majority of the Jews in Egypt were ineligible, and thousands thus remained stateless.

From 1948, the Egyptian Government's anti-Jewish measures were aimed at them as Zionists, irrespective of their citizenship. On May 15, 1948, King Fārūq proclaimed a state of emergency in the country, and during the same month a number of orders were issued which, although not containing any legal restrictions against the Jews, affected them in particular. On May 25, all citizens were prohibited from leaving Egypt without a special permit, and Jews were denied such permits. (Those who nevertheless left the country in July and August 1948 were foreign nationals whose consular missions exerted pressure to obtain exit permits for them.) A few days later, on May 30, an order was issued empowering the Government to confiscate the property of persons whose activities, in its opinion, were detrimental to the State, providing for the confiscated property to be transferred to a special appointee, and enabling employers of these property owners to dismiss them. In theory, this was not specifically directed against the Jews. Nevertheless, out of more than a hundred individuals and companies whose property was confiscated within a short period thereafter, the great majority were Jews. In August 1948, instructions were issued permitting only Egyptian nationals to serve as brokers on the Egyptian stock exchange. In September, a further directive made Egyptian nationality a prerequisite for engaging in medicine.[95] In this way, the number of those badly hit economically mounted rapidly.

During this period, hundreds of Jews were arrested, accused of Zionism or communism and placed in detention camps, despite the fact that Zionism was not prohibited in Egypt then. During the months of June to November 1948, a number of terrorist acts were perpetrated against Jews. On June 20, bombs were placed in the Jewish quarter in Cairo, demolishing 12 houses in the explosion, killing 34 Jews and wounding over 80. In reaction to the bombing of Cairo by the Israeli Air Force on July 16 (by mistake a civilian area was bombed instead of the royal palace at 'Ābidīn), an Arab crowd assaulted Jews in the streets, pulling them off buses and beating them, without police intervention. Following pressure exerted by the foreign missions, the crowds were dispersed by the police. During the four days of July 17–20, bombs were again placed in the Jewish quarter, killing and wounding 250 people. About 500 shops were looted.[96] On September 22, 1948, 19 Jews were killed and 62 wounded in further explosions. In October, Jews were murdered and robbed in Cairo and Alexandria, and on November 11 another bomb was placed in the Jewish quarter in Cairo.

Furthermore, the Jews were forced to contribute hundreds of thousands of Egyptian pounds to the Egyptian army, and the Chief Rabbi of Egypt, Rabbi Ḥayyim Naḥum, was compelled, on the eve of the establishment of the State of Israel, to proclaim the duty of Egyptian Jews to defend their country against Zionism.[97]

1949–1954

In August 1949 a surprising change occurred in Egyptian policy towards the Jews. That month, the need for a special exit permit to leave Egypt was cancelled, some scores of those imprisoned in May 1948 were released, their property returned to them, and they were permitted to leave. When the *Wafd* Government came to power at the beginning of 1950, Jews were released and by early 1951 the detention camps were emptied of Jews, except for those who were communists. The Jews remaining in Egypt renewed their economic activity and reopened their schools, although they feared harm to them by the Muslim Brotherhood. But no harm was done, the only incident being the placing of a bomb in the Ramla quarter in Alexandria, which caused no damage. In 1951, publication of a Jewish newspaper was even resumed and a *Maccabi* group played football matches.[98]

The revolution of July 1952 and the deposition of King Fārūq did not bring about any change. On the contrary, General Neguīb was friendly to them and although they could leave the State if they so desired, only few did so in the years 1951–1953. True, in November 1953, a number of young Jews were arrested, accused of spreading communist and Zionist propaganda and eight of them were sentenced to from three to seven years' imprisonment, but this did not seem to indicate a deterioration in the position of the Jews.

1954–1972

In November 1954 General Neguīb was deposed, to be replaced by Gamāl 'Abd-al-Nāsser, and that was the beginning of difficult times for the Jews. Within a few months, dozens were arrested, several of them accused of spying for Israel; in December 1954, a death sentence was issued against two of them, and they were hanged at the beginning of 1955, despite intervention on their behalf. From then on, the number of anti-Jewish publications increased in Egypt, some of them even being distributed by Government publishers. Among them was the Arabic translation of the *Protocols of the Elders of Zion.* Although the Egyptian authorities were not interested in harming the Jews, for they were anxious not to appear incapable of defending the State's residents, they nevertheless denied them the possibility of leaving the country. Emigration to Israel in 1954–55 was negligible for lack of exit permits.

Immediately after the Sinai Campaign, on November 1, 1956, a military order was issued authorizing the Director-General of absentees' property to manage the property of political prisoners and even to sell it. After a few days, hundreds of Jews were reported to have been arrested and their property transferred to the Director-General. Among the detained were some of the wealthiest and most respected members of the Jewish community. Thousands of Jews were thus suddenly left without anything. During the first days of November, orders were given for Jews to pack a small part of their belongings and leave the country within a few days. Each one was allowed to take with him, out of all his property, only 30 Egyptian pounds, jewels to the value of 140 Egyptian pounds and unlimited Egyptian goods (clothing and shoes).[99] Within three and a half months, from November 22, 1956 to March 6, 1957, 14,012 Jews were expelled from Egypt in this way, and by September 1957—a further 7,000. Jews continued to be expelled after that as well, and many left on their own initiative because they no longer had any source of livelihood. Altogether, by the beginning of 1960, about 36,000 Jews left Egypt for European countries. The majority proceeded to Israel from Europe, while thousands emigrated to the United States or to Brazil, or remained in Italy, France or England.[100] Thus, out of some 40,000 Jews living in Egypt in 1956, only 8,500 remained in 1960.

Those who left lost their property, except for British and French nationals who were assured of compensation by virtue of the agreements which Egypt had with Britain and France. In 1957, the non-movable property which the Jews left behind in Egypt was valued at 24.2 million Egyptian pounds (the price of 101,255 fedan of agricultural land and 2,807 buildings).[101]

Emigration continued; of the 8,500 Jews counted in Egypt in the 1960 census, only 3,000 remained in June 1967. During these years, and especially in June 1967, many were arrested; in that month hundreds, including the rabbis of Cairo and Alexandria, were sent to concentration camps. After only three years, in July 1970, all the Jews who had been detained in June 1967 were freed. For the past few years Jews have not been permitted to leave Egypt, managing to do so only through the intervention of foreign countries. Nevertheless, most of the Jews have left Egypt, and the number of those who remain, as estimated in mid-1972, is 300 people, mostly elders. In March 1972 the Chief Rabbi Ḥayyim Duwayk left for France. No other rabbi is left in Egypt.[102]

Rabbinical religious courts were abolished, together with the Muslim and Christian religious courts. A law passed on September 24, 1955 had laid down that matters of personal status would be judged before State courts in accordance with the special religious laws of the litigants. However, this law recognized the superiority of Muslim religious law, by providing that in the event of the litigants being of different faiths—such as for example, Orthodox Copt and Catholic Copt—they would be judged according to Muslim religious law. The law established further that if one of the litigants would convert to Islam, the two parties would be judged according to Muslim law, but if one of the parties converted to a non-Islamic religion, the trial would be conducted in accordance with the laws of his religion before conversion.[103]

In summing up the political changes that took place in Egypt in the last hundred years, as far as they affected the Jews, we note that up to the 'forties, the Jews enjoyed almost full civil equality, both in theory and in fact. With the emergence of the Palestine problem and the xenophobic nationalism to which it gave rise at the end of the 'forties, their situation changed for the worse, to the extent that the majority were expelled from Egypt or preferred to leave the country of their own accord.

Iran

In the 'seventies of the 19th century, foreign States began to intervene on behalf of the Jews in Iran, especially the British counsuls there. This intervention had some effect, particularly for the few Jews living in Teheran, and it was important because the legal status of the Jews in this country did not change before 1906. They remained without rights, clearly not citizens, their residence in the State dependent on payment of the poll-tax, as established by Muslim law on the emergence of Islam. In the Ottoman Empire this tax had been abolished in 1855.

In contrast to the Ottoman Empire, where religious law had given way to that of the Majalla, the juridical system in Iran remained in the hands of the Sharī'a courts. Under this law, as has previously been mentioned, the evidence of a Jew against a Muslim was not considered valid, and a Muslim was not put to death for the murder of a Jew, even if two Muslim witnesses had been found to give evidence against him. Fortunately for the Iranian Jews, the kings who reigned in this period (up to 1906) were enlightened, but they could do nothing about this method of passing judgment, which placed the fate of the Jews at the mercy of any Muslim desiring to inflict injury on them. There was, in fact, a higher court of appeal appointed by the Shah, whose judges rendered verdicts according to their conscience and not according to Muslim religious law, but the Iranian Jews, fearing Muslim public opinion and the Muslim religious functionaries, did not dare to apply to this court. Although the Jews in Teheran could turn to the Shah himself, in the other cities they could address themselves only to the representatives of the district governors, who were often religious fanatics not interested in protecting the Jews.[104] The religious functionaries who had great influence on the masses remained hostile, as they had been in the past. The theory among the Shī'ītes of impurity of non-Muslims continued to be a cause of humiliation and persecution, suffering and torture, until many of the Jews could bear it no longer and converted to Islam or to the Bahai faith.

In 1865, Jews from Baghdad addressed themselves to the *Alliance Israélite Universelle* in Paris in a memorandum in which they described the situation of the Jews in Iran. In 1873, in response to this and other memoranda which the Society received, it organized, in cooperation with the Anglo-Jewish Association in London, its first campaign on behalf of the Iranian Jews. That year, Nāṣir al-Dīn Shah, King of Iran (who ascended the throne in 1848 at the age of 17 and was murdered in 1896) visited Europe. Wherever he went—London, Paris, Berlin, Vienna, Amsterdam, Rome and Istanbul—representatives of the local Jewish communities and of the *Alliance* and the Anglo-Jewish Association met with him and presented him, orally or in writing, in almost identical terms, with a description of the tragic situation of the Jews in his kingdom, together with a request and suggestions for amending the situation. The memoranda and protocols of the conversations, including the verbatim replies of the King and his Viceroy, were printed in French and Hebrew by the *Alliance* in Paris. The Hebrew version , called "sending of (Purim) gifts" was despatched to the Iranian Jews.

It is of interest to examine the King's reaction to these complaints. The Anglo-Jewish Association's memorandum was answered, in the King's name, by his Viceroy, Malcolm Khan, on July 5, 1873; it stated that the King, "on his return to his kingdom, will give his attention to the matters placed before him with a view to improving the welfare of the Jewish community in the land of Iran, for the King has always found that they obeyed him and were faithful workers."[105] But a week later, when he arrived in Paris and a delegation of the leaders of the *Alliance*, headed by Adolf Cremieux, presented themselves before him, the King became excited about what he had heard and according to minutes of that meeting, he said, through Malcolm Khan: "all these complaints are lies . . . the lot of the Jews is as the lot of the rest of my people, all that has been told you is a lie, I testify to that." He then pointed to Malcolm Khan, referring to him as one who loved the Jews very much, to the extent that the Muslims envied them because of it. At the meeting with the *Alliance* in Istanbul on August 19, 1873, the King again denied that Jews were persecuted in Iran saying: "the situation of the Jews in Iran is not like the slanders which the journals in Europe publish about them. They have always had the benefit of my good will. And here is proof of that—this eunuch of mine—he is a Jew."[106]

Nevertheless, the complaints he heard in Europe must have impressed Nāṣir al-Dīn. On his return home he published a pamphlet in which he described his travels and, *inter alia*, mentioned the Jews in Europe who held posts as advisors, ministers and high dignitaries. The Jewish traveller, Ephraim Neumark, who visited Iran in 1884, related that he saw this pamphlet there but that the Shah was unable to curb the people's hatred of the Jews.[107] And, indeed, the Shah could do little to improve their lot. Not only the people's treatment of them but also their legal status remained unchanged. Members of the Jewish communities in Teheran and north-west Iran continued to send complaints to Europe, lamenting the oppressive measures of government representatives and reporting that they were unable to complain to the Shah for fear that their oppressors would take revenge on them.[108]

The Shah of Iran did make some attempt to amend the situation. In October 1878 he issued a royal decree introducing changes in administration, one of which was the transfer of Jewish affairs to the Foreign Ministry, a change which was considered beneficial to the Jews. In May–June 1880, he instructed all the Muslim judges not to transfer Jewish legacies to their relatives who had converted to Islam. Needless to say, however, an improvement in the Muslim people's attitude could not be expected within a short time. In 1881, the British Ambassador in Iran, who had been requested by the British Foreign Office to intervene on behalf of the Jews, reported that they were still prohibited from opening shops in the market and the practice of transferring Jewish legacies to their relatives who had converted to Islam was still in force.[109] Neumark had heard, so he recorded, that the latter practice would be disregarded only on the intervention of the British Ambassador. He explains, and correctly, that the King was unable to alter the inheritance law, for he had no religious authority, although he himself was good to the Jews. Moreover, Neumark states further, in addition to the poll-tax imposed collectively on the Jews of every city, the *Aghā-ī-Yahud* (Lord of the Jews), who was in charge of Jewish affairs, was often most avaricious, extorting from them as much money as he could and at times imposing on them all sorts of fines.[110]

Since the authorities could not improve the situation of the Jews, it is plain that the people did not change their attitude toward them. They still adhered to the idea of the Jews' impurity. Neumark refers to the following examples of this: a Muslim did not buy anything from a Jew except spices, textiles and utensils; he did not offer a Jewish guest tea or a nargillah; even if he received an honoured guest, he did not seat him on a carpet but laid out a mat for him. A Jew could not handle and select merchandise in a Muslim shop, but could only point to the article he wished to purchase and if the salesman was a decent man, he would sell him the goods he actually wanted. On a rainy day, the Jews were accustomed to stay at home, for whoever left his house on such a day was certain to receive blows from a young Muslim.[111]

In Teheran, where the Shah's rule was stronger, there were relatively few cases of harm to the Jews; but this was not so outside the capital, particularly in the areas near the Caspian Sea. In Bārfurūsh, for instance, where the son of the Mujtahid died in about 1874, after receiving medicine from a Jew who had converted to Islam, many Jews were massacred in revenge, and those who remained were compelled to convert. Only after appeals to Europe for help did the Shah dispatch an army to the place; he permitted the Jews to return to their religion and ordered the Muslims to recompense them for the goods looted from them.[112] There were also cases of Jews being murdered in various cities in Iran.[113] According to Morris Cohen of the Anglo-Jewish Association, who reported on the situation of the Jews in Iran during these years, the Jews had become accustomed to this kind of life, and the Muslims could not comprehend that a Jew was not an impure and dirty creature.[114]

In light of the many complaints sent to London, the Jewish Board of Deputies in Britain utilized the second visit of Naṣir al-Dīn to London in 1889 to submit a memorandum to the guest. In it they thanked the King for his efforts to treat the Jews well and urged that his instructions be implemented in the far-off provinces as well and that he permit the Jews to study in state schools.[115] As a result, in 1890 the Shah renewed his instructions of 1880 revoking the practice of transferring a deceased Jew's legacy to his proselytized relative.[116] But the attacks continued outside Teheran, and the British Government's representatives continued to intervene. One place where the Jews suffered particularly at the end of the century was in the city of Hamadhān. In September 1892, when a concession for the manufacture of tobacco was given to the British, the religionists led those opposing it, organizing strikes *(bast)* until they succeeded in having it abolished. Their success added to their self-assurance, proving, they believed, their great influence on the masses. Heading the religious leaders in Hamadhān was the Mulla Abdalla, who exploited this success to molest and humiliate the Jews. He summoned a delegation of the Jewish community leaders, informed them that they were enjoying too much freedom, and issued instructions designed to degrade them further. Only after several Jews succeeded in telegraphing the Shah about their situation, did an order reach the District Governor to send the Mulla Abdalla to Teheran. But this command was not obeyed and the Mulla again summoned a Jewish delegation, making its members affix their signatures to the terms on which they would live in the city. These included restrictions regarding their external appearance, intended to degrade them and facilitate their identification: a prohibition against wearing fine clothes—they were to wear only those made of cotton cloth of indigo blue colour, and on them they were to sew a red patch; their shoes were to be not of a pair—a slipper on one foot and a shoe on the other, or each shoe of a different colour; they were not to wear a coat, but to carry it on their arms; they were not to cut or shave their beards; and Jewish women were to cover their faces with a two-coloured veil. There were also prohibitions with regard to their houses: they were not to be beautiful—any such house would be demolished; they were not to be higher than a Muslim's house and the entrance door was to be very low. Other prohibitions restricted their movement: they were forbidden to go outside the city walls, and on a rainy day they were not to leave their houses; in walking in the street they were obliged to stand at the side of the road if a Muslim passed by, and Jewish doctors were not permitted to ride an animal. These instructions also contained details designed to degrade the Jews before Muslims: a Jew was to bow when addressing a Muslim, he was not to speak to him loudly, but only in a low meek voice; he was to keep a distance of at least five yards between himself and a Muslim walking in front of him; and if a Muslim should consider it right to curse him he was to bow his head in submission. Their food, too, was restricted: a Jew could not buy fruits of good quality; he could not drink alcohol or wine outside his home—if he did so he would be killed. These prohibitions indirectly granted permission to Muslims to beat and murder Jews, for a Muslim who beat a Jew could claim that the Jew did not keep his distance, or that he spoke in a loud voice. A Muslim could murder a Jew and afterwards claim that the man he killed drank wine or did something similar. The Teheran authorities, following British intervention, sent an army to Hamadhān to defend the Jews, but this did not prevent riots against them at the end of 1892. This time the Mulla was indeed brought to Teheran, but under pressure of the Hamadhānites, he was released and returned to Hamadhān at the beginning of 1894. The Prime Minister of Teheran explained this step to the British Ambassador by stating that the Mulla who succeeded Abdalla was worse than him. Despite the fact that the Mulla Abdalla had obtained his release by promising to prevent harm being done to the Jews, on his return to Hamadhān he renewed the brutal treatment. Later, complaints ceased to reach London from the Jews of that city.[117]

In 1896, Naṣir al-Dīn Shah was murdered, after a reign of forty-eight years, and his son, Muẓaffar al-Dīn Shah, took his place. With the changeover of kings, the religious functionaires dared to raise their heads and to molest the Jews even in the city of Teheran. In December 1896, the Mujtahid in the capital published instructions for the Jews to wear a patch on their chests, and to cut their hair, so that they could be distinguished from the Muslims. This led to the intervention of the British and French Foreign Ministries, following which the Shah issued an order prohibiting any harm to non-Muslims. But there are records of attacks on Jews in that same year in Tūisīrkān, and in 1897 on those in Shīrāz, Hamadhān and Kermanshāh. The Muslim religious leaders in Iṣfahān also imposed an economic boycott on the Jews of that city, prohibiting the purchase of merchandise from Jews, or its sale to them.[118] From then until 1906, Jews in various cities continued to suffer, particularly from this economic boycott.[119] Their plight improved somewhat in those cities where *Alliance* schools were opened, for example in Teheran by Joseph Cazes, in 1898, and in Hamadhān by Isaac Bassan in 1900. These men, as foreign nationals, were able to approach the authorities on behalf of the Jews—they were regarded by the Jews, and at times also by the Muslim masses, as ambassadors and their schools as embassies. This protection was important, for among the Iranian Jews there were only a few with foreign nationality (Russian or Turkish) and the majority did not benefit from the terms of the Capitulations.

1906–1925

In August 1906, the constitutional movement in Iran succeeded in forcing King Muẓaffar al-Dīn Shah to promulgate a constitution for the State, with a parliament to be convened within a brief period. The Constitution established equality of rights for all Iranians without distinction of religion. It may be said that from this date the Jews of Iran became citizens for the first time, legally at least, in a country where they had lived for centuries. In 1909, they were granted representation in the parliament *(Majlis)* by one deputy. The Jews in each city were to propose a candidate and from among these candidates one was to be elected to represent all the Jews of Iran in parliament, provided he gained the approval of the authorities. In 1909, a Jewish deputy, 'Azīz-Allah Sīmānī, was in fact elected, but he resigned shortly afterwards since he did not feel at ease among the Muslim deputies. In his stead a Muslim was chosen to represent the Jews.[120] Later, a Jew was elected regularly: from 1916 to 1922 Dr. Luqmān was the deputy, and from 1922 to 1925, Shmuel Hayyim. Under the Law, the Jews elected only their own deputy. During this period, too, they began to be appointed to local councils and several were accepted into the civil service.

Unfortunately, there was not much significance in this constitutional equality granted the Jews. Until Riza Shah Pahlavī was crowned King in December 1925, they were still obliged to pay the poll-tax,[121] the symbol of inequality of the minorities.

Needless to say, the Muslim masses' hostility to the Jews could not be eradicated within a short time, particularly in this period of anarchy, of financial and political crisis and of Russian and British competition for influence. Jews were again the target, and the authorities were unable to defend them, despite their good intentions. In 1907, Jews were assaulted in Shīrāz. In 1908 there were cases of looting and murder in Shīrāz, Hamadhān, Darab and Kermanshāh. In 1910, twelve Jews were murdered and about 50 wounded in Shīrāz. Less grave incidents also occurred in Seneh and Hamadhān.[122]

In 1921, following an army revolt, Riza Khān, one of the officers, seized power and tried to introduce law and order. In December 1925 he had himself crowned. Two cases of riots against Jews have been recorded as having occurred at the outset of his reign—in Teheran in 1922 and in Iṣfahān in 1925—both of which were quelled by the authorities. Up to 1925, there were still cases of proselytes being awarded the legacies of their Jewish relatives: the Jewish deputy in parliament, Shmuel Hayyim, complained about this in 1925.[123] There is no doubt that this period witnessed great progress in the legal and political position of the Jews in Iran, but only from 1925 on could one speak of the beginning of a brighter era in the history of Iranian Jewry.

1925–1971

By means of a military dictatorship, Riza Shah Pahlavī endeavoured to unite all the peoples dwelling in Iran into one nation and to introduce European civilization into his country. Aware of the fact that the religious functionaries constituted a serious obstacle to the attainment of his aims, he set out to crush them. The State indeed remained Muslim: in accordance with its constitution, its king and ministers were obliged to be Shī'ite Muslims, but the status of the religionists was reduced and the leaders were compelled to dress in European attire and to cut short their beards. In the days of Riza Shah, secular laws were introduced, civil marriage was permitted, and state schools were established to replace the religious schools. The Shah also encouraged the women to remove the veils from their faces, starting with his daughters.

As far as the Jews were concerned, the suppression of the religionists was a signal for putting into practice the equal rights which they had won in 1906, and indeed, Jews were now made equal to Muslims in all spheres; even the poll-tax was abolished. Two forms of legal discrimination remain: a non-Shī'ite Muslim cannot serve as a Minister in the Iranian Government, and non-Muslims may not participate in elections to parliament, except in the elections for their own representatives.

In practice, Jews began to be accepted as officials in the civil service, although not in the legal service and not in the Iranian National Bank, and it was difficult for them to be accepted as teachers in state schools. The military service law now applied to Jews, but they rarely attained officer rank, except in the medical corps; nor were they attracted to military service. Jewish children began to attend state schools, although here, too, some difficulties were encountered. The impurity belief and the humiliating practices accompanying it were prohibited by the authorities, but religious Muslims still consider Jews unclean: it is difficult to uproot by a sweep of the hand this belief of hundreds of years which has stamped upon it the mark of religion. Not everywhere may Jews use the city bath-houses, at times they are forbidden to touch fruits in a shop before purchasing them, and they are not served drinks in a Muslim cafe. Fortunately, these restrictions are rare today, with the growing number of educated Muslims in the State.

As part of Riza Shah Pahlavī's attempts to unify the inhabitants of Iran into one nation, citizens were forbidden to set up organizations of a foreign nationalist trend, and so Zionism was prohibited. The king's attempts to minimize the influence of religion and the religionists on the life of the State also limited the possibilities of expanding religious consciousness among the Jews in Iran. The fact that it was forbidden to import books relating to Jewish religion and culture[124] was another factor. True, the synagogues were not closed, as they had been in Turkey, and religious studies in elementary schools were permitted, but only at hours fixed by the Ministry of Education.

In the summer of 1941, Riza Shah Pahlavī, because of his sympathy for the Axis powers, was compelled to resign by the Russians and the British who had seized control of Iran, and he was exiled from his kingdom. In his stead, his son, Muhammad Riza Shah became King of Iran. The new, young king, who is still reigning in Iran, is not as extreme as his father was in the struggle against religious fanaticism and in the attempt to unify the Iranians and transform them into one nation. The Jews have therefore been permitted to establish a Zionist organization and to expand religious study and the study of the Hebrew language.

In the last twenty years, hatred of Jews has diminished, but has not disappeared entirely, and it is precisely the descendants of the forced converts in Meshed who are particularly hated. The Muslim population in Meshed exploited the evacuation of the city by the Russians in 1946 to carry out a massacre of these "Marannos". Those who remained in Meshed do not dare to this day to reveal their Jewishness.[125]

On the eve of the establishment of the Jewish State, active propaganda was conducted against Jews and leaflets circulated calling on the faithful to impose an economic boycott against the Jews in Iran. Leading the propagandists was Sayyid Abū al-Qāsim Kāshānī, who, during the Second World War, had been imprisoned because of his Nazi sympathies. A short time later, in March 1950, twelve Jews were murdered in Kurdistan for unknown reasons, with the result that most of the Jews of the area left for Teheran, and from there many went on to Israel. The Government instructed the local authorities to do all they could to defend the Jews there. In 1951, after Dr. Muhammad Moṣṣadegh became Prime Minister of Iran, religious and anti-Jewish propaganda was intensified, for Moṣṣadegh was supported by the religious leaders and the nationalists, although he himself could not be considered an anti-Semite. On his downfall, the Shah again curbed the religionists and the Jews' position improved.

To sum up, it may be said that the political situation of the Jews, especially of those living in the capital, improved vastly over the last 40 years. The fact that during this period, and especially from the end of the 'thirties, many more moved from the provinces to Teheran, and that there was also considerable emigration from the Kurdish region and from the small communities to Israel, led to the transformation of the Iranian Jewish community from a minority scattered over various cities, in not all of which they gained the protection of the ruling power, into a minority concentrated for the greater part in the capital city.* In Teheran and other big cities the number of educated Muslims increased, which contributed to the improvement of the situation of Jews. The present generation of Jews has also been trying not to isolate itself from the Muslims. Jews now give their children Persian names rather than Hebrew or Jewish names. The young Jews have begun to speak the Muslim-

* See further, p. 81.

Persian dialect, which differs from the Jewish dialects spoken in the various cities of Iran. The Jewish population which had been concentrated in its own quarters has begun to move to mixed quarters in Teheran, now that large numbers of them have become wealthy. The young Jew, like the educated young Muslim, was also drawn into party activity, especially into the communist *Tūdeh* party. Within this party, the Jewish Cultural and Social Society was established, with its own communist organ in the Persian language, called *Nīsān*. A few Jews also joined the Democratic Party of Ahmad Qavām al-Salṭaneh. It appears, however, that their party activity diminished, especially on the suppression of the communist party after the fall of the Moṣṣadegh Government in 1953.[126]

In no other country in the Middle East did relations between Jews and non-Jews improve within such a short period as they did in Iran. Because of this emigration from Iran to Israel was not on a mass scale. In the years 1948 to 1966, about 49,000 Iranian Jews emigrated to Israel, but about 62,000 were still living in Iran according to a 1971 estimate. One cannot know, however, what tomorrow will bring.

The Yemen, Aden and the Arabian Peninsula

A short time after the occupation of San'a by the Ottoman army in 1872, a Jew from one of the townships of the Sakfān district wrote, in September of that year, to the new Turkish Governor of San'a, Mukhtār Pasha, informing him of the improvement which had already taken place in the situation of the Yemenite Jews. In April 1875, four Jewish religious court judges from the Yemen capital wrote to the Anglo-Jewish Association in London in the same spirit.[127] And indeed, there were some improvements. In 1875 Jews in San'a were permitted to set up a new quarter south of their existing one, and the Ottoman authorities even allowed them to build new synagogues there. They were also exempted for a brief period from their assigned task of collecting animal carcasses.*

On the other hand, the poll-tax was not abolished in the Yemen, as it had been in the other parts of the Ottoman Empire, and the Ottoman rulers did not even reply to the Jews' request to reduce its rate. The Ottoman Governor in San'a saddled the population, and particularly the Jews, with the task of grinding flour for his soldiers against a small payment. The poll-tax and the milling obligation embittered the Jews and to a certain extent contributed to their growing desire, evident from the 'eighties, to emigrate to Palestine. The Muslim population's treatment of the Jews, including the humiliations they inflicted on them, did not change, and at

* See above p. 5.

times the Jews suffered at the hands of the Turkish soldiers as well.[128] Years of famine, resulting from siege and drought, aggravated their plight. The famine was very severe in 1898[129] and again in the years 1900–1903. In 1904, Imam Ḥamīd al-Dīn died and was succeeded by his son, the Imam Yahya. The new Imam was anxious to rid the Yemen of Ottoman rule, for he considered the Turks unbelievers. He stirred up a revolt, which spread to all the towns of the Zaydīs, a Shī'ite sect, and at the beginning of 1905 the latter set out for the capital and laid siege to it. During this siege, many of the inhabitants of San'a died of famine; not a few of them were Jews.[130] At last, in April 1905, the Turkish ruler surrendered and Yahya entered the city as victor. The Jews were compelled to express their loyalty to him. He, for his part, promised them protection provided they would do their duty towards his regime. In a decree handed out to their leaders in 1905 he set out some of their duties as required by Muslim law, emphasizing that these instructions had been in existence for a long time but had not been implemented by the Ottoman unbelievers. Owing to the importance of this decree, which is unique in the eastern countries in the 20th century and which remained in force until the mass emigration in 1950, it is quoted in full below.

THE IMAM YAHYA'S DECREE OF 1905:[131]

"In the name of Allah the merciful and the compassionate. . . . This is a decree which the Jews must obey as commanded, and they are under the obligation to observe everything in it. They are forbidden to disobey it. It is intended to remind them of what the governors of the State, the Ottoman governors, abolished, which caused the failure of the previous Imams . . . and that is: These Jews are obliged to pay the *jizya* [poll-tax]—every adult man. [The rate] of this tax is 48 'Qafla' on the rich which is 4 riyāl less a quarter, and the person of moderate means—24 'Qafla', which is two riyāls less an eighth, and the poor man—12 'Qafla' which is one riyāl less half of an eighth.[132] Thus they are made safe and will enjoy our protection. It is forbidden to them to avoid paying it, and they must do so before the year is out. It shall be paid to whomever we have ordered to receive it. This is a command given by Allah in a clear manner in Allah's Book [in the Qurʿān]. They must also [pay] half of a tithe [five per cent] of their commerce, on the amount that will reach the quota [about 19 riyāl] each year, and they shall not pay on something which does not reach this quota. It is their duty to pay the aforementioned poll-tax and half of the aforesaid tithe.

"It is also forbidden to them to help each other against a Muslim, and they shall not raise their houses above the Muslim houses [a Jew's house may not be higher than a Muslim's],[133] and they shall not disturb Muslims in their path and shall not encroach on their occupations, and shall not slight the religion of Islam, and shall not curse any prophet, and shall not irritate a Muslim in his belief, and shall not sit on saddles, but sideways [both feet at the side], and shall not wink, and shall not point to a Muslim's nakedness, and not display their Torah outside their synagogue, and not raise their voices while reading, and not sound the shofar loudly—a low voice is sufficient for them. They are also forbidden to engage in shameful things which bring a curse from Heaven.* It is their duty to exalt the Muslim and honour him.

"The Jews of San'a have chosen the protected Jews Aharon Cohen, Yahya al-Kāfiḥ, Yahya Isaac and Yahya al-Abyaḍ to correct that which will be done wrongly, and they will judge between them, in accordance with the laws of their religion. Members of the Jewish religion are commanded to obey them and to listen to their orders, and they [the four] must guide them on the right way, and not by tyranny, and shall not change anything of their law, and shall not draw them away from it for the sake of extortion, so that the weak shall not be downtrodden by the strong. And they shall not prevent anyone who will seek it [to be judged] by the laws of Muhammad.

"We have also appointed from among them Yahya Danokh to be president, and he shall convey the instructions which we have commanded to be given in San'a, and the Jews shall conduct themselves in accordance with what is required . . . and shall avoid what is required to be avoided. He is the man and his orders shall be carried out in respect of those under the protection of the prophet—under our protection."

This decree, with the exception of the last parts dealing with spiritual and secular leadership, established the relations between the Jews, the authorities and the local population. Its importance lies in that it was, in practice, the law of the State. But these prohibitions were not new, and they had been in force previously. The Imam did not even include all the prohibitions which existed before that in respect of the Jews, such as those about riding a horse or a camel, about riding within the city altogether, and about bearing arms. Further, the oath and evidence of a Jew against a Muslim, although not referred to in the above decree, was never accepted in the State courts.

The Imam Yahya himself saw to the strict implementation of his decree. His first act was the demolition of several synagogues in San'a which had been built during Ottoman rule. However, he saw to it that no harm should be done to the Jews in a way that was contrary to Muslim law. Yahya had not been long in power in San'a when the Ottoman forces conquered the city. In 1908, Yahya returned and besieged the capital, a siege which, as usual, led to severe famine, suffering and death among

* Hinting at prostitution. See p. 159 and note.

the population. Not until 1911 did Yahya succeed in forcing the Ottomans to agree to his rule in the city, albeit under their symbolic protection. On September 22, 1913, the Sultan in Istanbul published a firmān confirming that Muslim religious law would be in force in the Yemen.[134] In 1918 the Ottoman forces left the Yemen. During his long rule, which lasted till February 1948, Yahya saw to it that his 1905 instructions were implemented fully, and in 1921, he even revived a decree of previous centuries—the orphans decree.* Although there are no data on the Jews who converted to Islam, undoubtedly Yahya concerned himself with the conversion of Jewish orphans,[135] something which oppressed the Jews more than the laws humiliating them. In the early 'twenties, Yahya forbade Jews to travel to Palestine.[136]

Despite these injustices, in the period of Yahya's rule the life of the Jews was assured, the Imam hearing complaints and judging in their favour if he saw that they were being oppressed contrary to Muslim law. The Yemenite Jews remembered him favourably.

On February 17, 1948, Yahya was murdered, and Abdalla al-Wazīr took control of the capital. After four weeks of siege, Crown Prince Ahmad, Yahya's son, succeeded in breaking into the city and taking over the reins of power. Ahmad's soldiers took to looting, as was customary in the Yemen, and the first to be plundered were the Jews. Money, jewels, clothes, utensils and sleeping mats were stolen. Only after the intervention of Prince Abbas, the Imam's brother, did the looting cease. The Imam Ahmad afterwards ordered that the injured be compensated with a small sum so that they could resume their work, and there was some hope that the Jews' political situation, too, would be improved. The establishment of the State of Israel that year, however, led to incitement in the capital. In December 1948, Jews were even accused of throwing two Moslems into a well. As a result, 60 Jews were arrested in San'a for several months, being released only after paying a large fine.[137]

At the beginning of 1949 the Imam Ahmad, who was more open to Western influence than his father had been, permitted the Jews to leave the country. He was the first Arab ruler to do so. He even forbade the collection of taxes or other payments from them, although there were cases in which money was extorted from the departees by local governors.

Generally speaking, the Jews living in all parts of the Yemen suffered from degrading treatment until their mass immigration in 1950. A Jew was required to be the first to greet a Muslim and he had to address him as *sīdī* (my lord), while a Muslim would not greet a Jew first nor would he respond to a Jew's greeting, only saying *al-ḥamdlillah* (thank God), or something to that effect. A Jew could not ride an animal in the city, not even during the period of Ottoman rule,[138] and if he rode a donkey outside the cities, he could do so only with his two feet on one side.

* See further, p. 168.

On meeting a Muslim he had to descend from the animal and to ask permission to continue on his way. A Jew was forbidden to live among Muslims and to mix with them, lest he contaminate them, for the majority of the Yemenite Muslims were Zaydīs-Shī'ites. Muslim children would sometimes tease Jewish children, and even old men and rabbis, throw stones at them and insult them. A Jew could not even shout at the children, he could only appeal to an adult Muslim to rescue him from them. When Muslims talked among themselves and mentioned a Jew, they would add the word *ḥāshākūm* (beneath your dignity) as if they were referring to an animal. As a matter of fact, the Jews used to do the same when talking about a Muslim!

So as to avoid provocation, the Jews would dress very modestly. They celebrated their Sabbaths and Festivals in the Jewish quarter, and did not appear in fine clothes outside their neighbourhood. They did not wear a turban on their heads, for the *atarot* decree* remained in force.[139]

The Jews in towns were completely isolated from the Muslim population: they lived in special quarters, and their only contact with them was to transact minor business, such as selling or buying foodstuffs, or selling their handiwork (jewellery, etc.). The Jew could be distinguished from the Muslim by his outward appearance, his sidelocks, and his clothes. The Arabic spoken by the Jews was different from the Muslim Arabic, both in vocabulary (the Jews included Hebrew and Aramaic words as well) and in accent.[140]

The Jews in the villages were not so completely cut off from the Muslims. Sometimes there were good neighbourly relations between them, and it even happened that Jewish and Muslim children played together. A particularly good atmosphere prevailed south of San'a and Dhamār, where tribes less hostile to the Jews dwelt. Shmuel Yavnieli, who was in the Yemen in 1911, points out that in the south and east of the Yemen, Jews were living dispersed over many villages, with single Jewish families in each village, so that good neighbourly relations were established between them and the Muslims. He mentions the satisfactory relations in the villages of Dal'am, Ḥabīl, Ḥubaysh, Khiarya, Doram and Bayḍa. In the last village, Jews even carried a knife *(shufra)* as the Arabs did, and in 1911 they were not at all inclined to emigrate to Palestine. But in other villages, such as 'Aqīrī, Ba'dān, Dhamār, Dharāḥ, and Qurna, Yavnieli found the Jews persecuted by the local governors and sometimes also by the people.[141]

Finally, it should be pointed out that just as the Yemen lived in almost complete isolation from the world, and no political changes occurred there, there were also no changes in the legal position of the Jews during the years 1873-1951. In such circumstances, small wonder that the Jewish exile in the Yemen was a difficult one indeed, and most of the Jews there were always ready to leave the country; as soon

* See above, p. 4.

as the possibility presented itself in 1949-50, they left for Israel en masse. Only very few Jews remained there.

ADEN AND THE REST OF THE ARABIAN PENINSULA

There were small Jewish communities in the vicinity of the Yemen, concerning whose political situation almost nothing is known, and in the case of some of them, their very existence was unknown. A few Jews lived in Bahrein, at least from the middle of the 19th century, and they, too, lived peaceful lives, until on November 4, 1947 riots broke out against the community in the capital, Manāma. A young Jewess was killed and several Jews wounded. The only synagogue in the city was plundered and demolished. Thirty-five of the forty-two Jewish houses were looted. Later on, the inhabitants proclaimed an economic boycott against the Jews, being encouraged by frequent calls in the newspapers to do so.[142] Since 1948 some of the Jews have left the country, but some scores of them still live in Bahrein.

In the Aden Protectorate, there were a few small sultanates which were subject in theory to Britain, but in fact to the native Sultans. In some of these Sultanates a few small Jewish communities existed. There is nothing to indicate that they were oppressed. As the Muslims in the Protectorate were Sunnis, Jews in the region had a better life than their Yemenite brethren for at least they were not considered impure. Living there for hundreds of years they adapted themselves to the conditions prevailing there. Like the local residents, they were accustomed to grow beards and shave their moustaches, but their sidelocks distinguished them from the Muslims. On the establishment of the State of Israel, news reached them about the possibility of emigrating to Israel, but the local sultans sometimes made it difficult for them to leave. The Sultan of Lodar, for example, did allow them to go but forbade his subjects to buy the departees' belongings, and so the Jews left behind their meagre possessions receiving nothing in payment for them. The Governor of Ḥabbān prohibited the Jews' departure, because the Muslims complained that they owed them money and had not repaid their debts. The Jews acknowledged the debts, but claimed that the sum was smaller than that demanded. The emissary from Israel, Joseph Ẓadoq, who was then in the Yemen, travelled to Ḥabbān, and thanks to the gifts which he distributed among the Sultan and his secretaries, the latter persuaded the creditors to compromise and settle with the Jewish debtors for a small sum. When they agreed, the Sultan gave the Jews permission to leave.[143]

As to the Jews in the city of Aden, whose number was augmented by those who came there from the Yemen at the time of the British conquest of 1839, their legal and political position was better than that of their brethren in the Yemen. They were not discriminated against by the authorities. Several were even accepted in the civil service and their children in state schools, and, above all, they did not suffer harm at the hands of the local inhabitants, though they were insulted by the local Muslims and a number of cases of looting has been recorded.[144] The most serious incident in the last hundred years occurred, according to available records, on the days of December 2–4, 1947, when a pogrom was carried out in the city. As in other Arab countries, and despite the fact that Aden was not independent, but under British rule, demonstrations were staged on December 2, following orders issued by the Arab League to arrange strikes in protest against the decision to partition Palestine. In the demonstrations held the morning of that day, no harm was done to Jews, but in the afternoon, stones were thrown at them and a rumour was spread that Jews had killed Arabs. As a result, the Jewish quarter was assaulted. A Jewish school in the city was set on fire, and Jewish shops looted. The British, who maintained a small force in Aden, comprised mostly of Arabs, did not suceed in preventing the riots from spreading, and in certain cases Arab police even participated in the attacks on the Jews. During the ensuing two days the riots continued, leading, according to an announcement by the Aden authorities, to 82 killed and 76 wounded. This announcement also indicated that a synagogue, school and houses had been set on fire and most of the Jewish shops looted. Only when military forces arrived from outside did the riots cease. The British Government appointed an investigation committee consisting of one man. From his report it emerged that the riots were caused by incitement from outside Aden, which found ready ears, especially among the many unemployed Yemenite Arabs hanging around the city.[145]

The Jews who had been robbed did not receive any compensation, so that within a few days many of them were penniless. As a result, and also out of fear that the riots might be repeated, many endeavoured to leave Aden. From May 1948 until the end of 1955, about 3,500 Jews who were born in Aden, arrived in Israel.[146] This number included hundreds of children born in Aden of Yemenite parents who had been delayed in the city on their way to Israel.

Some of the few hundreds who remained resumed their trades, but suffered in 1958 and again in 1966 from the disturbances which broke out there against the British. Several were murdered and much Jewish property looted. The few Jews left, about 150 in number, were evacuated in July 1967 after the Six-Day War in the Middle East, when the Arabs were preparing to massacre them. Thus the Jewish community in Aden came to an end.

Except for the attacks on the Aden Jews in the years 1947 and 1967, and on those in Bahrein in 1947, no other anti-Jewish riots occurred in all the States and Principalities of the Arabian Peninsula. It is most revealing that attacks occurred precisely in those places where the Jews were less degraded than in the Yemen. It seems that the Muslims in Aden and Bahrein were more susceptible to incitement from outside than were those in the Yemen.

Chapter Two
DEMOGRAPHIC EVOLUTION

One of the fundamental questions in studying the history of the Middle East Jews in our day is that concerning their number. Unfortunately, there is no reliable material on this subject; with the exception of Egypt, where a population census was conducted in 1882, in no country of the Middle East was such a census taken prior to the last few decades: in Turkey—in 1927, in Iraq—in 1947, and in Iran—in 1956. In the absence of population censuses, it is obvious that data on birth-rates, death-rates, infant mortality and natural increase are non-existent for any of the countries in the region, both as regards the 19th century and in our day. All the data available on the number of Jews in this area before the aforementioned censuses are based on estimates made by travellers and tourists of the number living in the important cities and some of the townships and villages. Not only do these not include all the localities in a particular State where Jews reside, but generally speaking, it is not possible to rely on the data provided. Often substantial differences exist between the estimate given by one traveller and that of another who followed him after a short time, and it is difficult to know whether this was due to emigration, or to the occurrence of plagues, or only to inaccurate estimates by one, or both, of the travellers. Hence, it cannot be said with certainty whether the number of Jews in a particular country increased or decreased in the past hundred years and for what reasons. Moreover, data are lacking on the dimensions of Jewish emigration from villages and small towns to the main cities, from one country to another, and from the countries of the region to overseas. There undoubtedly was much movement of Jews in all these directions and less from other countries to those of this region. Particularly large-scale emigration took place from Turkey and Syria to Egypt, Europe and America, and from all the countries of the region to Palestine. As to immigration into the region, it was relatively large to Egypt and Turkey from East Europe before the First World War, and insignificant thereafter.

On the whole, and despite the above reservations, the number of Jews in the countries of the region may be estimated to have been 400,000 in 1917, 460,000 in 1947, 115,000 in 1968 and 104,000 in 1972. Their distribution among the various countries can be seen in the following table:

TABLE A-1: JEWS IN THE MIDDLE EAST COUNTRIES, 1917–1972

	1917	1947	1968	1972
Iraq	85,000	125,000	3,000	400
Egypt	60,000	66,000	2,500	300
Syria and the Lebanon	35,000	35,000	6,000	5,000
The Yemen and Aden	45,000	54,000	500	300
Iran	75,000	100,000	65,000	62,000
Turkey	100,000	80,000	38,000	36,000
Total	400,000	460,000	115,000	104,000

This table shows that in the thirty years between 1917–1947 there was emigration from Turkey and Syria and a not inconsiderable number left Egypt (the increase from 60,000 to 66,000 Jews is less than the natural increase), while there was less emigration from Iran, the Yemen and Aden. But after 1952, most of the Jewish communities in the Arab countries of the Middle East dwindled and the number of Jews in the Lebanon, Iran and Turkey was very much smaller. The majority of the emigrants went to Israel, although several tens of thousands made their way to Europe and America.

Proportionally more Jews from Egypt left for Europe and the United States. Following the passage of a bill in 1957 which changed the immigration laws of the U.S. by providing for the entry of 25,000 refugees, Jews from Egypt who emigrated to Europe following the Sinai War of 1956, and had not settled into permanent jobs or had other reasons for leaving Europe, took advantage of this alteration in the law and immigrated to the U.S.

Despite the absence of exact data we may conclude that in this period Middle Eastern Jewry was in the process of urbanization. As a result of the movement to the main cities, the decisive majority of the Jews of the Middle East had become city dwellers. But there was a difference between the percentage of city dwellers in Egypt (96% in 1947 in Cairo and Alexandria) and Iraq (about 75% in Baghdad and Basra) and Iran (about 50% in Teheran and Shīrāz), while in the Yemen. only some 15% of the Yemenite Jews lived in the Capital.

This process of concentrating in the main cities of the State, where most of the government and community institutions were to be found, greatly influenced the Jews' economic, educational, health and organizational development, and, to a certain extent, also their relations with the other inhabitants.

A third point to be noted is the decrease in the mortality rate in most of the countries in the region, except, perhaps, in the Yemen. As regards Egypt, it may be deduced, from the limited data available, that the birthrate also fell. It is difficult, however, to know the exact rates of decline.

As a result of the development of educational institutions, which from now on also embraced a not inconsiderable proportion of the women, and as a result of the rise in the average economic level, the average marriage age also became higher. Again, there is no possibility of examining the extent of this in the various countries of the Middle East.

Egypt

Egypt was the only state in the Middle East which conducted a population census regularly from 1882; these were carried out with increasing efficiency and detail, until it was possible to ascertain from them a limited number of basic facts about the demographic changes occurring among Egyptian Jewry.

In the middle of the 19th century, there were about 5,000–6,000 Jews in Egypt, the majority in Cairo. From then on, their number began to be augmented, at first slowly, and later by many more immigrants from Syria, Turkey and East Europe, until by the time of the 1897 census, the number had grown to 25,200. Jewish immigration to Egypt continued until 1917, after which a gradual departure began, taking on the form of a mass exit after 1948, until today no more than 300 Jews remain there.

TABLE A-2: THE JEWS IN EGYPT, 1897–1972[1]

Year	Cairo	Alexandria	Other Places	Total	Surplus of Females	% of Foreign Nationals
Estimate 1840	—	—	—	5,000	—	—
Census 1897	11,608	9,831	3,761	25,200	—	49.6
Census 1907	20,281	14,475	3,879	38,635	-825	—
Census 1917	29,207	24,858	5,516	59,581	+41	58.1
Census 1927	34,103	24,829	4,618	63,550	+976	49.1
Census 1937	35,014	24,690	3,249	62,953	+1,123	36.0
Census 1947	41,860	21,128	2,651	65,639	+1,047	22.5
Census 1960	5,587	2,760	214	8,561	+183	—
Estimate 1968	—	—	—	2,500	—	—
Estimate 1972				300		

A study of the above table reveals the following:

Up to 1917 there was considerable immigration of Jews to Egypt. Until 1907, there was a larger proportion of men among the immigrants (847 more men than women in the age group 20–49), while in the years 1907–1917, there were more women. From 1917, when the Jews began to leave Egypt the emigrants were mainly men, creating a large surplus of Jewish women. The majority of those leaving were young men aged 15-29, so that the larger number of women was particularly conspicuous in this age group. Thus, as had occurred in other countries, young men were the first to come to Egypt and were also the first to leave.

Among the principal reasons for the large influx of Jews into Egypt was the economic development which had begun in that country in the 'sixties of the previous century, and the privileges granted to foreign nationals by the Capitulations. The terms of these Capitulations attracted some of the Jews of Turkey and Syria, where the economic situation had deteriorated, as well as thousands of Jews from East Europe, who were fleeing from the successive pogroms. During the First World War, thousands of Jews expelled from Palestine also reached Egypt; some of them made their permanent home there and others left after a brief stay.

After the War, economic conditions in Egypt ceased to attract masses of immigrants, and there were also local residents who preferred to leave for foreign countries for economic reasons or to further their education. In the 'forties the Muslim population began to display hostility towards the Jews; this was another important factor leading to their departure in larger numbers from Egypt for Palestine and other countries, and by the time the State of Israel was established, thousands had gone there. At the end of 1956, after the Sinai campaign, tens of thousands of Jews were expelled from Egypt.

Another fact emerging from Table A-2 is that the Jews were concentrated in the two main cities of Egypt, where 85% of them had lived in 1897. In 1917, the proportion rose to 90%, and in 1947, 96% resided in Cairo and Alexandria. In no other Middle East country had there been such a high concentration of Jews in the two chief cities. Since the educational, health and economic institutions were all to be found in Cairo and Alexandria, the Egyptian Jewish Community's concentration there had a favourable effect on their development.

A third fact revealed by this table is that up to 1917 there had been a high percentage of foreign nationals among the Egyptian Jews: those coming to Egypt retained their foreign nationality for the Capitulations made it advantageous. Moreover, even persons born in Egypt endeavoured, sometimes with success, to obtain foreign nationality. But after the First World War, some of the foreigners—Jews and non-Jews alike—left Egypt, while others lost their nationality (e.g., Syrians who were nationals of the Ottoman Empire; when the Empire broke up, only few of these obtained Syrian or Turkish citizenship). Later, pressure was put on the foreigners, by means of propaganda, until many waived their nationality. Incidentally, not everyone who surrendered his foreign nationality was granted Egyptian nationality.* Thus, the total number of foreign nationals in Egypt declined in the years 1927–1947 from 225,000 to 146,000, and among the Jews, from 29,000 to 13,000.

* See above, page 50.

Many of the Karaites with foreign nationality left Egypt during this period. They numbered 1,848 in the year 1927, and 322 in 1947, while the number of Karaites of Egyptian nationality rose from 2,659 to 3,164. The total number of Karaites in Egypt fell from 4,507 to 3,486. It is impossible to ascertain what happened to more than 1,500 of them before their emigration to Israel.

The following table presents the data gleaned from the Egyptian censuses, which indicate that the Egyptian Jewish Community consisted of older age groups, owing, no doubt, to the emigration of the young men in the 'twenties.

TABLE A-3: JEWS IN EGYPT, 1907–1947, ACCORDING TO AGE (IN PERCENTAGES)

Age Group	1907	1937		1947	
	Total	Total	Karaites	Total	Karaites
0–4	11.8	8.1	9.0	10.3	13.5
5–14	22.8	21.3	22.0	16.1	19.9
15–29	30.7	28.7	28.9	27.3	27.2
30–49	24.4	27.4	27.4	28.7	25.4
50–59 } 60+ }	10.3	8.2	7.2	9.2	7.8
		6.3	5.5	8.4	6.2

It can be seen from this table that the Jewish Community in Egypt grew older during the 40 years 1907–1947, particulary the Rabbinate Jews (as distinct from the Karaites). This can be explained by the emigration of the youth, and by the fall in the birthrate. While in 1907 there were 442 children aged 0–4 for every 1,000 Jewish women of child-bearing age (15–49), in 1937 the number of infants per 1,000 women of this age fell to 278; it rose again to 357 in 1947. It should be noted that for every 1,000 women of child-bearing age emigrating to Israel from Iraq in the years 1948–1952, there were 576 infants. It may be assumed, despite the deficiencies in the statistical data, that the birthrate among the Egyptian Jews, at least in the 'thirties, was declining. This decline in birthrate stems from the improved economic, educational, sanitary and health conditions under which the Jews lived. As regards the improvement in their health, it may be said that among the immigrants to Israel from Egypt no special diseases were found; even eye diseases, which had been prevalent among them up to the beginning of this century[2], seem to have become less common among the younger generation.

Iraq

In contrast to Egypt, no official authoritative population census was held in Iraq before 1947, and even this census is not entirely satisfactory.[3] The estimates of the number of Jews who lived in this country in the 19th century cover only a number of localities, and are therefore not reliable. In addition to the 1947 census, official estimates for all Iraq exist for the years 1904, 1919 and 1932. According to the first estimate, in 1904 there were 61,435 Jews in the country, and according to the second, made during the period of the British occupation, there were 86,488 out of a total population of 2,694,282 (3.2%). Several years later, in 1932, a new population estimate was made, which came to 2,857,077, of whom 72,783 were Jews (2.5%). The population census of 1947 produced a figure of approximately 4.8 million inhabitants, of them 118,000 Jews (2.5%).[4] As against these figures, it should be remembered that in the years 1948–1951 about 123,500 Iraqi-born Jews emigrated to Israel, and during the same years thousands went to other countries, for example, Iran, England and the United States. At the end of 1951, approximately 6,000 Jews remained in Iraq, and if it had not been for this emigration, the Jews in Iraq would have numbered about 135,000 by that year. Accordingly, it may be assumed that their number in 1947 was approximately 125,000 and not 118,000. The 1932 official estimate, too, is incorrect; it appears that at that period the Iraqi authorities were interested in minimizing the proportion of the minorities in a State about to receive its independence. The 1919 estimate, on the other hand, seems reasonable—about 86,000 Jews. It is impossible to make any estimates for earlier periods, not only because we don't know the rate of natural increase, but mainly because we are unaware of the extent of Jewish departure from Iraq to India, to the Far East and to Europe which began in the 'thirties of the 19th century.

These calculations, together with estimates made by travellers and tourists who visited Iraq in the previous century, reveal the extent to which the Iraqi Jews were dispersed throughout the country, and moved about from place to place.

After the plague in 1831, which caused many fatalities among the residents of Basra, only a few dozen Jewish families remained in that city.* In the 'sixties Jews began to move there, their number rising gradually and reaching 4,000–5,000 souls on the eve of the First World War.[5] They were drawn to Basra mainly because of the economic development of southern Iraq, and the fact that Basra was an important port. During the First World War, more Jews streamed into this city, especially young people fleeing from military service in the Ottoman army since Basra had already been conquered by the British in November 1914. In 1919, 6,928 Jews were to be found in the Basra district; in the 1947 census they numbered 10,537.

As a result of the development of Basra port and the greater security in southern Iraq created by the Ottoman governor, Midḥat Pasha, who ruled in the years 1869–1872, people began to move from central Iraq to the south, among them Jews, a number of whom settled in Basra; others stayed in places where until then there

* See above, p. 12.

had been no Jews, such as 'Amara, Qal'at Ṣāliḥ, 'Alī al-Gharbī and Musayyb (in the Ḥilla district). The small Jewish settlement in Ḥilla also expanded. While in the middle of the 19th century there had been only two small Jewish communities in all of southern Iraq, in Basra and in Ḥilla, by the end of the century these communities had grown larger and additional communities had appeared.[6] After the First World War, however, not only did movement to the cities of the south cease (except for Basra), but many Jews left, until, according to the 1947 census, in four of the southern districts ('Amāra, Ḥilla, Muntafiq and Dīwāniya) there remained only 5,473 Jews as compared to 10,755 estimated in 1919. The main reason for emigration from this district was economic; non-Jews also left southern Iraq for Baghdad.

In the middle of the 19th century, a total of about 500 Jews were to be found in all the five southern districts of Iraq; in 1919—about 17,700; in 1947 about 16,000; and only a few score have remained there since 1952.

The largest Jewish community in Iraq in the last hundred years was that in the city of Baghdad, it having been estimated, in 1848, by the traveller Benjamin ben Joseph, to comprise 3,000 families; at the end of the century the number was reckoned to be 30,000–40,000 souls;[7] in 1919—50,300, and according to the 1947 census —77,542. Despite the fact that these are only estimates, there is no doubt that the number of Jews in Baghdad increased, not only as a result of a large natural increase due to improved sanitary and medical conditions, but also following immigration into the city in the second half of the 19th century, from Iran and from the Kurdistan region, and, after the First World War, also from southern Iraq. In the remaining central districts (Diyāla, Dulaym, Kūt and Karbala) there were 4,670 Jews in 1919, and 4,681 in 1947, according to the census taken that year.[8]

With regard to northern Iraq, many scores of small Jewish communities were scattered over that area, the largest of them being in the city of Mosul, with 450 families (according to Benjamin ben Joseph in 1848), which remained at approximately the same strength—2,000–3,000 souls[9]—until the beginning of the 20th century. Apparently the decline in the economic standing of Mosul following the opening of the Suez Canal contributed to the departure from this city for Baghdad and Europe. After the First World War there was movement of Jews to other cities in the region—Arbīl, Sulaymānīya and Kirkuk. Migration to Kirkuk followed the development of the oil industry there. According to an official estimate in 1919, there were 13,835 Jews in all the northern districts of Iraq (Mosul, Arbīl, Kirkuk and Sulaymānīya), and according to the 1947 census—19,767. In 1919 about 66% of the Jews in Iraq lived in Baghdad and Basra. According to the 1947 census, about 74% resided in those two cities, about 22.5% in other cities, and the remaining 3.5% in the areas defined by the Iraqi authorities as rural. Most of the rural Jews were to be found in the area of Kurdistan in northern Iraq as well as in Khāniqīn, a town in the Diyāla district, near Baghdad. On the other hand, in the other nine districts of Iraq the few Jews in the rural areas were not permanent residents, but were there in connection with their jobs. This is illustrated by the fact that the majority of the Jews in the rural areas of southern and central Iraq were men, as indicated in the following table:

TABLE A-4: JEWS IN IRAQ ACCORDING TO PLACE OF RESIDENCE, 1947

	Kurdish areas (Mosul, and Kirkuk Districts)		Other Districts		
	Urban	Rural	Urban	Rural	Total
Males	5,222	1,312	52,568	862	59,964
Females	5,527	1,393	50,657	459	58,036
Total	10,749	2,705	103,225	1,321	118,000
Percentage of rural	20.1		1.2		3.5

It is important to note that in the two main districts where Jewish Kurds lived—Mosul and Arbīl—20.1% lived in rural areas, as compared to only 1.2% of the Jews in the nine southern and central districts. This is the source of the economic and cultural differences existing between the Babylonian and Kurdish Jews.

It may be assumed that the percentage of rural dwellers among the Kurdistan Jews in the middle of the 19th century was larger than in 1947, while we cannot surmise that any substantial change occurred in that respect among the Babylonian Jews, most of whom were urban dwellers.

The population census taken in Iraq does not yield information on the age composition according to religion; the only source from which anything may be learned about the age structure of the Iraqi Jews is the data gathered by the Israel Immigration Department during the mass immigration of the Iraqi Jews in the years 1948–1952.

TABLE A-5: IMMIGRANTS ACCORDING TO AGE, 1948–1952, IN PERCENTAGES[10]

Age	From Iraq	From the Yemen and Aden	Egyptian Jews 1937 Census
0–4	13.5	12.3	8.1
5–14	25.5	28.1	21.3
15–29	29.1	26.3	28.7
30–49	17.9	22.1	27.4
50–59	6.8	5.9	8.2
60+	7.2	5.3	6.3

The high percentage of children among the immigrants from Iraq stems from the high birthrate and the low infant mortality rate. This is indicated by the fact that for every 1,000 women aged 15–49 who came from Iraq in 1948– 1952 there were 576 children aged 0–4, as compared with 473 children per 1,000 women from the Yemen and Aden, where the infant mortality rate was high.

The high percentage of persons aged 60 and over who came to Israel from Iraq leads us to believe that there was a decline in the mortality rate and an increase in life expectancy among the Iraqi Jews after the First World War. The fall in the deathrate is the result of improved sanitary and medical conditions and the better economic and cultural circumstances of the majority of Iraqi Jews. Like the immigrants from Egypt, the Iraqi immigrants to Israel were not found to be suffering from any special diseases, although there had not been any medical restrictions on this immigration to Israel.

Turkey

In contrast to the situation in other Middle East countries, large-scale departure of Jews from Turkey dates from the end of the 19th century, most of them going to Egypt, the American continent and a small number to Palestine. From the time of the First World War, the destination was mainly Palestine. True, at the end of the 19th century, Turkey received Jews from East Europe, but their number did not exceed several thousands, and over the last 70 years the Jewish community in Turkey gradually shrank. At first this was due to economic factors: the small communities in the southeast of the State were adversely affected by the diversion of international trade to the Suez Canal. After the First World War, however, there was also a political reason: the rule of the Greeks in many cities in western Turkey led to the flight of thousands of Jews, especially from the city of Izmir. In the 'thirties, the European Turkish Jewry also suffered, and in 1942, as a result of the heavy property tax imposed particularly on members of the minorities in Turkey, many of the Jews were ruined and decided to leave the country. In the years 1948–1950, 33,000 Turkish Jews arrived in Israel.

The number of Jews in Turkey in 1904 stood at about 147,000[11]; the first census conducted in the Turkish Republic in 1927 included 81,872 Jews, the second 78,730 (1935), and the ensuing ones—76,965 (1945), 45,995 (1955), 43,929 (1960), and 38, 267 (1965). Their number today is estimated at about 36,000.

At the same time as thousands of Jews were leaving Turkey, those remaining began to concentrate in a few cities. The European Turkish cities, Adrianople, Churlo, Burgaz, Kirkkilise and others, gradually became depleted of their Jews. The exit from them started during the Russo-Turkish War in 1876 and continued after the Balkan War and the First World War. Thus, only 5,712 Jews out of the main community were left in Adrianople in 1927 (according to the census of that year), compared with 15,000–17,000 who had been there before the First World War.[12] A further decline in the number in this city and in all of European Turkey (except Istanbul) occurred after the riots against the Jews in Adrianople in 1934*; out of the 24,000 Jews estimated to have lived in European Turkey in 1904, only about 1,000 remain today.

The Turkish Kurdistan region, too, as well as most of the small Jewish communities in Asiatic Turkey were practically depleted of Jews, very few remaining in Urfa, Diyarbakir, Nusaybin, Mardin, Antioch and Iskenderun (Alexandretta), owing to both the economic crisis and the Greek occupation in the years 1919–1922.[13]

The second largest community in Turkey, that of Izmir, had grown in number from 25,000 in 1904 to 35,000 in 1913, when Jews residing in the vicinity moved to Izmir because of the economic crisis. However, many more left immediately after the First World War and the Greek conquest of the city. The population census of 1927 counted only 16,501 Jews in Izmir.[14] Their number diminished further, especially after the large-scale emigration to Israel in the years 1948–1950; by the time the 1955 census was taken, there were only 5,382 Jews in the city, and the 1960 and 1965 censuses reported 4,885 and 4,062 Jews respectively. Today there are only 4,000 Jews in Izmir.

In Istanbul, too, emigration occurred after the economic crisis of the 'twenties, when non-Jews also left[15]; afterwards the number remained stable, as Jews moved to Istanbul from the various Turkish cities. The 1904 estimate showed 65,000 Jews living there; the 1927 census—47,035 and that of 1935—47,135.[16] After 1948, however, the number of Jews in Istanbul decreased substantially, the majority going to Israel. In the 1955 census, only 36,914 were counted, in 1960—35,368, and in 1965—30,831. Today their number is estimated at 30,000 souls.

The fluctuation in the number of Jews in Turkey may be summarized in the following table:

TABLE A-6: NUMBER OF JEWS IN TURKEY, 1904–1965[17]

City	1904 Estimate	1927 Census	1960 Census	1965 Census
Istanbul	65,000	47,035	35,368	30,831
Izmir	25,000	16,501	4,885	4,067
Adrianople	17,000	5,712	438	298
Others	40,000	12,624	3,235	3,071
Total	147,000	81,872	43,926	38,267

* See above, p. 21.

In other words, 84% of all the Jews in Turkey today live in Istanbul, while in 1927, 57% resided there and in 1904, less than 45%.

One of the outstanding phenomena among the Turkish Jews since the First World War is the larger proportion of women, although this is dwindling, as can be seen from the following:

TABLE A-7: JEWS OF TURKEY, ACCORDING TO SEX, 1927–1965[18]

Year	Male	Female	Total	% of Males	Surplus of Women
1927	38,103	43,769	81,872	46.5	5,666
1935	36,813	41,917	78,730	46.7	5,104
1945	36,247	40,718	76,965	47.1	4,471
1955	21,299	24,696	45,995	46.3	3,397
1965	18,210	20,057	38,267	47.6	1,847

It is interesting that only in the three large cities—Istanbul, Izmir and Adrianople—has the proportion of Jewish women been so high. According to the 1927 census there were 37,332 Jewish women and 31,661 men there (5,671 more women), while in the remaining smaller localities in Turkey the numbers of women and men were equal.[19] The 1935, 1945, 1955, 1960 and 1965 censuses also revealed more Jewish women than men in the main cities. Without knowing the number of Jews according to age, it is impossible to explain this surplus of women. According to the population census taken in 1960 in Turkey, there were 948 Jewish males and 1,885 Jewish females in the 0–5 age-group, i.e., 33.5% and 66.5% respectively. Moreover, only 6.45% of all Jews living in Turkey that year were aged 0–5 years. This is a very low percentage compared to all other Jewish communities in the Middle East. For this reason one might even suspect the authenticity of this census.

In the absence of data it is also difficult to ascertain the rates of natural increase among the Turkish Jews, or the mortality and birthrates.

Syria and the Lebanon

Very few demographic data are available concerning the Jews of Syria and the Lebanon, and it is doubtful whether what does exist is correct. It is therefore difficult to study the demographic changes in these communities over the last hundred years. Nevertheless, it may be said with certainty that during this period and up to 1958, there was a steady rise in the number of Jews in Beirut, while numbers in Damascus, Aleppo and Sidon were constantly diminishing. Emigration from Syria began in the 'eighties of the 19th century, at first to Egypt and afterwards also to Latin America, the U.S.A., England, the Lebanon and Palestine[20]; since the First World War, it has been principally to Palestine and the Lebanon. Initially, the Jews left because of the economic decline of Aleppo and Damascus following the opening of the Suez Canal, and later, particularly during the 'twenties, because of the deterioration in the political situation in Syria. As a result of the Druze revolt in October 1925 and the assaults on the Jews in Damascus, about 3,000 Jews fled from there within a few days; in April 1926, only 6,635 remained in the city.[21] Emigration was resumed when the Muslims in Damascus and Aleppo began to display hostility towards the Jews, especially after the riots against the Aleppo Jews at the end of 1947. In 1904 the number of Jews in each of these two cities had been estimated as 10,000 souls, and on the eve of the First World War as 12,000.[22] There are no estimates of the number in Qāmishlī in Eastern Syria, but it appears that it was very small; only in 1926 did some hundreds of Jews move to this city from Nusaybin in southern Turkey.[23] The total in all of Syria, therefore, according to the census taken in 1932, was 26,250. A second census, in 1943, revealed 29,770 Jews in all of Syria.[24] Immediately afterwards came the mass illegal immigration to Palestine from Syria, which continued until 1947; since then many Syrian Jews succeeded in fleeing to the Lebanon and Turkey, and from there emigrated to Europe and America or found their way to Palestine. Today, there are an estimated 3,000–4,000 Jews in Syria.

As to the Jews of the Lebanon, the community which had been settled in Sidon remained, until the middle of the 19th century, the most ancient and largest community, with about 25 families. In addition, there were two other small communities, in Tripoli and Beirut, of about 15 families each (1824).[25] In the second half of the 19th century, the number in Beirut and Sidon increased: in 1904 it was estimated to be 610 souls in Sidon and 3,000 in Beirut. Shortly afterwards, they began to leave Sidon for Beirut and America, until in 1913 there were an estimated 530 souls remaining in Sidon and 5,000 in Beirut.[26] Although this last estimate was apparently exaggerated, in any event the census conducted in the Lebanon in January 1932 revealed 3,060 Jews in Beirut and 458 in Sidon. As a result of the continuous movement from Syria to the Lebanon, the number of Lebanese Jews grew to 5,666, according to the 1944 census, and in 1947 their number was estimated to be 5,950 (2,833 men and 3,117 women), of whom 5,288 were in Beirut.[27] After the establishment of the State of Israel, the number rose—a 1958 estimate showed 9,000 in the Lebanon. The Lebanon, therefore, was the only Arab State in which the Jews increased in number after 1948, despite the fact that from there, too, Jews went to Israel or to Europe and America. But after 1958, the flow of refugees from Syria slowed down and departure from the Lebanon was on a larger scale, so that the Jewish population in this country shrank to 5,000 souls in 1967. Immediately after the June 1967 war in the Middle East, emigration from the Lebanon was resumed. In 1972 about 1,000 souls remained, the majority in Beirut. The small Jewish community in Tripoli came to an end before 1947, and of that in Sidon only about 50 souls were left. There were no permanent Jewish communities living in other cities, although synagogues were to be found in Zaḥla, in Bḥamdūn and in 'Aley. These synagogues had been established for the use of Jewish summer campers.

It would appear, therefore, that the number of Jews in Syria and the Lebanon never reached more than 35,000 souls during the last hundred years, most of them dispersed among three communities—Aleppo, Damascus and Beirut—with some single families in other cities. Obviously the small size of the communities in the Levant countries was the reason for the lack of Jewish institutions such as hospitals and secondary schools, which were to be found in bigger oriental communities.

Iran

In Iran no population census was conducted before November 1956, and all the existing data on the number of Jews there before this date are estimates which do not include all the small places throughout the country where Jews lived. Several of the estimates included Jews who had converted, they or their fathers, to Islam or to the Bahai religion. The fact that some of the proselytes or their children considered themselves Jews, makes it difficult to determine the total number of Jews. During the 50 years 1875 to 1925, the estimates fluctuated between 40,000 and 50,000, in the 'thirties between 50,000 and 70,000, and in the 'forties between 80,000 and 100,000. After about 29,000 Jews emigrated to Israel in the years 1948–1956, 65,232 Jews remained in Iran, according to the first population census.[28]

There is some doubt as to the accuracy of these figures. It may be assumed that in 1920 there was a total of about 80,000 Jews in Iran, which rose to 100,000 in 1948. According to the first population census taken in 1956, 65,232 Jews were living in Iran. One may suspect the authenticity of this figure. A more accurate estimate puts their number that year at 72,000; of them some 20,000 emigrated to Israel in the years 1957–1966. With the addition of the natural increase, the Jewish population in Iran was estimated at 61,000–62,000 in 1966. Actually, in the second population census taken in 1966 there were 60,681 Jews in Iran. As a result of the small percent of emigration to Israel, some 62,000 Jews still live in Iran today (1972).

In view of the inadequate demographic data available on the Jews of Iran, it is difficult to determine the extent of their wanderings in the 19th century, but it may be said with certainty that the number of Jews in Teheran was constantly on the increase.[29] After the First World War, Jews moved to Teheran in increasing numbers and in 1935 there were 11,000 in that city.[30] During the Second World War, and immediately afterwards, their number was greatly augmented by many new arrivals, transforming Teheran into an important centre of Iranian Jewry, with 40,000 out of the 100,000 Jews in the country living in the capital in 1948. Following extensive emigration to Israel, 39,700 out of a total of 61,000 Iranian Jews resided in Teheran in 1966, according to that year's census. From these figures it can be seen that it was only in the last 30 years that a large proportion of the Iranian Jews —more than 85%—was concentrated in one city. In all the other Middle East countries, with the exception of the Yemen, the Jews had been concentrating in the main cities a long time before this. This is one of the reasons why other Jewish communities in the East achieved economic, social and cultural development earlier than did the Iranian community.

In the last 30 years many more Jews settled in southwest Iran, following the development of the oil industry in Abadān and the laying of the Trans-Iranian railroad connecting the Persian Gulf with Teheran and the Caspian Sea. In Abadān, in Khorramshahr and in Ahwāz, hundreds of Iraqi Jews also made their homes, and in 1956, over 3,000 were living in the main cities of the Abadān district. In the same period the number of Jews in the Iranian Kurdistan region in Hamadhān and Iṣfahān was dwindling, as they moved to Teheran or emigrated to Israel.

Despite these changes in the demographic map of Iranian Jewry in the past 30 years, and despite the emigration to Israel of many whole communities, it is revealing that even in 1966, Jewry in this country was dispersed over many locations, only 77% living in the two largest cities, Teheran and Shīrāz.[31] One can imagine how much more widely dispersed they were 30 or 40 years previously.

With regard to the age structure of the Iranian Jews, the 1956 and 1966 censuses inform us that among the remaining Jewish community the percentage of elders was high: over 10% were aged 55 and over. Undoubtedly this was due to the emigration of many young people to Israel. In the years 1948–1952, persons of the 55 and over age group coming to Irael from Iran represented only 5.5%, as can be seen from the following table:

TABLE A-8: JEWS OF IRAN ACCORDING TO AGE, IN PERCENTAGES

Age	Immigrants from Iran 1948–1952[32]	Jews in Iran	
		1956 Census	1966 Census
0–4	13.9	22.2	10.8
5–9	12.8		12.6
10–19	28.8	24.8	25.0
20–29	17.3	41.4	14.7
30–54	21.7		26.6
55+	5.5	11.6	10.3

Old age today constitutes one of the gravest social problems in the Jewish community in Iran, and it is being aggravated by the continued emigration of young people.

From the available material it is difficult to determine the extent of decline in the death rate and infant mortality rate among the Iranian Jews. It is more or less certain that these have indeed fallen in recent decades, as a result of improved sanitation and health conditions in Iran, and the better cultural and economic circumstances of those remaining there, following the emigration of a considerable proportion of the poorer classes. Nevertheless, the birth rate should still be high. According to the 1966 population census there were 457 children aged 0–4 to every 1,000 Jewish women between the ages of 15 and 49.

The Yemen and Southern Arabian Peninsula

A population census was never taken in any of the countries in the Arabian Peninsula, with the exception of the Bahrein Islands and the city of Aden. It is not known, therefore, how many Jews lived, at any one time, in the Yemen, in Najrān in Saudi Arabia, in Southern Yemen (the former colony and protectorates of Aden) and in Kuwait on the shores of the Persian Gulf. Even the exact total of all the inhabitants there is not known.

Nevertheless, it is evident that a hundred years ago there were several tens of thousands of Jews in the Yemen, and only small communities of some hundreds of souls elsewhere in the Arabian Peninsula.

Estimates of the number of Jews in the Yemen are available only from the 20th century, and these refer to only some scores or hundreds of Jewish communities scattered all over the country. These estimates are not necessarily inaccurate, but they do not include many additional hundreds of communities. Two calculations made in 1904 fixed the number of Yemenite Jews as 30,000–50,000.[33] Yomtov Sémach, an emissary of the *Alliance Israélite Universelle,* who reached the Yemen in 1910, reported a figure of 12,026 Jews scattered over 139 localities; according to him, there were 3,000–4,000 more in other communities, making a total of about 15,000–16,000, besides about 4,000 in the city of Aden. This estimate did not seem reasonable to Shmuel Yavnieli, who visited the Yemen a short time after Sémach; in 1911, Yavnieli reported that there were more than 30,000 Jews in the Yemen and a further 3,000 in Aden.[34]

On the other hand, the number of Jews in the Yemen and in Aden in 1949 can be calculated to a greater degree of exactitude, by the number who came to Israel in the years 1949–1950. In these two years 44,072 Jews born in the Yemen and 3,028 born in Aden reached Israel;[35] by adding the 4,000 approximately who remained in both countries in 1951, a total figure of about 51,000 Jews must have been there in 1949. We do not know what was the rate of natural increase among the Jews of the Yemen and Aden, but if we recall that in the years 1910–1948 about 19,000 came to Israel, we may conclude that in 1910 there were not 20,000–30,000 Jews but about 45,000–50,000. It is difficult to estimate how many Jews lived there in earlier periods, since up to 1910 the Yemenite Jews suffered a high death rate, as a result of famines, plagues and wars. With regard to Aden, however, we know that the number of Jews there rose considerably from the time of that city's conquest by the British in January 1839 , when about 250–500 Jews lived there. According to the census conducted there in 1901, they numbered 3,050 souls,[36] and in 1910 there were estimated to be 3,000–4,000 souls; in 1931 it was reported that there 4,151 Jews, in 1946 —7,723, and in 1947—8,550, of whom 4,750 were local residents and 3,800 refugees of Eastern Aden (the majority in the Principality of 'Udhālī) and some hundreds in the Western Protectorate (mainly in Ḥabbān).

The large increase in the number of Jews in Aden was the result of the influx of Jews from the Yemen, some of whom had come there to benefit from the more favourable political conditions in Aden, and others to find their way to Palestine —the latter were delayed in Aden for many years before they succeeded in reaching Palestine.

After the establishment of the State of Israel and the mass departure from the Yemen and Aden in the years 1948–1955—about 50,000 Jews left for the new Homeland—about 2,000 remained in the Yemen and a further 831 (according to a 1955 census) in the city of Aden.[38] Since then, hundreds more have come to Israel from this area; at the beginning of 1967, only about 150 were still to be found in Aden, all of whom left the colony following the riots there in June 1967, after the Six-Day War between Israel and the Arab States. It may be that some hundreds may still be found in the Yemen itself.

We may assume that the greater part of the small Jewish community in Bahrein has also left. In 1948, there were about 400 Jews in the Bahrein Islands, and a population census taken in that state in 1950 included 250 Jews and 149 in the census taken in 1959[39]—the lower figures being due to the departure from Manāma, the capital, after the anti-Jewish riots in December 1947.* The small Jewish community which existed in Kuwait after the First World War also left that country before the 'thirties, emigrating to Iraq, where they were known as al-Kuwaytī (Kavietī).

There is no evidence to indicate whether the Jews moved from one place to another within the Yemen during the last hundred years, or whether in 1949, they were concentrated in a smaller number of localities than they had been a hundred

* See above, p. 67.

or even fifty years before that. Even if they had undergone a process of urbanization, its dimensions were undoubtedly smaller, for at the beginning, and also the middle, of the present century, they were scattered in many places, with sometimes only a small number of Jewish families in each. Yomtov Sémach reported that in 1910, 2,744 Jews lived in the capital, San'a, 1,832 in the four cities, Rada', Dhamār, 'Amrān and Shaybām; he reported 7,450 Jews in 134 other localities[40] or an average of 56 Jews in each small locality; an average of 86 individuals lived in each of the 139 places to which he referred. Shmuel Yanvieli assumed that in addition to these localities there were 7,000 Jews in 130 other small localities (and a further 11,000 in many others)[41]; hence, according to Yavnieli's estimate, a total of 19,000 lived in 269 localities, or about 70 individuals in each. Since many other small communities were doubtless to be found in those days which were not recorded by these two travellers, the average community must have comprised even less than 70 persons. There are no signs indicating that the situation has changed since then. It would appear that the emigration of about 19,000 Jews from the Yemen and Aden in the years 1910–1948 did not lead to the complete break-up of many communities, but only decreased the number in each. S.D. Goitein, who studied the origin of thousands of Yemenite Jews who reached Israel in the years 1949–1950, came to the conclusion that they had been scattered over more than 1,000 communities[42]; in other words, 50,000–53,000 Jews of the Yemen and Aden lived in communities comprising an average of 50 souls.

From the data available on the mass immigration from the Yemen and Aden in the years 1948–1952 we may ascertain that this Jewry was young in age (see Table A–5), a fact which may be attributed to the high birthrate, and the short life span. We may also assume that even in the middle of the 20th century the infant mortality rate was still high. For every 1,000 women aged 15–49 who came to Israel from the Yemen and Aden there were 473 children aged 0–4, which is a low rate taking into consideration the fact that among a similar group of women coming from Iraq there were 576 infants per 1,000 women. As a result of the high death rate, the number of persons in a Jewish family coming to Israel from the Yemen in 1949–1950 was small—3.8.[43] This number is almost identical with Shmuel Yavnieli's partial data of 1911—3.66 per familty.[44]

Considering the high percentage of Jews in the Yemen who lived in the small localities, the few children in their families (1.7–1.8 on an average) was an important factor in determining educational possibilities. In many places where there were not more than ten families, the number of children of school age did not exceed an average of eight or nine, since the girls did not study. This is one of the significant factors in the great dispersion of so many small communities over so many localities. This dispersion also affected the economic, political and religious situation of the Jews in the Yemen.

Chapter Three
ECONOMIC TRANSFORMATIONS

No research has as yet been carried out on the economic position of the Jews in any of the Middle Eastern countries—neither on the present situation nor on what it was fifty or a hundred years ago. Most of the material available on this subject is based on impressions gained by travellers and tourists who visited various parts of the region and, for the greater part, deemed it sufficient to report briefly, referring to Jews as being rich people, persons of moderate means, or poor. At times they added some details on the major occupations of the Jews in the city which they visited. The definitions are not only general—and one cannot always be certain that the travellers' impressions were correct—but it has happened that two travellers who visited a particular place at brief intervals conveyed entirely opposing impressions, and there is no assurance that the difference is due to a change having taken place in the economic situation of that community during those years, or to subjective approaches on the part of the travellers in question. Undoubtedly it is impossible to determine, on the basis of these comments, whether the economic circumstances of the Yemenite Jews differed from those of the Iranian Jews, even if it was said of both communities that they were destitute.

As to the occupations of the Jews, official material is available only with respect to the Egyptian and Turkish Jews, based on government censuses. There is nothing on the occupations of the Jews of Iran, Syria and the Lebanon, while with respect to those of Iraq, the Yemen and Aden—who emigrated in masses in the years 1949–1952—the Immigration Department in Israel has data based on declarations made by immigrants. Although this material is not always exact, it can be used as a basis for obtaining a general idea. On the other hand, it is not possible to compare the occupations of the immigrants from these countries with those of the Egyptian Jews because of the varying descriptions of occupations; Egypt, for example, included the merchants' clerks among the merchants, but the Israel Immigration Department classified merchants and clerks separately.

Nevertheless, it may be said that in the middle of the 19th century the majority of the Middle Eastern Jews were poor, although even then there were differences between the Jews of Syria, Iraq and Egypt, among whom were some merchants and very wealthy individuals, and those of Iran and the Yemen, where poverty was more prevalent. Following the opening of the Suez Canal and political and economic changes, there was considerable improvement in the economic position of most of Middle Eastern Jewry, with the exception of those living in the Yemen and Turkish, Iraqi and Syrian Kurdistan. During the last 100 years, there was a larger percentage of middle class Jews, particularly among those in Iraq, Turkey and Egypt, as a result of the development of educational institutions, which created new occupations for Jews: those of clerks and the academic professions. It is almost certain that the relatively small gap between the economic position of the Jews in the various countries of the Middle East widened in the last 100 years. Generally speaking, in the middle of the present century Egyptian Jewry was the richest and best established; Iraqi Jewry came next, particularly the Babylonian Jews, and the Lebanese community third; Turkey, Syria and the Yemen followed, with a vast difference between the Jews of Egypt and those of the Yemen.

These dissimilarities in the economic circumstances of the various communities are also perceptible in Israel, despite the fact that very few of the extremely rich came to Israel from any of these countries, and if they did, it was after they had been forced to abandon a considerable part of their wealth in their countries of origin.

The Jews who immigrated to Israel from Turkey and Iran were mainly from the lower economic strata and their economic position at the time of their arrival in Israel does not reflect that of the community in the country they left. Moreover, during their years in Israel, great changes took place in the economic standing of the Jews from the Middle Eastern countries. In general, however, the gap which had existed between those coming from one Middle Eastern country and those from another remained. Those who immigrated, for example, from Egypt, Iraq and Lebanon, being privileged culturally as well as financially, could concentrate in the large cities of Israel and earn their livelihood from commerce or by working as officials, while the immigrants from Kurdistan and the Yemen, settled mainly in villages in Israel and became farmers and artisans.

Since most of the Jews in the Middle East—except the Yemenites and Kurds—were veteran city-dwellers, their occupations were typical for people living in cities: commerce, crafts, and services. The average per capita income of Jews was higher than that of the non-Jewish city-dwellers since most of the Muslims living in the big cities were mostly newly urbanized populations who had moved to the cities after the First World War. These Muslims were employed in service occupations and as unskilled workers. Hence, it is not certain whether the occupations and the economic position of the Jews were different from those of veteran non-Jewish city-dwellers.

Nevertheless, since many Muslims lived on small and unstable incomes, they were easily agitated against the Jewish firms and shops. In the 'forties, during the anti-Jewish disturbances which took place in Egypt, Iraq, Syria, Aden, and Bahrein, these masses pillaged Jewish property. In most of these countries, some of the young, educated Muslims, without suitable jobs, were easily aroused, out of jealousy, against the Jewish minority.

It seems that this fact contributed much to the anti-Jewish agitation in Muslim countries. Because of the Palestinian problem, this agitation developed into blood-hatred of the Jews. In Turkey and Iran, where Muslims are not politically minded regarding Palestinians, there is no serious anti-Jewish hatred.

Egypt

In the mid-1800's, the great majority of Egyptian Jews were described as destitute, but in comparison with the general poverty of the population, they were better off. At that time, there were already merchants and big bankers among the Jews.[1] The number of Jews in Egypt was then small; it was only from the 'sixties onwards that Jewish immigration on a relatively large scale began. In 1863, when the Khedive Ismā'īl came to power, he began to carry out large-scale economic development plans: industries were established, roads paved and lines laid for a railroad, and the Suez Canal was opened. The tempo of development was fast and wasteful, and within a number of years the country was sunk deep in debt. In 1876, Ismā'īl was forced to accept Franco-British instituted missions to control his revenues and expenditures so as to collect their debts. This control accelerated the immigration of foreign nationals, including Jews, from various countries. The foreigners enjoyed not only equal rights, but also privileges, including practically no payment of taxes to the State Treasury. The conquest of Egypt by the British in 1882 extended the privileges of the foreigners, who played a large part in the economic development of the country. The Jews contributed to the development of the sugar industry and the railroad, and participated in the founding of the National Bank of Egypt and the cotton exchange. They were among the directors of the large credit companies, such as the Belgian Bank, the International Bank, the Land Bank and Crédit d'Orient. Among the families who played an active part in these enterprises were the families Goar, De Menasce, Hazzan, Tilche, Harari, Suares, Cicurel, 'Adah, Politi and Mosseri. The latter was a veteran Egyptian family which founded two banks and several commercial companies for industry and agriculture.[2] From among these families there emerged a group of Jewish millionaires, whose number, although not large in itself, was quite considerable in proportion to the total number of Jews in Egypt. In the years 1863–1920 the middle class also expanded; its members engaged in the cotton business, in foreign trade, and, as a result of the development of educational institutions, now included doctors, lawyers, engineers and clerks. Despite the fact that a poor class remained, as well as pedlars and craftsmen, on the whole this Jewry was transformed, within 60–70 years, into the richest of all Eastern Jewry.

After Egypt became an independent state, and after an educated Muslim class had grown up in it, the Egyptian authorities began, in the 'twenties and 'thirties, gradually to restrict the foreigners' influence on economic life, until immigration to Egypt, including that of Jews, practically ceased. In 1937 the Capitulations were abolished in accordance with the convention of Montreux, and the economic privileges of the foreign nationals were discontinued. Since the Jews were already well established economically, these first steps did not affect them adversely. Ten years later, on July 29, 1947, the Egyptian Company Law was promulgated: its purpose was to oust the foreigners. This law (with slight amendments made in 1954) established, *inter alia,* that at least 40% of the members of the Board of Directors of every share company must be Egyptian nationals, that the number of employees with Egyptian nationality must be not less than 75%, and that these must receive not less than 65% of the total salaries. This law affected the Jews in particular, of whom only 15% were Egyptian nationals, the rest having foreign nationality or being stateless.* Many Jews who worked in banks and commercial companies were dismissed.

TABLE B-1: OCCUPATION OF JEWS IN EGYPT AGED 15 AND OVER, 1937–1947, IN PERCENTAGES[3]

Occupation	All Egypt, 1937		Cairo and Alexandria, 1947	
	Jews	Non-Coptic Christians	Jews	Non-Coptic Christians
Mining, agriculture and fishing	0.6	1.1	0.4	0.8
Industry and crafts	21.1	30.6	18.1	28.4
Building	—	—	1.0	1.9
Communications	2.4	6.7	2.5	7.4
Commerce	59.1	29.8	58.9	34.3
General administration and public service	10.4	15.6	12.2	6.2
Personal services	6.3	16.2	6.9	21.0
Total	100.0	100.0	100.0	100.0
In absolute figures	20,298	79,693	21,376	42,605
Unproductive and unemployed	37,535	125,534	15,395	29,401
Housewives (estimate)	—	—	19,700	47,000
Total aged 5 and over	57,833	205,227	56,472	119,000

* See above, p. 49.

With the establishment of the State of Israel, many of the Jews ruined by the law left Egypt; some went to Israel and others to European and American countries. Some lost their jobs, others their property, although some of them succeeded in smuggling their wealth out of the country before they themselves left. Many of those who remained were compelled, in November 1956–December 1957, to leave the country without taking more than a few pounds sterling. Thus, Jewish property to the value of millions of pounds fell into the hands of the Egyptians, and the small Jewish community remaining in Egypt today plays practically no part in the country's economy.

The occupations of the Egyptian Jews, which were examined in the population census of 1937 and again in that of 1947, can be compared with those of the non-Coptic Christians in Egypt, who, like the Jews, were mostly city dwellers and foreign nationals.

From table B-1 it may be seen that practically no Jews engaged in farming, and, in comparison with the other Jewish communities in the East, relatively few were in industry and crafts (18–19% including directors and clerks in industrial enterprises). Most of the Jews (59.1%) were engaged in commerce; some of them were clerks in commercial companies.* Compared with the non-Coptic Christian minority, more Jews were engaged in commerce, general administration and public service (including medicine, law, etc.).

The Egyptian statistical data reveal further that more than a third of all the Jews were breadwinners, and each breadwinner had to support 2.1 persons only. The number of dependents in Egypt was therefore less than in any other Jewish community in the East. This may be attributed to, *inter alia,* the low birthrate, few illiterates and the fact that the percentage of breadwinners among the women was higher among Egyptian Jewry.**

Iraq

In the middle of the 19th century, the Jews in Iraq were engaged in crafts, hawking and small commercial businesses, and in the Kurdistan mountains also in agriculture. There were few in foreign trade, since not only was Iraq almost cut off from Europe, but its agriculture and industry were backward and its commerce weak.

* By sampling 20% of the Jewish men born in Egypt, who were in Israel in 1961, it was found that only about 30% of them had engaged in real commerce in their countries of origin (Central Bureau of Statistics, *Population and Housing Census 1961,* Publication no. 27, Jerusalem, 1965, p. 12). It may be assumed, however, that in Egypt the percentage of Jews engaged in commerce was higher, since it is almost certain that proportionately many merchants did not emigrate to Israel.

** See p. 175.

True, there were Jewish bankers in Baghdad in the Middle Ages, but from the 14th century up to the end of the 18th, their number was not significant. At the end of the 18th century, a few rich Jewish merchants were to be found in three Iraqi cities: in Baghdad, the administrative centre; in Mosul, the continental port of Iraq through which part of the transit trade passed from Europe to the Far East; and in Basra, which began to develop as a port city. But the number of prominent Jewish merchants and bankers was still small. From the time of the opening of the Suez Canal, however, Iraq—and particularly the cities of Baghdad and Basra—began to occupy an important place in trade with the Far East. From then until the First World War, the Jews gradually acquired an important share in the country's foreign trade, until they displaced Muslim, Christian, and even European merchants, including the British who had settled in Iraq. The latter found it difficult to compete with the local Jewish merchants, and local Muslims were compelled to take Jewish partners.[4] Their knowledge of foreign languages and the fact that at that time Iraqi Jews had settled in both Manchester and India[5] were important factors in helping them to obtain control of foreign trade.

No change took place in this period in the economic situation of the Kurdistan Jews, while that of those in Mosul gradually declined, following the deflection of the transit trade from Europe to the Far East through the Suez Canal instead of by way of Aleppo and Mosul. On the eve of the First World War, the Jews of Mosul had become the "poorest and most backward of the inhabitants," according to the first director of the *Alliance* school in Mosul, Maurice Sidi.[6] The Mosul Jews and those of the Kurdistan area suffered badly from the famine prevailing in the region at the end of the 19th century, and required financial assistance from abroad; in 1884 the number of needy in the *wilāyit* (district) of Mosul was estimated to be 1,782 out of the 4,732 Jews there.[7]

Up to the First World War, the economic position of some of the Jews in Baghdad and the south had improved, but most of the Iraqi Jews were artisans and hawkers and many were destitute. Despite the impressions of several travellers, few were merchants.[8] There were very few in the free professions, for it was not until the beginning of the 20th century that the first Iraqi Jews concluded their studies at schools of higher education, in medicine, law and pharmacy.* Only a few were clerical workers, for, in contrast to Egypt in this period, there were still few foreign companies and banks in Iraq, and since the majority of the Iraqi Jews could not read and write Turkish,** only a few individuals found employment in the civil service. Iraq at the time remained an underdeveloped country. The Ottoman governors, except Midḥat Pasha (1869–1872) did not display any special interest in devel-

* See pp. 124–125.

** See p. 119.

oping the country. Moreover, Iraqi Jews did not enjoy, as did their brethren in Egypt, the privileges provided by the Capitulations, for they were not foreign nationals.

The period of the British occupation and Mandate, which began in 1914 in southern Iraq, in 1917 in the centre, and in 1918 in the north, and ended when Iraq received its independence in 1932, changed matters considerably for the Jews. With the development of commerce, the Jews, with their knowledge of European languages, their contacts with relatives in Europe and the Far East, and the loyalty to British rule, became more active in foreign trade and in the wholesale business. Many of them became rich when they were appointed as army contractors, providing for the thousands of Indian and British soldiers encamped in the country. This also accounted for a larger number of Jewish clerks in commercial companies and in the British administration. Soon there were many more Jewish officials in the civil service as well, until in 1934 some government ministries began to limit their number, although at no time were these jobs closed to Jews. Even during the Palestine war, Jews continued to work in the Iraqi civil service. They had a large share in commercial companies, in the banks, in the administration of the railroad, in the Basra port and in the Iraqi oil companies. With the expanded educational network and the larger number of Jewish academicians, the percentage of those in the free professions also rose. On the other hand, the number of Jews engaged in farming declined. Jews in the central and southern regions of Iraq were not engaged in farming, although it was a customary occupation among the Jews of Kurdistan. It may be assumed that when some of the Kurdish Jews emigrated to Palestine and others moved to Baghdad and the cities of northern Iraq, the percentage of farmers among those remaining was lower. On the whole, therefore, the years 1914–1951 witnessed the expansion of the middle class, a group which had hardly existed previously.

The first population census taken in Iraq in 1947 did not furnish information as to occupations according to religion, and we do not know, therefore, how the Jews were employed. With the mass immigration to Israel in 1950–1951, those aged 15 and over were asked what they had done in Iraq; a summary of their replies is presented below.

There is a possibility, of course, that some immigrants made incorrect declarations about their occupations in Iraq, since their statements were recorded without any checking. But if this were the case, it may be assumed that the number of such incorrect replies was small, in view of the revealing fact that the occupations of immigrants arriving in 1950 and in 1951 were similar. True there was a small percentage of merchants among the 1950 arrivals compared to those of 1951, but this may be explained by the fact that those with medium and large businesses required time to liquidate their affairs, and so delayed their departure, or that these mer-

TABLE B-2: OCCUPATIONS OF IRAQI-BORN IMMIGRANTS, 1950–1951 IN PERCENTAGES[9]

	1950	1951	Total
Number of breadwinners	8,236	21,904	30,140
Breadwinner whose occupation was known	8,219	21,792	30,011
Professional and technical	5.8	5.9	5.9
Administrative and clerical	15.9	15.8	15.8
Commerce	24.8	28.5	27.5
Agriculture	3.3	3.3	3.3
Crafts and industry	35.8	30.6	32.0
Transport, building, mines and unskilled work	10.9	11.2	11.1
Personal services	3.5	4.7	4.4

chants intended to remain in Iraq. When, in March 1951, a law was promulgated placing Jewish property under control, the merchants joined in the mass exit.

If the above data do not accurately reflect the occupations of the Iraqi Jews in the middle of this century, it is more likely to be due to the fact that some members of the free professions, merchants with large businesses and officials were not among the immigrants to Israel (if they left Iraq they went to other countries), while most of the unskilled labourers, craftsmen and farmers came to Israel. Nevertheless, taking into consideration the fact that in these two years about 90% of all the Jews of Iraq left for Israel, the occupations of the 1950–51 immigrants, as recorded, may be considered as reflecting fairly closely the actual situation in Iraq at the beginning of 1950: despite the changes that occurred in previous decades, about 48% were still engaged in crafts and services, 28% in commerce and 24% were clerical workers or members of the free professions. The percentage of those in crafts and services before the First World War was probably much higher, when only a few were clerical workers and members of the free professions. It is impossible to compare these data with those of Egypt because of the dissimilar descriptions of occupations, but undoubtedly a higher percentage of Egyptian Jews were engaged in commerce, as clerks and in the free professions.

The Israel statistics for 1950–1951 give us the following breakdown of those in crafts and industry: clothing and textile branches—12.3% of all the earners; gold- and silversmithery—4.7%; shoemaking and tanning—4.7%; foodstuffs, beverages and tobacco industries—3.1%; woodwork—about 3%.

Details about occupations according to sex reveal that a considerable proportion of those engaged in the clothing and textile industries were women; a large percentage of the women were also teachers. The total number of Jewish women breadwinners, however, was small (7.6% of all breadwinners), compared to those who worked in Egypt (13.8%) in 1937, which may be one of the reasons for the larger number of dependents among Iraqi Jews than among Egyptian (3 against 2.1). The higher birthrate among the Iraqi Jews was, of course, the main cause of this larger proportion of dependents.

To better discern the changes which occurred in the occupations of the Iraqi Jews, a breakdown of the above table is necessary, showing immigration from the Kurdistan areas separately. There is no doubt that among the Babylonian Jews there were no farmers, and the percentage of farmers among the Kurdish Jews was probably higher than 3.3—it may have been as high as 20%. There were very few Kurdish Jews (and no women at all) employed as clerks and in the free professions. It is estimated that 27–28% of the Babylonian Jews were to be found in these occupations. They also engaged more in commerce than the Kurds, while the opposite was true with regard to industry, transport and porterage, building and services. But it is difficult to make firm estimates without checking the immigrants' personal questionnaires and classifying them according to region of birth.

It is clear that a considerable improvement occurred in the economic situation of the Babylonian Jews, and little change in that of the Kurdistani Jews.

Iran

According to the available evidence about the economic situation of the Jews in Iran, it is apparent that, up to the 16th century, they included important merchants who acted as middlemen between their country and India and Turkey. But from that time on, these few began to be displaced by the Armenians. The Jews were then reduced to hawking, brokerage, selling antiquities, tailoring, weaving and dyeing. Some also earned their livelihood as dancers, singers and musicians and doing any other work which the Muslims considered unsuitable or beneath their dignity. Thus, there were not many very rich Jews, and the few who were rich were hit by the inheritance rulings if they did not convert to Islam. Reference has already been made to this practice, which afforded Jews who had converted the right to any inheritance left by any relatives who had remained Jewish. There were no prominent bankers among the Jews. The discriminatory laws, which had been collected in a codex in the name of the Shah Abbas the First (1557–1628) and called *Jāmi'-i-Abbas*, and the heavy taxes impoverished them; anarchy added to their misery.

In the 19th century, most of the tourists who visited Iran painted a dark picture of the depressing economic position of the majority of the Jews there, particularly after the famine in 1870, which caused so many fatalities among the heads of families that World Jewry had to come to the assistance of their destitute dependents. Nevertheless, in several localities there were a number of rich Jews. It would be desirable, therefore, to classify the places of Jewish settlement in Iran by geographical area in order to understand the variations in the circumstances of the Jews in each area and the changes that took place up to our time.

A. MESHED

From the time the Jews of Meshed were compelled to convert, in 1839, they were able to reveal their commercial ability and preserve their wealthy. They engaged in internal trade (with Teheran, Iṣfahān, Shīrāz) and external trade (with Afghanistan, Bukhara and Kurdistan). Dealers in carpets and skins, in particular, became rich; others, of more moderate means, have remained part of the Iranian middle class up to the present, whether they stayed on in their own city or moved to another, or emigrated to Palestine. However, some poor Jews were to be found as well.[10]

B. KURDISTAN REGION

Most of the travellers who visited several cities in this region in the 19th century did not describe poverty among the Jews there, and in certain cases even referred to rich Jewish merchants. The only destitute Jews in this region were those who lived in places which were not situated along the international trade route from Syria and Turkey to Iran and the Far East.[11]

After the evacuation of parts of Kurdistan by the Russians in 1917 (which they had occupied two years earlier), anarchy prevailed in the region, and many of the Jews there were adversely affected. In 1922, the Kurds revolted and some of the Jews were compelled to emigrate to Iraq and to other Iranian cities. Generally, however, those who remained recovered. Dr. A. I. Brawer indicated, in 1935, that the Kurdish Jews in Iran were better off, from the economic and cultural standpoint, than their brethren in Turkey and Iraq. He alleged that he did not see Jewish beggars in Seneh or Sanandaj, that their clothes did not betray poverty, and although he found only few well-to-do, the Jews made an impression of being in comfortable economic circumstances.[12] With all the diversity of description by various travellers, the Kurdistani Jews in Iran were apparently never considered poor over the last 100 years, and in any case they were believed to be wealthier than the majority of Iranian Jews. In 1950, several thousands of Jews from the Iranian Kurdistan area emigrated to Israel, only some hundreds remaining, who were by no means destitute.

If the good economic position of the Jews of Meshed may be attributed to their conversion to Islam, even if that conversion was only apparent, the relatively good economic position of the Kurdish Jews in Iran may perhaps be attributed mainly to the fact that the Muslim Kurds were Sunnis and not fanatic Shī'ites like the other Iranian Muslims; the Sunnis did not feel themselves contaminated by Jews and were not such religious extremists as to wish to degrade them.

C. SOUTHWEST IRAN

In the 19th century, most of the Jews in Kermanshah were poor, although a few rich could be found among them.[13] Jews were not settled anywhere in southwest Iran apart from Kermanshah, but at the end of the century, when the Suez Canal was opened, with the resultant development of commerce in southern Iraq,* the position of the Kermanshah Jews improved and Jews, mostly from Iraq, began to settle in the cities of Khurramshahr (Muḥammara) and Ahwāz, as well. Travellers who visited the vicinity after the First World War indicated that the Jews in these three cities were well established materially.[14] After the Second World War, however, and following the completion of the Trans-Iranian railroad which connected the Caspian Sea with the Persian Gulf, the Jews of Kermanshah,[15] Ahwāz and Khurramshahr were badly hit; only in Abadān are Jews still working for the oil companies.

D. THE LARGE CITIES

The economic position of the Jews in Hamadhān in the 19th century was generally good.[16] As far back as the early 'seventies, they were permitted to maintain shops in the market, in contrast to the restrictions in the other Iranian cities.[17] Hamadhān in the 19th century was a commercial centre through which merchandise sent from Iraq to Teheran passed, and Jews from Iraq as well came to settle there. But from the time of the First World War the Jews were not so well off and most left the city; only about 820 were left in 1966, compared to some 8,000 thirty years earlier.

The Jews of Teheran were described as poorer, although among them, too, were to be found merchants dealing in silk, diamonds and precious stones.[18] After the First World War they too suffered economically, owing to the Government monopoly of foreign trade instituted in 1925 by Riza Shah Pahlavī. Later, the world economic crisis also affected Iran. The development of communication routes impoverished the pedlars, since the villages in the vicinity now needed them less. It is true that a few rich Jews in Teheran left the Jewish quarter, but the masses who lived in the neighbourhood were mostly destitute and starved.[19]

* See above, p. 90.

After the large-scale emigration from Teheran to the State of Israel, many poor Jews still remained there. The poor who had left for Israel were replaced by others from the small towns, who are concentrated in the old quarters.[20]

Throughout the entire 19th century and the first half of the 20th, the Jews in Shīrāz had been regarded as very poor.[21] But it seems that in the past 10–15 years there has been a change for the better, the Jews remaining there having become rich through the development of commerce in Shīrāz, which attracted more Jews to this city, and the community of Shīrāz has become the second largest in Iran, after Teheran.

All those visiting other cities of Iran, such as Yazd,[22] Iṣfahān,[23] Būshīr, Kāshān,[24] —in the 19th century as well as in our day—have referred to the great poverty of the Jews, with only some few individuals being in circumstances described as good or moderate. After the mass emigration of Iranian Jews to Israel, no considerable change took place in the material position of those remaining there. In Iṣfahān, for example, it was estimated in 1952 that among the 960 Jewish families in that city, only 3% were in satisfactory economic circumstances; the rest were living in frightful poverty.[25] The other communities in Iran today are small, since the majority of their members left for Israel or moved to neighbouring cities, especially Teheran.

Unfortunately there is no way of studying the occupations of the Iranian Jews during any particular period, since the data on this subject gathered in the population censuses of 1956 and 1966 were not classified according to religion. The Immigration Department of Israel did publish such data with respect to the immigrants from Iran who arrived in the years 1950–1951, but these obviously do not include data concerning those who remained in Iran. The figures regarding those who arrived in 1950–1951 showed 12.6% as having been employed in agriculture, 10.9% in the free professions and as clerical workers, 26.2% in commerce; those remaining worked in crafts, building and services.[26] These data were collected from the Kurds and the poorest strata of the other Iranian communities. Since it was only in the Kurdistan region that the Jews engaged in farming,[27] it may be assumed that the Jews in Iran today include a large percentage of merchants and members of the free professions, and less craftsmen, with very few farmers among them, if any.

Turkey

If it was possible to establish that in the last hundred years a considerable change for the better occurred in the economic circumstances of the Jews in Egypt and Iraq, and only a slight improvement in those of the Iranian Jews, it is difficult to arrive at any definite conclusion as to the extent of the change that took place in this period with respect to the Jews of Turkey.

According to the evidence of various travellers who visited Turkey in the 19th century, the majority of Jews there were indigent, engaged in various crafts, with a few individuals among them rich merchants. The Jews of Turkish Kurdistan suffered particularly,[28] owing to the absence of a stable regime in the area.

The small communities in the south, for the greater part, were also impoverished. Although Bursa and Aydin prospered economically, most of the Jews there were poor, for commerce was concentrated in the hands of the Armenians, who employed only members of their faith.[29]

Competition on the part of the Armenians and the Greeks, and the absence of modern education among most of the Jews in the small towns, considerably retarded their economic development, and there is no evidence to indicate that the situation improved after the First World War. On the other hand, it is known that many Jews moved to the large cities or emigrated to Palestine. It may be supposed, therefore, that the few Jews now living in the small Turkish towns are not numbered among the poor.

With regard to the large communities, a few merchants and even a number of wealthy Jews could be found in Adrianople in the mid-1800's, although the greater part of the Jewish population there was destitute. In the 20th century matters became worse. The Turko-Greek War, the First World War, the Turkish War of Liberation, and then the Second World War, as well as the closing of the Bulgarian border, brought the city's commerce to a standstill and led most of the Jews to leave Adrianople. Today only a small community remains.

In Istanbul[30] and in Izmir,[31] there were thousands of jobless and destitute; the rest were mainly craftsmen, including tailors and shoemakers, and a few brokers, bankers and merchants. In Istanbul there were some who had managed to take over part of the country's foreign trade. A few were civil servants and a small number earned their livelihood as doctors, pharmacists, lawyers, and in similar occupations.

With the rise of the Young Turks, many Jews began to replace the Greeks and the Armenians in commerce, for the Christians were considered by the authorities to be lacking in loyalty. When thousands of Greeks left Turkey in 1922, the Jews acquired a larger share of Turkish commerce. Owing to the spread of education among the Jews, more academicians and clerks appeared among them, most of them working for merchants and the banks. Fewer were employed in the civil service, for, in the eyes of the authorities, the Jews remained a foreign minority. The Jews of Istanbul and Izmir continued to grow rich until 1942, when a mounting wave of hatred against foreigners began to be felt. In November 1942 the Varlık Vergisi Law (Property Tax Law) was promulgated. This Law provided for the imposition of a tax on the property of every Turkish subject at the rate of one percent of the value of his property. The property value was fixed by local committees, whose decision was final and excluded any right of appeal. These committees generally assessed the property of the minorities at several times its real value. Property owners were sometimes compelled to sell their property to pay the tax, and at times even the payment received—prices having had to be reduced radically because of the properties offered on the market—was insufficient to pay the one percent tax. In such cases, they were obliged to work at paving roads, clearing snow in the hills and similar jobs, against a government wage of three Turkish pounds a day, half of which was deducted to pay the property tax, a quarter to pay income tax, a quarter remaining for the worker's subsistence. This tax brought 456 million Turkish pounds into the State coffers, 280 million (61.4%) of which had been collected from 270,000 members of the minorities.[32] Many families among the minorities were dispossessed of all their property; hundreds of Jews were brought to work camps, after all their property had reverted to the Government. They were released in April 1944, when the Varlık Vergisi Law was abolished. Many subsequently left Turkey, most of them for Palestine.

The emigrants to Palestine included many of those who had suffered from the Property Tax and many from the small towns, so that it may be assumed that the Jews remaining in Turkey were on the average better established than they had been in the 'forties. Most of those who remained were merchants, officials and members of the free professions, with some service workers and only a small number of destitute.

TABLE B-3: Occupations of Jews aged 15 and over in Turkey, according to sex (1960) in percentages[32a]

	Men	Women	Total
All breadwinners	13,840	1,474	15,314
Breadwinners whose occupation was known	13,081	1,446	14,527
Professional and technical	5.7	7.7	6.0
Administrative	34.4	40.5	35.0
Commerce and salesmanship	35.7	9.9	33.1
Agriculture	1.1	1.9	1.1
Fishing and mining	0.2	—	0.2
Transport	1.2	0.5	1.1
Crafts	15.3	19.4	15.7
Manual labour	2.2	3.1	2.3
Services	4.2	17.0	5.5

According to the population census conducted in Turkey in 1960—the first to indicate occupation according to religion—a considerable percentage (35%) of Turkish Jews were shown to be officials and administrative workers, and 33.1% of all the Jewish breadwinners were engaged in commerce, as can be seen from the above table.

In the absence of data for earlier periods, it is difficult to know what changes took place in the economic position of the Turkish Jews in the last few decades, but it is almost certain that before the emigration of thousands of Turkish Jews to Israel in the years 1948–1960, the percentages of those engaged in crafts and manual labour was higher.

Syria and the Lebanon

The differences between the Jewish communities in Damascus, Aleppo and Beirut were remarkable in all fields, and especially in the economic sphere. It is desirable therefore to discuss each of the three main communities of these two countries separately.

There was a conspicuous economic dissimilarity between the Jews of Aleppo and those of Damascus as far back as the 16th century. Aleppo, which was then a transit city for trade between Europe and the Far East, began to lose its standing at the beginning of the 17th century, when the English began to trade with Iran through Basra and the Persian Gulf. At the end of that century, they made fairly serious efforts to divert their trade through the Red Sea. In 1789, following the French Revolution, all French international trade, and in particular that going through Aleppo, declined. In the first half of the 19th century, the efforts of Muhammad Alī, the ruler of Egypt, to develop the continent's trade through his country, hit Aleppo's economic standing. Several years after the opening of the Suez Canal, Aleppo was almost entirely removed from the scene of international trade.[33] Nevertheless, travellers who visited Aleppo in the 'eighties spoke of very rich Jews there, pointing out, however, that there were fewer than there had been previously.[34] Since then, the Jews continued to suffer an economic decline and increasing numbers emigrated to the Lebanon, Palestine and England, but especially to Egypt and America. Most of those who remained were poor, and the number requiring assistance increased, reaching 40–65% in 1942.[35] Of the small amount of property retained by the community some was looted in the riots against the Aleppo Jews at the end of 1947,* after which the few rich emigrated, for the most part, to

* See above, p. 46.

the Lebanon or to Europe and America. The small community now in Aleppo is decreasing in number and lives in great distress, aggravated by the Damascus Government's denial of freedom of movement.

In contrast to the Jews of Aleppo, most of those in Damascus in the 16th century were craftsmen: cobblers, goldsmiths and matmakers. There were also many hawkers among them, who were compelled to wander to the neighbouring villages to make a living. At the same time, there were also a few who had become rich by trading with Palestine, Egypt and Venice.[36] Some eminent wealthy Jews were also to be found in Damascus in the 19th century. The convert Moses Margoliouth, who visited the city in 1848, described at length the wealth of some of the Damascus Jews, their houses overlaid with marble, with large and beautiful pools in their courtyards. He pointed out that these houses were surrounded by mud walls and the doors were simple, so as not to attract attention.[37] Ephraim Neumark, too, who was in the city in 1884, recorded that he found distinguished rich men among the Jews of Damascus, but pointed out that their economic position was adversely affected in the 'seventies as a result of the decline in the international standing of the city. Neumark reported further that from the economic viewpoint "Damascus has fallen from the stage, is sitting on the chair, but not on the ground." He also found that most of the city's Jews were earning their livelihood from crafts: goldsmiths and silversmiths, tailors, shoemakers and watch repairers, while others were labourers in workshops. Most of the silk, wool and cloth-dyeing industries were concentrated in the hands of Jews.[38] Because of the damage to the economic standing of Damascus after 1890, some Jews left for America and Egypt.[39] Their departure was not on the same scale as that of their brethren, the merchants in Aleppo, since being labourers and artisans, they were not so severely affected by the opening of the Suez Canal. On the eve of the First World War, the Jews were still engaged in goldsmith and silversmith work, weaving, dyeing, spinning and woodwork, but their share in foreign trade had dwindled, and their influence on the Damascus market was negligible.[40] They suffered a serious economic upheaval after the political events of 1925, which led to much unemployment and to the departure of many from the city,* while many of those remaining became dependent on funds collected for them, mainly among the Syrian Jews in New York.

Data available for the year 1926 reveal that from among the 6,635 Jews of the city, 2,275 were breadwinners, that is, one breadwinner to every three persons; 32% were artisans (including copper workers, weavers, tailors, shoemakers and labourers), 17% were clerks, 4% worked as maids and servants, 14% were hawkers, 9% merchants and goldsmiths or silversmiths, 1% rabbis, and the remaining 23% were engaged in various occupations, the majority apparently in the services.[41]

* See above, p. 45.

Yomtov Sémach, who visited the city at the end of 1929, also had the impression that most of the Damascus Jews were artisans.[42]

During the ensuing years, their economic situation deteriorated as the demand for handwork decreased; most of the Jews who remained in Damascus in the 'forties were poor. Along with them suffered those Jews who had been dismissed from the civil service and from companies and enterprises in 1947.[43]

The situation in Beirut was just the opposite to that in Aleppo and Damascus. Jews, particularly those from Syria, moved there mainly because of its development as a port city. The Jewish traveller, Ludwig August Frankl, who visited Beirut in 1856, indicated that most of them were engaged in commerce. Sidney Samuel, who was there 23 years later, related that among the thousand Jews of Beirut there were very few poor and most were well-off financially.[44] As the city's economy developed, Jews took part in the Lebanon's internal as well as foreign trade, in banking and in tourism. There are no details available as to their exact occupations, but it can be assumed that most of them were merchants and clerks, with a few artisans. The Jews in Beirut enjoyed full economic freedom, even after the establishment of the State of Israel, and their position improved until June 1967, when the country's economy was hit by the war in the Middle East. Since then, thousands of Jews have left Beirut, and many others intend to leave. They are permitted by the Lebanese to transfer their money freely.

The Yemen and Aden

While the economic position of the Jews in Egypt, Iraq, the Lebanon and perhaps also in Iran, improved in the last century, the impressions of travellers who visited the Yemen indicate that the majority of the Yemenite Jews were destitute and remained so up to 1950. Most of them were engaged in handicrafts, mainly as goldsmiths, and a few in small retail businesses. Only a few individual rich Jews were to be found in San'a.[45] They did not engage in foreign or the wholesale trade. The hawkers and craftsmen were at times compelled to wander far to earn a meagre livelihood, and their sources were easily impaired. Drought and wars, which were frequent up to the First World War, led to less income for the merchant and artisan, for they could not expect customers at such times. The Jews of San'a were particularly badly affected, frequently suffering from starvation.

Owing to the general poverty in the Yemen, the Jews became accustomed to living very meagerly. As a rule, they did not eat more than twice a day, and even then their food was inadequate. Their main meal consisted of flour, maize and coffee from the coffee shells. Meat was eaten only on Sabbaths and festivals or at meals given in connection with religious ceremonies. In the city they ate a piece of wheat bread with oil and vegetables. The quantity of their food, on the whole, was insufficient for sustenance. Only a few wealthy individuals had meat, milk, honey and eggs in their diet. The Yemenite Jews' poor nutrition accounts for their being thin and short, although they were not sickly.[46]

This was the general situation, though there were regions where the economic conditions were particularly depressed, as in 'Aqīrī, Ḍālī', Rawḍa, Qa'ṭaba and in the capital. On the other hand, the Jews in Bayḍa, Ṣaūma'a, Dhū Shfāil and Ba'dān, and a section of San'a, earned a relatively good livelihood. From the impressions of travellers, it appears that few Jews in the Yemen were farmers.[47]

Several rich Jews could be found at the beginning of the century in Aden, but there, too, most were merchants-hawkers and craftsmen.[48]

There is no way of assessing the average income of the Jews in the Yemen, nor is occupational structure clear, since, as already stated, no census was ever taken. It is not known whether any changes occurred in their occupations in the last five decades. Two sources, however, one of 1910 and the other of the mid-century, may give us some idea as to the main occupations of the Yemenite Jews.

Yomtov Sémach, who was in the Yemen in 1910, compiled a list of the men's occupations in 139 localities. Besides being deficient in that it does not cover the entire community, the material is also incomplete in that it lacks a detailed classification of occupations. The persons included were classified into three groups: craftsmen; shopkeepers and pedlars; various professions, including teachers, rabbis, scribes, and unemployed. No explanation was given as to the classification of those who were engaged in two occupations, such as handicrafts and commerce, or handicrafts and teaching. Nevertheless we can deduce the following from Sémach's data:

a. Most of the Yemenite Jews were craftsmen (among them, twenty, or 0.6% of all the breadwinners, engaged in farming).

TABLE B-4: OCCUPATIONS OF JEWISH MEN IN 139 LOCALITIES IN THE YEMEN, 1910, IN PERCENTAGES[49]

Occupation	San'a	Rada', Shaybām, Dhamār and 'Amrān	134 Localities	Total
Total	657	460	2,164	3,281
Craftsmen	51.4	59.6	85.5	75.0
Pedlars and shopkeepers	32.0	28.1	11.5	17.7
Miscellaneous	16.6	12.4	3.0	7.3
Total	100.0	100.0	100.0	100.0

b. The proportion of craftsmen was small in the big cities and large in smaller localities.

If the occupations of the Jews in the hundreds of places where small communities existed but were not visited by Sémach approximated the occupations of the Jews in the above 134 localities, it can be assumed that in 1910 over 75%, and perhaps closer to 80%, of the Jews in the Yemen were craftsmen, and close to 15% were merchants and pedlars, while 5% were engaged in miscellaneous occupations.

The second source is the data of the Immigration Department in Israel. Immigrants from the Yemen and Aden were questioned on their arrival, as were all immigrants, about their previous occupations. Since the migration was on a mass scale, the data obtained provide a unique source of material.

TABLE B-5: Occupation of immigrants born in the Yemen and Aden aged 15 and over, 1948–1950,[50] in percentages

Occupation	Men 1948–49	Men 1950	Men 1948–50	Both Sexes 1948–50
Total number of immigrants	18,759	4,299	23,058	47,170
All breadwinners	3,919	1,131	5,050	5,246
Breadwinners whose occupation was known	3,634	1,131	4,765	4,952
Crafts and industry	45.4	45.4	45.4	46.1
Building, transport and mines	5.1	1.3	4.2	4.1
Agriculture	12.5	24.1	15.2	15.2
Unskilled work and personal services	0.1	2.2	0.7	0.7
Professional and technical	2.5	3.2	2.7	3.0
Administrative and clerical	0.7	0.8	0.7	0.7
Commerce	33.7	23.0	31.1	30.2

Surprising in this table is the high percentage of those engaged in farming, which contradicts the reports of travellers who visited the Yemen and of some Jews who had lived there. It is difficult to explain why fewer farmers, and more building and transport workers, came to Israel in 1949 than in 1950.

If the immigrants from the Yemen did not make incorrect declarations, either in error or for other reasons, there were more Jewish farmers in the Yemen than in any other Jewish community throughout the world, except for Kurdistan in Iraq.* The great majority of Yemenite Jews were engaged in handicrafts, building, transport and the services, and not a small percentage in commerce.

* See page 93.

However, as has been noted, there are reservations concerning the data, and no conclusions are possible concerning changes in the occupations of the Yemenite Jews in the years 1910–1950, apart from the knowledge that most were artisans; second place was taken by merchants-hawkers; there were some members of the liberal professions (mainly rabbis, beadles, cantors, etc.) and only a few clerks, owing, no doubt, to the lack of modern education and the possibilities of employment for Jews.

Chapter Four
EDUCATIONAL PROGRESS

Undoubtedly, one of the most important changes for the better in the history of the Middle East Jews during the last hundred years took place in the field of education. Illiteracy, common at the beginning of the period, was gradually eliminated in most of the countries, especially among the young. The number of graduates of secondary and higher education schools throughout the period, and of women attending schools, was constantly on the increase. On the other hand, there was a parallel decline in the number of religious schools and in the number of pupils attending such schools.

The extent of the improvements varied from one country to another, being most outstanding in Egypt, followed by Turkey, Iraq, the Lebanon and Syria in that order, and less so in Iran and Aden. In the Yemen, there were no changes.

The uneven progress is due to the varying political, economic and demographic conditions under which the Jews lived. While their political situation in Egypt, Turkey, Iraq, Syria and the Lebanon was on the whole good after the 'sixties of the last century, it did not begin to improve in Iran until 1906, with real progress being made only after 1925. As stated, there was no improvement whatsoever in the Yemen throughout the entire hundred years. Economically, the Jews in Turkey, Egypt, Iraq and the Lebanon began to be better off from the middle of the last century, while in Syria, Iran and the Yemen their lot was only slightly improved. And above all, the concentration of the Jews of Egypt, Turkey, the Lebanon and Babylonian Iraq from the end of the last century, chiefly in the principal city or in the two largest cities of the respective countries, where the state, foreign and Jewish schools were located, enabled them to further their education. The Jews of Kurdistan and Iran began to concentrate in the main cities only in the last few decades, most of them having remained, up to then, in places where even government elementary schools were non-existent. Only about 15% of the Yemenite Jews, up to their mass emigration to Israel, lived in the capital, and even there they received no modern education.

Although the population census taken in Israel in 1961 did not furnish details about the prior education of immigrants, it does give us some indication as to the differences between groups born in the various countries.

TABLE C-1: PERCENTAGES OF LITERATE PERSONS AMONG MIDDLE EAST-BORN JEWS IN ISRAEL (AGED 14 AND OVER), BY COUNTRY OF BIRTH, SEX AND AGE AT IMMIGRATION, AND MEDIAN YEARS OF STUDY[1]

Country of birth	Age at time of immigration			60+	Median years of study
	15–29	30–44	45–59		
Egypt and the Sudan	94.7	90.2	75.6	62.1	–
Turkey	84.1	68.3	54.7	34.3	–
Syria and the Lebanon	76.0	58.3	46.9	48.8	–
Iraq	69.5	52.9	39.2	27.8	–
Iran	63.7	47.2	31.5	23.0	–
Yemen and Aden	45.0	35.5	28.6	30.8	–
		Men			
Egypt and the Sudan	95.6	92.2	83.4	78.9	9.3
Turkey	89.4	79.4	71.3	56.6	6.6
Syria and the Lebanon	87.2	83.4	68.8	71.7	–
Iraq	82.7	75.7	62.2	51.3	7.4
Iran	81.3	70.5	52.3	38.2	6.4
Yemen and Aden	74.5	64.5	56.5	57.1	6.0
		Women			
Egypt and the Sudan	93.9				
Turkey	78.4	58.1	42.1	22.5	5.3
Syria and the Lebanon	65.0	37.4	30.1	22.5	
Iraq	56.1	28.5	14.2	6.8	2.9
Iran	46.5	21.5	8.4	(3.2)	1.0
Yemen and Aden	18.1	4.9	2.5	(1.8)	0.8

The fact that there were fewer illiterates among Egyptian Jewry, including women, than among any other Jewish community in the region, has been true since the end of the last century. Since then, additional progress was made, the few illiterates remaining being mostly the elderly. Great advances were made, too, by all the other Jewish communities in the Middle East, although in the Yemen and Aden, and in Iraqi and Iranian Kurdistan, the number of women receiving any education was insignificant.

Outstanding roles in education were played by the *Alliance Israélite Universelle* and the foreign schools, where the majority of the Jewish children studied in Egypt, Syria and the Lebanon during the entire period surveyed, and in Iraq, Iran and Turkey before the First World War. In all of these schools they were taught according to foreign curricula, so that they left school without a command of, and at times barely able to speak, the language of the country where they lived. Learning European languages drew the young people closer to European countries as far as their political aspirations and cultural values were concerned, and made them a foreign body in the local society.

Another interesting fact is that although the education the young people received differed from that of their parents, no chasm seems to have been created between the young and their families and environment, as might have been expected. It did alienate them from religious observance, but did not lead to assimilation or conversion.

It was not only in the *Alliance* and in the foreign schools that the study of foreign languages was stressed, but in schools of the local communities as well. From the age of six or seven, the children learned two languages, and sometimes three, at the same time. Considering that in the early period of Jewish education in the Middle East, most of the pupils left school after four or five years of study, it is not surprising that they were fluent in several and literate in none. Later, when many young people continued studying for seven or eight years, or even more, they succeeded in acquiring a good knowledge of several languages. This enabled some of them to gain admission to European institutes of higher learning, or to obtain appointments as senior officials in the civil service, in banks and in commmercial companies, where people with a knowledge of foreign languages were much sought after.

Children in the Eastern countries began learning at a tender age—at three or four—in the *ḥeders,* and even when modern schools were subsequently established, this practice continued. At first kindergartens were part of the schools, and here the children began to read and write. When the kindergartens were separated from the schools (in Egypt at the end of the last century, in Iraq only at the beginning of the 1940's) children's games, songs, music and handicrafts were introduced. This meant that the children spent more of their very early years in studying, with little time for the joys of childhood. Social and psychological significance attached to this fact.

All the teaching was done by rote, and this remained unchanged throughout the period. Discussing ideas and analyzing problems were, and remained, uncommon in schools of the Middle East, including the Jewish schools.

Publications by the Middle East Jews in the second half of the 19th century were restricted almost entirely to religious works; in the 20th century, hardly any religious treatises were written by their rabbis (unless they sent their works to be published in Palestine). Instead, Jews in the Middle East wrote scientific, literary and other books in Arabic, Persian, Turkish and in European languages. Many newspapers, too, were founded, written in various languages by Jews for Jews. Some of them were not of a high level, and frequently they did not last long, owing to distribution difficulties. The 450,000 Jews who lived in the Middle East had no common language, so that each group, sometimes several groups in the same country, required a paper in its own language. Even the Arabic they used was not uniform, and not all who spoke it were able to read the literary form. This is one of the reasons that Jewish theatres did not develop in the region, although some Jews joined local non-Jewish theatrical societies. The few groups of Jewish actors that did emerge did not remain on the scene for any length of time.

Music was almost the only art which Jews of this region including Yemen were active in. Musicians and composers were found among the Jews of Iran, Turkey, and Iraq. Their songs were not only religious, but they were also lay songs, popular among non-Jews as well. Since the 'thirties, classical Western music has been heard and adopted by some Jewish youth in Egypt, Turkey and Iraq.

Egypt

The first Jewish communities in the Middle East to receive a modern education were those in Egypt and Turkey. As early as the 1830's a few children, most of them of rich families, attended Christian schools. In Egypt, the majority, however, continued, up to the 1860's, to study in *ḥeders* and other religious schools in Cairo and Alexandria, and also in those small localities where teachers were available. The teaching at these institutions was of a low standard, and the subjects taught were confined to reciting the prayers and the weekly Portion of the Law, without any comprehension of content.[2]

In the 'sixties, most of the *ḥeders* and other religious schools underwent a fundamental change. The study of several foreign languages was introduced, and less Hebrew and religious subjects taught. Actually, they may be considered as the first modern educational institutions of the Jewish communities, for most of them were administered by the communities and not by private individuals or groups. Although they were still called *ḥeders* it can be said that the traditional educational institutions ceased to exist in Egypt in the 1860's. Teaching of religious law continued, of course, in some Jewish schools, but the number of pupils was on the decline, and certainly fewer hours were assigned to these subjects. Thus many Jews did not study in Jewish schools; they were unable to recognize a letter of the Hebrew alphabet, and had practically no knowledge of Jewish religion or history. These changes came about without any pressure being exercised by the authorities, being the result of the parents' own wishes.

By the beginning of the 20th century, interest in Jewish education had become restricted to a few Jews, despite the efforts made then by several Zionists in Egypt. That is why no Yeshivas could exist in Egypt for a long period. The *Ẓafnat Pa'neyaḥ Yeshiva,* opened in Alexandria in 1915,[3] was shut down after a short time. In 1939 a new attempt was made to set up a religious institution, and Dr. Moshe Ventura, the Chief Rabbi of Alexandria, founded the Rambam Institute, in which he himself lectured and gave lessons in religious law and the Hebrew language. Despite all this institution's importance in a community in which many members had neglected the study of their religion, it was not a Yeshiva, because of its small number of students, and the few lectures given a week by the founder.[4] Even in Turkey, where religious education was greatly restricted by the authorities, it never declined to this extent. It was only in the 1930's that Jewish youth started to evince an interest in studying the Hebrew language, through the Zionist groups founded in Cairo and Alexandria.

While traditional Jewish education was losing ground, modern education was being expanded. The Christian secular and missionary schools were the first to be opened to Jewish pupils. In 1857 twenty Jewish children attended the Catholic Frères school in Cairo, and five in their school in Alexandria. In 1883/4, in Alexandria, 801 children attended Christian schools, or some 40% of the Jewish children of school age, while only 497 (or 25%) studied in Jewish schools. (Some 35% of the Jews of school age did not attend any school). It is of interest to note that in that year the majority of the Jewish girls in Alexandria who attended school studied in Christian institutions, while the majority of the boys attended Jewish schools, or non-missionary Christian schools, as indicated in the following:

453 Jewish boys and 44 girls attended 10 Jewish schools;

97 Jewish boys and 289 girls attended 8 Christian schools;

231 Jewish boys and 184 girls attended 14 non-religious Christian schools.[5]

The above figures can apparently be explained by the indifference of the Egyptian Jews to religious educations in general and to such education for girls in particular. Moreover, some Jewish parents' preferences for Christian schools for their children can be attributed to the fact that they included secondary school classes. They thought it right to send their children to an institution in which they could continue with their studies, for there were no Jewish secondary schools in Alexandria. It was not until 1925, when a teacher at the Catholic Frères school in Alexandria told his pupils that the Jews were using blood for baking *mazzah* for Passover, that the Jewish Community established their own secondary school. Afterwards, other such schools were opened, which no doubt led to fewer Jewish children attending Christian schools.

The first modern Jewish schools were set up in Cairo and Alexandria in 1840, at the initiative of A. Cremieux, who visited Egypt in connection with the blood libel in Damascus, but they were closed after two years, mainly because the rich Jews preferred the Christian institutions.[6]

In 1854, a school called *Aghion Talmud Tora* was opened in Alexandria, and it was followed by additional Jewish schools in the two large Egyptian cities. In all of them, Hebrew, Arabic, French and Italian were taught. In 1896, the *Alliance Israélite Universelle* entered the education scene in Egypt, when it founded a boys' school in Cairo, and a year later a school for arts and crafts; then another school, for boys and girls, in Alexandria (the sexes were separated in 1900). In 1898 it established a girls' school in Cairo, and in 1902 a school for boys and another for girls in Cairo. They turned over the latter two schools to the Jewish Community in 1912 and the remaining ones, in Cairo and Alexandria, in 1919. Since then, only two schools in Ṭanṭa remained under the direction of the *Alliance*. In the 1930's, they were amalgamated into one co-educational school which remained open until 1956, when a Jewish Community no longer existed in that city.

TABLE C-2: PUPILS IN ALLIANCE SCHOOLS IN EGYPT, 1900–1956[7]

Year	Boys	Girls	Total
1900	427	195	622
1905	723	584	1307
1910	726	547	1273
1913	822	301	1123
1922*	105	172	277
1936*	171		171
1950*	408		408
1956*	533		533

* In these years the *Alliance* had schools only in Ṭanṭa and some of the pupils were non-Jewish; in the 'fifties most of the pupils were non-Jewish.

In fact, the duration of the *Alliance*'s services to Jewish education in Egypt was shorter than in any other country in the East; and in this period, too, only a small proportion of the Egyptian Jews attended these schools, as may be seen from the following Table:

TABLE C-3: JEWISH PUPILS IN EGYPT, 1907–1946[8]

Year	Boys	Girls	In Jewish Schools		% of Jews in foreign schools
			Boys	Girls	
1907/08	4,000	3,194	906	504	80.3
1912/13	4,523	3,815	1,154	744	77.2
1924/25	7,461	6,230	4,097	3,119	47.3
1930/31	7,928	6,621	4,542	3,969	41.5
1936/37	7,635	6,657	4,474	3,960	41.0
1945/46	6,733	5,374	2,883	2,056	59.2

These figures do not include Jewish pupils attending state schools, whose number was on the increase, especially in the 'forties.

There are no details available on the level of the schools attended by Jewish children, but it is evident that many attended Christian secondary schools up to 1925, when a Jewish junior secondary school was established in Alexandria, and another later in Cairo. During the years, further Jewish secondary schools were opened in the two cities, but none of them included all the classes, and those who wished to complete their studies were compelled to transfer to a state or Christian school.

The data available show an increasing attendance of Jewish pupils at schools in Egypt from about 3,000 in 1883/84 to about 15,000 in 1938, and illiteracy decreased correspondingly. Only the non-Coptic Christians (most of them Europeans) could pride themselves on a smaller percentage of illiterates.

TABLE C-4: LITERACY AMONG JEWS IN EGYPT, AGED 5 AND OVER, 1907–1947[9]

Year	Male	Female	Total
1907	63.3	35.5	49.7
1927	81.7	63.9	72.7
1937	83.3	67.7	75.4
1947*	89.7	75.9	82.2
1947* Non-Coptic Christians	90.2	80.4	85.0
1947* All communities	56.1	30.6	43.8

*Only in Cairo and Alexandria.

These statistics show a gradual decline in illiteracy, especially among the Jewish women; of the latter those still unable to read and write in 1947 were no doubt in the age-group of 50 and over. It is doubtful whether in the 6–15 age-group there was much illiteracy, even among the girls.

Egyptian Jewry made much progress in the first half of the 20th century in higher education as well, as shown by the official Egyptian census of 1947, which provided data of the kind of certificates held by the residents according to religion. (Such details are unique in the Middle East.)

TABLE C-5: SECONDARY AND HIGHER EDUCATION, SCHOOL GRADUATES, CAIRO AND ALEXANDRIA, 1947[10]

Sex	Population aged 16+	Holders of diplomas of at least secondary school		Population aged 20+	Holders of diplomas of higher education schools	
	Number		%	Number		%
Jewish Men	21,967	2,340	10.7	19,842	801	4.0
Jewish Women	23,246	740	3.2	20,842	126	0.6
Total Jews	45,213	3,080	6.8	40,684	927	2.3
Non-Coptic Christians	99,726	6,472	6.6	90,808	2,638	2.9
Total Population	10,849,519	103,065	5.7	1,577,365	34,781	2.2

Despite the progress made in overcoming illiteracy among Jewish women, not many proceeded beyond elementary school; even in the 'forties many parents did not permit their daughters to complete secondary school, and certainly not institutes of higher education.

Even more than favourable political and economic conditions the concentration of the Jews of Egypt in the two major cities contributed to the educational and cultural progress; here the Jewish, foreign, and highly developed state educational institutions were located, as were the universities, which admitted Jews without restrictions.

Finally, most Egyptian Jews indeed spoke Arabic. Although they tended to be contemptuous of Arabic, it was taught in their schools, albeit as a foreign language, a few hours a week. In the Christian schools the children learned mainly French, Italian and English. Thus, Egyptian Jews, including those born in Cairo and Alexandria, were like strangers in the land not only in the eyes of the Muslims, but also in their own eyes. Most of the Egyptian Jews displayed a similar lack of interest in the Hebrew language.

LITERATURE AND CULTURE

With this negative attitude to Hebrew and Arabic, it is easy to understand why the Egyptian Jews lacked writers, poets, journalists and scholars writing in these languages. Among the few who published in Arabic, reference should be made to the satirical journalist, Jacob Sanu' (1839–1912), who wrote in spoken Arabic and was active in the Egyptian National Movement against the Khedive Ismā'īl and against the British regime in Egypt.[11] Later on came the famous Karaite writer and poet Faraj bey Murād, who wrote poems and many articles, especially on the legal status of the Karaites in Egypt. Another journalist, Sa'ad Jacob Mālkī, published the newspaper *Al-Shams,* in Arabic, which appeared during the years 1934–1948. With this exception, all the newspapers belonging to Egyptian Jews, and they were many, appeared in French.

A few religious works were published in Egypt in the last hundred years, most of them by non-Egyptian Jews, such as Shlomo Ḥazzan, Eliyahu Ḥazzan, Rafael Aharon ben-Shim'on, and Mas'ūd Ḥay-ben-Shim'on. The latter wrote a book, in two parts, *The Gates of Justice,* in Arabic (Cairo 1912, 1918). On the other hand, there were Egyptian Jews who wrote scientific books on various subjects, all of them in French. Among the Jewish researchers and historians, besides Turkish-born Rabbi Ḥayyim Naḥum, and Jerusalem-born Bension Taragan, mention should be made of Maurice Fargeon, who wrote two books on the Jews of Egypt, Noury Farhi,[12] René Cattaui,[13] A. Harari,[14] and Josef Cattaui.[15]

Since the Jewish community in Egypt was small and polyglot, there were no specifically Jewish theatrical groups, although some Jews took part in local theatrical activities. A number of young Jews distinguished themselves in various branches of sports.[16]

Iraq

From the 13th century, when the Babylonian Yeshivas ceased to exist, up to the 19th century, the Jews of Iraq were educated only in the *ḥeders*. It was not until 1840 that the first Yeshiva was founded in Baghdad. In December 1864, the *Alliance Israélite Universelle* began to function in Iraq, and soon after the Jews began to attend state schools as well. Towards the end of the century, the first Jews completed secondary school, and some went on to universities outside Iraq. Thus began a struggle between traditional and modern education, the latter steadily gaining ground. Unlike what had happened in Egypt, however, traditional education was not cast aside entirely and only few children attended missionary and other Christian schools. Moreover, in the second half of the 19th century, the Jews receiving a modern education were confined to Baghdad alone, and there, too, the number was small. It was only at the beginning of the present century that Jewish schools became widespread.

In the middle of the 20th century, there were no young Jews who had not attended school for at least a few years (except among the Kurdish Jews). More and more completed secondary school—among them some few girls as well—each year, and the number of those graduating from universities in and outside Iraq was constantly increasing. There was a considerable difference, however, between the Babylonian Jews, who, as indicated, were concentrated in the centre and south of Iraq, and the Kurdish Jews, who were scattered over villages and small towns, where, for the most part, there were no state schools, and certainly no Jewish schools, because of the small size and poverty of the communities.

TRADITIONAL EDUCATION

Up to the First World War many *ḥeders* existed all over Iraq, attended by a large number of pupils. In most cases, one of the rooms in the teacher's house served as the *ḥeder,* while in the hot summer months, his courtyard was used. The room was bare, the pupils sitting on mats, or sometimes on simple benches without backrests. There was no blackboard or any furniture in the room, but the teacher's punishment cane was most prominent.

Children from the age of 3–4 up to 12–13 attended the *ḥeder* together, without any classification as to age or knowledge. The teacher called up each child in turn, taught him a letter of the Hebrew alphabet, or a word, or a sentence, according to the child's knowledge, and if he had reached the stage of writing, he would write letters or sentences in the child's copybook, and the child was obliged to copy these lines according to the teacher's example. A child who did not read well or write beautifully was punished by blows or by having to rewrite the material. Since there were often more than 50 pupils, not infrequently it happened that each of them was called before the teacher not more than once a day. While one child was being taught, the others would be up to mischief; the teacher's helper who was supposed to supervise them was not very effective.

The child in the *ḥeder* started his schooling by learning the Hebrew alphabet, then words and sentences, until he was able to read fluently from the Holy Scriptures, with different tunes for the different books of the Bible. At a more advanced stage, if his studies were not interrupted, the child also learned to translate certain chapters of the Bible, and only after that, also writing and even arithmetic. Older children would study the writing of commercial letters in Arabic but with Hebrew characters. They were not taught Hebrew as a spoken language. Even the translation they learned was in an old Arabic dialect which they did not always understand. In the *ḥeder* no Talmud or religious rules were taught. In the Kurdistan mountains, the conditions were similar, except that the children generally learned to read from handwritten texts because of the lack of printed books, and most of them left the *ḥeder* before they reached the translation stage, or even before they succeeded in reading fluently.

The children in the *ḥeder* did not learn very much, since they studied for a few years only, and were taught by a teacher who not only had had no pedagogic training but whose own knowledge was scanty. The salary he received was low and he had to engage in some other occupation—as the cantor or the ritual slaughterer, for example—sometimes during the instruction hours.

A child who did not study as he should or was mischievous was struck by the teacher's cane on the palms of his hands, or received a slap in the face, or was stood in a corner with his face to the wall, and in grave cases publicly whipped on the soles of his feet, older boys holding his feet while the teacher beat him, and the rest of the children watching.

The Iraqi *ḥeder* was co-educational, although only few girls attended it.[17]

In the Talmud Torah schools (religious schools) founded in Baghdad—the first in 1832 and the second in 1907—the children were taught the same subjects as in the *ḥeder*, except that only boys studied there. They were divided into classes according to their knowledge, with a teacher for each class. They were not private like the *ḥeder* but directed by a public committee or by a Jewish Community committee. In each of the two Talmud Torahs in Baghdad the child could complete not more than four elementary school classes. Children were admitted to these schools from the age of four, and only few remained until the age of thirteen. In 1880, there were about 1,000 pupils; in the years 1920 and 1925—2,300; in 1930—2,049; and in 1950—1,880.[18]

Contrary to the practice in the religious schools in other Middle East countries, there was much opposition to teaching secular subjects in the Talmud Torahs in Iraq. The decision against introducing such subjects adopted by Rabbi Joseph Ḥayyim (died 1909) was strictly adhered to. An attempt, made in the 'twenties, to persuade the Rabbis in charge of the schools to teach some secular subjects failed. Therefore many parents, eager to give their children a modern education, to prepare them for the new conditions prevailing in the country, withdrew them from the Talmud Torah. In their efforts to halt this tendency, the Rabbis abolished the attendance fees, but even this step did not help much.

But the Talmud Torahs in Iraq had other drawbacks as well. The teaching standards were very low, as attested to in a report submitted by the School Committee of the Baghdad Jewish Community as recently as 1950. Some of the teachers were old and their methods outdated. The School Committee, under whose supervision the schools were placed in 1942, succeeded in replacing only part of the staff. The classes of the Talmud Torahs were very large; indeed they were as overcrowded recently as they had been in 1879; in 1920 the average number of pupils in a class was 59, and in 1950 it was 62.[19]

That it was the desire for a modern education for their children and not their opposition to a traditional education which led them to foresake these inadequate Talmud Torah schools is shown by the fact that when a modern Talmud Torah was opened in which both religious and secular subjects were taught, many parents sent their children to the new school. This modern Talmud Torah, opened in 1935 and named after Menashe Ṣāliḥ, was attended by 953 children in 1935/36, 1,241 in 1941/42 and 1,250 in 1949/50.[20] Here the state school curriculum was followed so that the children completing six grades could take the entrance examinations for a secondary school, and at the same time were provided with a fair knowledge of Jewish religious matters.

In the Talmud Torah in Basra, the number of students grew from 200 in 1903 to 320 in 1910, despite the opening of an *Alliance* school in the city in 1903. But this religious school lasted only until the beginning of the 'twenties. The Midrash (i.e., Talmud Torah) in Ḥilla was also shut down in 1907, when the *Alliance* school was opened there. When the latter school was closed in 1914, the Midrash was revived, but it, too, was shut down finally in 1924, with the opening of a modern Jewish Community school. In northern Iraq, there were Talmud Torahs in Mosul, Zākho, 'Amādiya and some other cities, most of which existed up to 1950.

Pupils who completed their studies at the large Talmud Torah in Baghdad and distinguished themselves were eligible for admittance to the Zilkha Yeshiva (Beit Midrash), which was founded in 1840 and which had about 60 students in 1848, 30 in 1863, and 20 in 1879.[21] Despite declining attendance a second Yeshiva was founded in 1908 in the name of Meir Eliyahu. In 1945 the first Yeshiva had three classes, and the second had two. In these two institutions of advanced traditional studies, the curriculum included only religious subjects. From among the students, rabbis, ritual slaughterers and religious court judges were appointed for the various Iraqi cities (especially in the centre and south of the country), some also emigrating to the Far East to undertake similar work for the Jewish communities there. There was a third Yeshiva in Arbīl, which furnished Rabbis and religious ministrants (beadles, cantors, etc.) for the Kurdistan villages. Unlike the Yeshivas in Baghdad, where the young people spent the whole day studying and received financial support, here they studied only on Sabbaths and in the evenings. Besides these Yeshivas, groups for the study of Talmud existed in Baghdad and even in the smaller cities, such as Ḥilla and 'Amāra.

Young intellectuals who in the 'twenties attempted to introduce reforms into religious life proposed setting up a seminar for Rabbis (Theological Seminary), in the belief that the Rabbis who would graduate from it would be more liberal.[22] A suggestion was also made to send young men to the Rabbinical Seminary in Istanbul, but it was not carried out. In 1932 one young man from Basra travelled to New York to study in a Yeshiva there, but returned at the beginning of his studies; no others followed him.

This extreme conservatism in matters of religious education in Iraq contributed significantly to the decline in the status of traditional education; in the last few generations no Rabbis of stature emerged who were capable of leading the Jewish community in a more progressive traditional way. Since the larger part of the Jewish public was eager for more modern education and progress, and this was not attainable in the conservative traditional educational institutions, they turned to the modern schools available in Iraq.

As more and more Jews studied in modern schools, their attitude to Jewish religion underwent a change; they began to look upon the religious duties observed in their parents' homes as superstitions.

MODERN EDUCATION

In the second half of the 19th century, while the traditional educational institutions were still widespread in Iraq, only few Jews sent their children to other schools. In the 1860's a small number were studying in missionary schools,[23] in state schools and in the one school founded by the *Alliance* in Baghdad in 1864. Not more than 200 pupils ever attended the latter school, the only *Alliance* school in Iraq at the time up to 1890; during the years 1864–1886 about 150 Jewish children completed its four classes,[24] all boys. The Iraqi Jews' piety and their Rabbis' opposition to modern education was an obstacle to Jewish education in this period.

Towards the end of the 19th century, the *Alliance* started to set up a network of educational institutions in Iraq. In 1890 it opened a vocational school for girls, and in 1893 a first regular school for girls in Baghdad (the first state school for girls in the country was opened only five years later). In 1893 there followed a boys' school in Basra. At the beginning of the 20th century, another school for girls in Basra and schools in Mosul, Ḥilla, 'Āmāra and Kirkuk were added. In 1902 the Jewish community in the capital, and later the communities in other cities of Iraq, founded their first modern schools. Gradually, the *Alliance*'s institutions played a smaller part in the education of Jewish children in Iraq, most of them attending the schools founded and administered by the local Jewish communities.

In 1920 there were altogether 12 Jewish elementary schools in Iraq—six in Baghdad and the remainder in the various other cities—only three comprising all six classes. The rest had three to five classes, so that their pupils wishing to obtain a school-leaving certificate had to go on to another school to complete their elementary school studies. In the course of the years, the Jewish network of schools was expanded, in 1936 reaching 17, six of them complete elementary schools. Later, other schools were added, some of them private; in the 'forties there were three complete secondary schools, two in Baghdad and one in Basra, besides several intermediate-secondary *(mutawassiṭa)*. After the First World War an increasing number of Jewish children also attended state schools.

Accordingly, more and more Jewish children were by this time completing elementary and secondary schools, and going on to institutes of higher education. From the 'thirties, girls, too, began to finish secondary school, and in 1941 the first Jewess graduated from Law School in Baghdad.

There are no exact data on the number of Jewish children who attended all the educational institutions in Iraq, the figures available being only for those supported by the *Alliance*. From the following Table it is interesting to note the increasing number of girls attending their schools:

TABLE C-6: CHILDREN IN ALLIANCE SCHOOLS IN IRAQ, 1880–1947[25]

Kind of school	1880	1900	1910	1913	1922	1939	1947
For boys	183	296	2,290	2,726	720	1,835	–
For girls	–	166	429	1,194	969	2,998	–
Co-educational		–	–	–	1,039	458	–
Total	183	462	2,719	3,920	2,728	5,291	5,225

In 1949/50, 4,026 pupils attended the *Alliance* schools in Baghdad alone, and 6,400 attended the Jewish community schools there, with another 2,300 approximately, in private schools, 1,300 in private vocational girls' schools and a few hundred in state and foreign schools. Thus about 15,000 Jewish children in all attended school in Baghdad that year. About 3,000 attended state and Jewish schools in other Iraqi cities, including about 2,000 in schools supervised by the *Alliance.* Altogether, therefore, about 18,000 Jewish pupils attended schools in all of Iraq in 1949/50, a third of them girls: about 2,000 in kindergartens, 11,000–13,000 in elementary schools (of six classes), about 3,500 in secondary schools (of five classes) and about 500 in institutes of higher education, a few of the latter outside Iraq.

In 1926 only 52 of those attending Jewish elementary schools in Baghdad passed the government examinations. Even if we add those graduating from non-Jewish elementary schools in Baghdad and elsewhere in the country, it is doubtful whether the number that year exceeded 100. By 1938 however, the indications are that about 500 passed, and at the end of the 'forties about 800–1000 each year. As for secondary school education, taking into consideration the drop-outs, the number of Jewish children who graduated from secondary schools in the 'twenties may be estimated at no more than a few score, and at the end of the 'forties in the vicinity of 300–400. Very few of the pupils attending elementary and secondary schools in Iraq were children of Kurdistan Jewish families—the majority were Babylonian Jews.

Illiteracy, too, was widespread among the Kurdistan Jews, even in 1950. Among the Babylonian Jews there was little illiteracy among the youth, including the girls, but there were still many illiterates to be found among the older people, particularly the women.

We have noted the following changes in Jewish education in Iraq: less traditional education, substantial increase in modern education, a growing number of girls at school and Jewish children spending many more years at the school-bench. But there were also further changes, as we shall indicate below.

Up to the beginning of the present century, no kindergartens existed in Iraq, and children of kindergarten age went to *ḥeder.* And when kindergartens were set up at the beginning of the century, they were attached to the schools and, in many respects, did not differ from the school classes. The children attending them even learned two languages—taught them by the regular teachers, none of whom had the slightest training in dealing with children of such tender age. In the kindergartens attached to the five Jewish community schools in Baghdad, an average of 19 hours a week were devoted to the study of Hebrew, 13 to Arabic and only 5 to handicrafts and drawing.[26] Games, songs and plays were rare. Not until the 1930's did the Iraqi Government begin to establish separate state kindergartens in Baghdad and several other cities. The Jews sent their daughters to these kindergartens, but not their sons. In the 'forties two Jewish kindergartens were opened in Baghdad, and there the children enjoyed playing games and singing, with a few hours devoted to lessons. But even then, it was mostly lessons and little play for the majority of the Jewish children of kindergarten age.

Another very important improvement was made in the curriculum. During the second half of the 19th century, Jewish children attended mainly *Alliance* elementary schools, where, within four years, they learned not less than five languages! In the first and second school year they were taught Hebrew, Arabic and French, and in the third and fourth Turkish was added, and for some pupils, English as well—all this apart from the general subjects such as arithmetic, geography and history. Considering the few years the child spent at school, the effort he had to make to learn five languages was undoubtedly not easy, and it may be assumed that the level of achievement in all of them was not very high. A question asked of the *Alliance* Central Committee in Paris on this matter received the reply that in the East many languages were required and that the pupils learn them quickly. The *Alliance* Committee in Baghdad then suggested to the Central Committee that at first Hebrew be taught as the primary language, Arabic as the second, followed by French and then English. The Baghdad Committee further proposed that the number of hours for the study of the European languages be increased gradually.[27] Nevertheless, five languages continued to be taught at *Alliance* schools in Iraq up to the First World War. After the British occupation of the country, they were reduced to four,[28] since there was no longer any need for Turkish. It should be noted here that actually only a few hours a week had been assigned to the study of Turkish, so that the children barely learned to read and write it[29]. Hebrew and Arabic, too, were not studied sufficiently, so that those finishing elementary school had a good knowledge of French, knew some English and had acquired only the rudiments of the other three languages. At any rate, the knowledge they gained of European languages enabled the *Alliance* school graduates to be taken on as clerks by commercial companies and banks, and when the British occupied the country, many of them served in the administration.

After the British occupation, the three languages taught in the first class of Jewish elementary schools were Hebrew, Arabic and English. The *Alliance* schools added French in the second class. In the 'twenties, some of the Jewish community schools began to change over to the government curriculum, with most of the teaching being done in Arabic. After Iraq obtained its independence, in 1932, they all did so, with the exception of the *Alliance* and Shammash schools, which taught in French and English respectively. This change was made to prepare the pupils for the government examinations, so that they would be eligible for admission to secondary and higher education schools.

Since the overwhelming majority of the Iraqi Jews, in contrast to the Egyptian, had attended at least elementary Jewish schools, up to the middle of the 20th century, only a few grew up in that country without learning at least a little Hebrew. Some Jewish young people could undoubtedly be found who could not recognize a letter of the Hebrew alphabet, but they were not many.

Teachers' qualifications were apparently satisfactory in the *Alliance* institutions and in the Shammash school, while in the other Jewish schools in Iraq, they were most inadequate up to the 1930's. Many of the teachers had not even completed secondary school, and only a few had pedagogical training. They were accepted as teachers without regard to their qualifications. There were some among them, however, whose personal experience had raised their standards of teaching. A report of the Baghdad Jewish Community's School Committee states that in 1920, at the four community schools, there was only one teacher who held a diploma (the nature of the diploma was not defined) and at the two *Alliance* schools in the city there were eight. Later, the situation improved: in 1930, there were twelve teachers with diplomas at the six community schools and eighteen at the Shammash and the two *Alliance* schools.[30] Most of the qualified teachers at the *Alliance* and Shammash schools taught in the secondary school classes.

In 1934–35, the Community School Committee decided not to engage new teachers for their elementary schools if they had not completed a secondary school (it was not until 1940 that the Iraqi Government issued a similar directive), so that by 1950, out of 172 teachers there were only five who did not meet this qualification, the rest holding secondary school or other certificates. But even in 1950 only eight out of 172 teachers had had pedagogical training and held teachers' seminary diplomas. To raise the standard of teaching, the Jewish School Committee decided, in 1949, that teachers must take special courses in instruction, and that those not doing so would be liable to dismissal. But this proposal had come too late—a year later the mass emigration to Israel started. With a view to raising teaching standards, the Menaḥem Daniel school in Baghdad had decided to send in 1947, at its own expense, two secondary school girl graduates to London each year to study pedagogy for three years, on the condition that they would return and teach at this institution for at least five years.[31] Because of the prohibition clamped down on the Jews at that time against leaving Iraq, it is doubtful whether a single girl was able to leave the country.

There was no textbook problem at the Jewish schools since, for the most part, they followed the government curriculum. At the *Alliance* institutions and at the Shammash school, foreign textbooks were used, although their contents were not always suitable for pupils living in an Arab environment. But all the Jewish schools were confronted with the problem of textbooks for teaching the Hebrew language. Up to 1906, Hebrew was taught from the Bible: from 1906 to 1927 a number of books were printed for the study of the Hebrew language.[32] In the 'twenties, several textbooks were brought in from Palestine, but not until 1947 did the authorities permit the use of the textbook, *Alpha-Beta,* drawn up by Ezra Ḥaddad for the study of the Hebrew alphabet. The Ministry of Education also approved Ḥaddad's second book, *Chapters from the Bible,* in Arabic. Further textbooks which he was about to publish, for more advanced classes, did not appear,[33] for the exodus to Israel had already started.

Most of the Jewish schools which had been opened up to the beginning of this century were housed in small buildings and when the number of pupils increased, the available space became inadquate and unsuitable. After the First World War new buildings were erected, or at least new wings added. In some, playgrounds and laboratories were also provided, and in the 'forties the Community School Committee finally put in new benches to fit the children's height. Most schools now also had libraries.

Despite the enlarged buildings, the average class remained greatly overcrowded. The two Talmud Torahs had, as already stated, about 60 pupils in each class, the other Jewish community schools in Baghdad 50 in 1920, 52 in 1941/42 and 50 in 1948/49.[34] The classes in the private Jewish schools, too, were much too large.

In view of the teachers' lack of pedagogical training and the overcrowded classes, it is not surprising that instruction was poor, as compared with that in schools in Britain and in Palestine, although it was better than in Iraqi state schools. In the 'twenties, standards improved in the Jewish schools. Especially outstanding was the Shammash secondary school: several of its pupils sat for Iraqi and London matriculation examinations. During the six years 1934–39, 24 boys and one girl[35] from among the Shammash school pupils passed the London matriculation examinations, in 1940–1944, 97 boys and 14 girls and in 1945–49, 144 boys and 21 girls.[36] These figures do not include pupils from the Jewish secondary school Frank 'Eyni who passed the same examinations; from 1948 this school, like the Shammash, prepared its pupils both for the Iraqi and the London matriculation examinations.

This improved educational level in the Jewish schools was the result of a larger proportion of the teachers graduating from higher education schools in Iraq and abroad. Another contributing factor was the law providing that any pupil who did not pass the examinations in two subjects at the end of the school year remained in the same class without any possibility of sitting for examinations at the end of the school vacations (anyone failing one subject was obliged to take a second examination at the end of the vacation period, and if he failed, he remained in the same class). A secondary school pupil who was held over for two years in the same class and did not succeed in the examinations at the end of the second year was unable to continue, and was expelled from school. Since only successful pupils could go on to higher classes, no gap was created in the level of knowledge of the pupils in the same class. Moreover, as holders of an Iraqi matriculation certificate were released from army service, the Jewish students made special efforts to obtain it; otherwise they would have been obliged to do regular army service for two years, or alternatively to serve three months and pay fifty dinars, in lieu of the full two years service. They did their best to avoid both possibilities.

VOCATIONAL EDUCATION

In Iraq, vocational education was not provided in the schools. Craftsmen learned their trade from their parents or by serving as apprentices to other craftsmen. A school for carpentry and blacksmithery opened by the *Alliance* in Baghdad was closed down on the eve of the First World War; it was reopened in the 'twenties, but did not last long. A second school for carpentry in the city, founded by a local Jewish philanthropist, was also shut down after several years. Only one Jewish elementary vocational school established in 1927—a school for the blind—held out until the mass exodus to Israel.

On the other hand, girls' schools for dressmaking, which were opened after the First World War, served their purpose for many years. In Baghdad, there were five such schools, and in Basra one, the latter existing for a short time. The Baghdad schools were attended by about 1,150 girls in 1925, and about 1,300 in 1950. The relatively small increase in the number of students is apparently due to the improved economic circumstances of the Iraqi Jews enabling them to give their daughters elementary and secondary education, instead of vocational.

BUDGETING AND SUPERVISION OF JEWISH SCHOOLS

The Ministry of Education supervised all schools, including Jewish, but the activity was more administrative and political than pedagogic, and no guidance or advice was offered the teachers. The government inspectors saw to it that in the Jewish schools Hebrew should not be taught for more hours than those assigned to it, and obligated the secondary schools to employ non-Jewish teachers for certain subjects, such as the Arabic language.

In Baghdad, supervision over Jewish schools was exercised also by the School Committee appointed in 1920 by the Jewish community. This Committee was not equipped to exercise professional supervision, so it had the services of a special advisor from London in the years 1927–1931. In the years 1931–1947, its task was limited to administrative and financial supervision; the Committee appointed in

1947 was the first to show initiative and make proposals for the advancement of education and for more social activity in the Jewish schools. Several of its suggestions were put into practice: it introduced some improvements in the religious schools; it dismissed a number of teachers who had grown to old for teaching and laid down a new system of classifying pupils in the classes. It also set up a Council of School Principals, which was later divided into two councils: secondary schools; it dismissed a number of teachers who had grown too old for teaching All three councils were required to meet once a month in the presence of one of the School Committee members, and the minutes of the meetings were submitted to the Committee. In this way, the School Committee was able to bypass the State law, which restricted its task to administrative supervision. Another innovation which the School Committee introduced was the establishment of sub-committees to deal with various phases of education in the Jewish schools, among them the Physical Education Committee, the Prizes Committee, the Health Committee (whose members were all physicians), the Laboratories Committee (which, after an investigation made recommendations for the establishment of laboratories in the schools). In 1949 further committees were added, one a Committee for Granting Permanency and Promotions to Teachers in the elementary schools.[37]

The School Committee in Baghdad supported and supervised an increasing number of schools, as indicated in the following:

TABLE C-7: SCHOOLS UNDER THE SUPERVISION OF THE JEWISH COMMUNITY SCHOOL COMMITTEE IN BAGHDAD[38]

Year	Number of Schools	Number of Pupils	Pounds Sterling
1920	8	5,511	
1930	11	7,182	22,900
1935	12	7,911	19,700
1945	14	10,021	57,500
1949	20	10,391	80,300

These figures do not include private Jewish schools in the capital.

Most of the expenditures were covered by the Community, for a large proportion of the children paid no fees (in 1920, 56%, in 1930, 64%), and a not inconsiderable number paid graded fees. As a result of the Committee's budgetary crisis in the 'thirties, the number of exempt pupils was decreased—in 1944/45 to 44% and in 1948/49 to 38%. In 1942, ten grades of fees were fixed for the paying children. Altogether, pupils' fees covered 30% of the schools' expenditures in 1930 and 63% in 1948/49. Most of the non-paying pupils were in the elementary schools: in 1948–49 only 3.5% of the secondary school pupils were completely exempt.

Poor children sometimes received lunch and writing materials free, and for pupils distinguishing themselves a number of funds were set aside for scholarships (in the name of Stafford Sason, Shaul Naqqār, Ezra Daniel and Henri David) to enable them to continue their studies in Iraq or abroad. In most of the schools pupils' committees collected contributions from children for their needy schoolmates. In 1948/49, these contributions brought in about £2,200.[39]

One doctor provided medical supervision starting from 1925; later, a number of physicians and nurses were available. Clinics were also established in the majority of the schools and destitute children received medicines free.

HIGHER EDUCATION[40]

There were no universities in Iraq until 1960, but in 1909 a Law School was opened, the first lawyers graduating from it in 1913. Immediately after the British occupation, schools for Pharmacy, Agriculture, Engineering and other professions were established, although they were not of university level, since they admitted students who had only partial secondary school education and the duration of study in some was only a few months. Most of them existed for only a short time.

In 1921, the Law School was reopened (after having been closed in the war years), and in 1927 a Medical School was set up, and in 1936 a School for Pharmacy and a Teachers Training School, followed in 1942 by an Engineering School, and in 1946 by a School of Economics. All these were now university institutions.

Jews attended these schools and also studied abroad. The first Iraqi-born Jewish university graduate took his degree in law from the University of Vienna in the 1880's. This was Yeḥezkiel Sason, who, in the years 1920–1925, served as Iraqi Minister of Finance. From the beginning of this century, Iraqi Jews graduated from the Faculties of Medicine, Pharmacy and Law in Istanbul. After the First World War, they began to study in universities in England, France, Turkey, India, Egypt, Syria, the Lebanon and the United States of America.

No exact statistics are available on the number of Iraqi Jews who completed institutes of higher education in Iraq and abroad in any year. In a special research project carried out by the Institute of Contemporary Jewry, the Hebrew University in Jerusalem, the names were collected of Iraqi-born Jews who completed university up to 1951. Although the list is not complete, the following information was gleaned from it:

a. In the first fifty years of the century, about 1,000 Jews completed institutes of higher education: 15 or so in the years 1901–1910 compared to about 550 in 1940–1950. In 1950 there were about 120 graduates.
b. In the first forty years of the century, all the graduates were men; the first woman to attend university graduated only in 1941. In the decade 1940–1950, there were 60 women graduates, 15 of them in 1950.

c. In the first thirty years (1901–1930) most of the graduates were from the major towns: Baghdad and Basra. Jews born in small cities graduated later.
d. The main profession studied by Jews was law, for several reasons: the Law Faculty was the first to be established, and in it it was possible to study in evening classes up to the late 'thirties; during most of the period, the authorities did not restrict the number of Jews applying for admission. Medicine came second, and after it, pharmacy, engineering and economics with a few in teachers' institutes. There were also some individuals who graduated in general humanities in Baghdad and elsewhere.

Several Jewish graduates were given positions as assistants and lecturers in institutes of higher education in Iraq, and since the mass exodus, some are serving as lecturers and professors in England, the United States and other countries.

LITERATURE AND CULTURE

Along with the changes in education, advances were also made in the sphere of literature. Up to the First World War, a number of rabbis, including Rabbi 'Abdalla Somekh and Rabbi Joseph Ḥayyim, had produced some religious works; and later, Ezra Dangoor, Moshe al-Ḥarīrī and others wrote essays on religious subjects,[41] most of which did not achieve publication. Apparently there was no interest in them on the part of Iraqi Jewry. After the First World War, however, a considerable number of Jewish writers and poets appeared on the scene whose works in Arabic were so similar to those produced by non-Jewish Iraqis that it was almost impossible to distinguish their Jewishness. Among these were Meir Basrī[42] (living up to the present in Iraq and continuing to write), Anwar Shaul[43] (left Iraq in 1971), Murād Mikhael,[44] Jacob Balbūl,[45] Shalom Darwīsh,[46] Abraham Jacob 'Ubadyah[47] and Sālim al-Kātib-Shalom Katav,[48] all of whom live in Israel, where the latter two continue to write.

In the second half of the 19th century, several Jews contributed articles and essays to Hebrew newspapers appearing in various parts of the world. Especially noteworthy is Rabbi Shlomo Bekhor Ḥazzan.[49] In this period, too, a Hebrew newspaper was issued in Baghdad called *Haddover*, or *Dover Mesharim* (1863–1871). After the First World War, at the same time that writers and poets started writing in Arabic, an increasing number of Jewish journalists founded newspapers: *Yeshurun* (1920, Hebrew-Arabic), *al-Miṣbāḥ* (1924–1929), *al-Ḥāṣid* (1929–1937), *al-Burhān* (1929–1938), *al-Barīd al-Yaumī* (1948), and others, all in Arabic.

From the 1920's, a number of Jews were prominent in the Iraqi theatre and some groups were organized and performed in Arabic. Most existed for only a short time. On the other hand, a large number of Jews distinguished themselves in music, as they had in Turkey and Iran, as singers, composers and players of Eastern instruments.[50] Other arts, such as painting, sculpture, and handicrafts, were not highly developed in Iraq, neither among the Jews nor the non-Jews.

EDUCATION AFTER 1951

After the mass emigration from Iraq, most of the Jewish schools were closed down, only two remaining, in Baghdad, to meet the needs of the thousands of Jews still there. Jews continued to attend state schools, some also the medical, pharmaceutical and humanities schools. Other Iraqi-born students studied in Israel, England and the United States.

Turkey

Jewish traditional education was also widespread in the territory comprising present-day Turkey. From 1850, however, the *ḥeders* and Talmud Torahs gradually became fewer, until in 1923, when the Turkish Republic was established, only a small number remained. In 1945 several traditional schools were reopened, but the generation that had grown up in the meantime received no Jewish or Hebrew education. On the other hand, from 1850 and especially after the First World War, when modern schools were established, there was a growing number of educated Jews in Turkey, among them some with secondary and higher education.

TRADITIONAL EDUCATION

Practically every Jewish place of settlement in Turkey, even the smallest, had its *ḥeders,* sometimes called Talmud Torahs. In each *ḥeder,* one *ḥakham* taught up to 60 children. In the large cities there were several Talmud Torahs, in which thousands of children received their education. Generally, the teachers, their methods of teaching and the housing facilities were of an inferior standard. The economic circumstances of most of the pupils was also such that only few of them studied for more than a few years, the majority dropping out at an early age,[51] before they had managed to reach the stage of reading Hebrew fluently, let alone understanding the material they had studied. Since they did not learn any foreign language or other secular subjects in the Talmud Torahs, they were not trained for any occupation; they left school able to do only the simplest work.

The opening of modern educational institutions—in 1850 in Adrianople, in 1854 in Istanbul and later in other cities—did not immediately result in a reduction of the number of pupils attending the *ḥeders* and Talmud Torahs; even when the first *Alliance* schools were established, many children still went to the religious schools. In 1889, about 2,500 Jewish children in Istanbul alone attended 28 *ḥeders* and Talmud Torahs.[52] The directors of the *Alliance* schools gradually brought these schools under their supervision. In 1879, the Talmud Torah in Izmir was transferred to the *Alliance* and a number of secular subjects were introduced, including the study of Turkish and French. This unification was ended in 1902. In January 1914, on the death of the principal of the Talmud Torah, the director of the *Alliance* school in the city tried to get control of the school, but was unsuccessful.[53] It was not until 1949, with the mass emigration of the Izmir Jews to Israel, that the two institutions were again merged. On the other hand, in 1902 the Talmud Torah in Bursa was merged with the local *Alliance* school, and in 1906 the two schools in Adrianople followed suit. The Talmud Torah in Tire had changed over to a modern school curriculum in 1901.[54] The other Talmud Torahs in Turkey shared the same fate, until on the eve of the First World War, only two such schools were left—in Istanbul and Izmir—and from 1949, not even one.

With fewer Talmud Torahs in Turkey, there were also fewer young people who could, or who wished to be, admitted to Yeshivas. Up to the middle of the 19th century, there had been many Yeshivas in Turkey, 18 in Izmir alone. This number was reduced in 1873 to 14 and in 1937 to four. In Istanbul, too, there had been six Yeshivas in 1889, although they were poorly attended at times, and in 1897 two more were added[55]; in 1941 only three remained. Yeshivas existed in other cities as well, some of which lasted until the Second World War.

These Yeshivas were intended mainly for adults, the curriculum including only religious studies. In 1892, an innovation was introduced into traditional education in the Middle East, with the opening of a Rabbinical Seminary in Adrianople to give Rabbis both a religious and a secular education. This Seminary, founded and directed by Abraham Dannon, had an organized curriculum, including some lessons in history and literature, taught partly in Turkish. It had ten students in its first year; when it was transferred, in 1898, to Istanbul, there were eleven. In 1910, eight students attended the Seminary, and sixteen its preparatory class.[56] A plan initiated in 1903 to expand the institution, in view of the demand for religious teachers and Rabbis, was not implemented; according to one version, this was owing to the fanaticism of the former Chief Rabbi, Moshe Levi, who vetoed the appointment of the institute's graduates to rabbinical posts.[57]

Despite all the difficulties it encountered, the Rabbinical Seminary continued to exist until the First World War. When the authorities began to relax their attitude towards religion, in 1944/45, it was reopened, in June 1945, with twenty students,[58] but functioned for only a short time because of a lack of students. On 6 February 1955, it was again revived, and this time with a larger attendance: 30 in 1959 and 44 in 1961. It was then decided to admit graduates of five-year elementary schools, with the Seminary period of study to be seven years. However, the graduates were not to be considered secondary school graduates and could not be admitted to universities, for the Turkish authorities regarded it as a religious-vocational school, similar to such schools for Muslim Imams. The institution's future is not assured, since the Jewish population has not grown in recent years, owing to emigration and to the fact that there is a growing lack of interest in religious studies. The economic position of the Jewish religious ministrants does not attract young Jews to the Seminary.

This process of decline in traditional education in Turkey in the last seventy-eighty years, and especially after the First World War, was caused by the same factors which contributed to the decline elsewhere. In Turkey, the policy of separating religion from the State and the hostile attitude of the authorities to everything connected with religious education for all faiths were additional factors. No other Jewish community in the Middle East had encountered such an attitude towards religious values. Despite the renewal of traditional education in recent years, it is unlikely that Turkish Jewry will ever again have the standing they enjoyed up to the First World War, when it furnished a number of Chief Rabbis to Iraq, Egypt, Libya, the Yemen, and Palestine.

MODERN EDUCATION 1850–1914

Some Jews in Turkey began to receive a modern education as far back as the first half of the 19th century. They studied in Christian schools, several reaching the Medical School in Istanbul before 1850. In that year, the first modern Jewish school was founded in Turkey, and the *Alliance* began to operate in 1867. From the 1860's, Jews were permitted to attend Turkish state schools.

During the second half of the 19th century, hundreds of Jewish children attended Christian schools, both in Izmir and in Istanbul, even after Jewish educational institutions became available. According to available statistics at the end of the century, 500 were to be found in the local Protestant schools in Izmir alone, 200 boys and 300 girls. In 1889, hundreds of Jewish children were being educated in institutions of the Catholic and Protestant Missions in Istanbul, despite the fact that part of this education was the compulsory study of the New Testament and despite the Mission's well-known attempts to convert the Jewish pupils. And, indeed, a few cases of conversion were recorded each year in Izmir alone, and many others who had attended these schools became indifferent to the religion of their fathers.

The Christian institutions attracted the Jewish children by exempting them from payment of school fees and by supplying them with free textbooks. At the same time, efforts were made to encourage Jewish parents to transfer their children to Jewish institutions; these met with only partial success, until, in 1905, the local Mission in Izmir decided to discontinue exempting children from payment of fees. The result was a smaller number of Jewish boys and girls attending its school, and more children enrolled in the *Alliance* schools.[59] Since the establishment of the Republic of Turkey, the number of Jewish children attending Christian schools gradually decreased, and today these schools do not constitute any danger to Turkish Jewry. Credit must be given, however, to the missionary schools for their contribution in providing a modern education for Jewish children in the 19th century, when modern Jewish schools were still very few and not of a high standard.

As to modern Jewish educational institutions, the first such school was opened in 1850 in Adrianople by the orientalist Joseph Halevi, who remained there for several years. Later, additional private schools were opened, but by 1902 none remained in existence, being replaced by the *Alliance* schools.

In Istanbul, a Jewish community school was opened in November 1854, with the assistance of the Vienna Rothschilds and with Albert Cohen as principal. Here Hebrew, Turkish and French were taught. The Rabbis opposed this institution and launched a hostile propaganda campaign against it, claiming that only a few hours were devoted to Jewish subjects. Although from 1859 three or four hours a day were devoted to the study of Hebrew, and morning and evening prayers were conducted with the students, the city's Rabbis, in 1867, proclaimed a ban and excommunication on the second director of the institution, Abraham Camondo. In 1858 another private school was opened, in Istanbul, under the management of a Mr. Bloch and with the support of the Camondo family,[60] followed by further private schools in the ensuing years. In one of them, founded in 1882, more hours were devoted to the study of the Turkish language. This school was of a satisfactory standard, twelve of its first graduates being admitted to the Medical School in 1889 after passing special examinations.[61]

In Izmir as well, from 1864, private individuals preceded the *Alliance* in founding modern schools, and they, as well as the Jewish community schools, continued to exist even after the *Alliance* opened its first school in 1867. In 1888, the Community accused the *Alliance* director of neglecting to teach Hebrew and Turkish, and in protest founded the Keter Torah school. The innovation in this school, which was directed by Moshe Fresco, was the introduction of Turkish as the language of instruction. For lack of budget, however, the school was closed down after four years. Further private schools were opened later.[62]

Private or Jewish community schools appeared in other Turkish cities as well, but most lasted only until the eve of the First World War; by the time the Republic of Turkey was established in 1923, not one of them remained in existence.

The fact that these private and Jewish community schools had been founded was an indication of the need felt to give the children a suitable education for life in Turkey. Although the private schools were closed down after a few years, because of lack of funds, nevertheless they did contribute something to the education of Jewish children. They did not, however, provide secondary school education and admitted practically no girls. In this period the only school open to Jewish girls were those of the Missions and the *Alliance*.

The greatest contribution to Jewish education before the First World War was made by the *Alliance* schools. Their first school in Turkey for boys was founded in Adrianople in 1867, and for girls in 1875, followed by two in Izmir and several in Istanbul. Towards the end of the century, they opened schools also in the small towns, as in Bursa, Aydin, Casaba, Tire, Bergama, Manisa, Tekirdağ (formerly Rodosto), in the Dardanelles, Gallipoli and elsewhere. They may indeed be proud of the number of pupils studying in the schools they founded in Turkey: in 1875 there were 773; in 1900, 7,267; in 1910, 11,101; and in 1913, 11,687.[63]

The language of instruction in their schools was Ladino in the first two grades and French in the higher grades. Hebrew was also taught, and from the third grade, Turkish and English as well. In Izmir, where many Greeks lived, the Greek language, too, was taught from the fourth class. Thus, in the fifth year of school, the children were learning four or five languages! Besides, they studied the Bible, history, geography, mathematics, bookkeeping and literature, and were also given lessons in religion.[64] In the third and fourth grades the number of hours assigned to Hebrew was reduced. Only a few hours a week were devoted to the study of the Turkish language, for according to an Ottoman Ministry of Education Order of 1867, the minority schools were obliged to teach Turkish only from the fifth class of elementary school.[65] As a result, the Turkish Jews did not have a command of the State language, not even those who attended the *Alliance* schools.

In view of the many drop-outs from school, the *Alliance* management deemed it advisable to teach the children a trade with which they could earn a living. In Izmir, Istanbul and other cities, they set up trade schools, or to be more exact, the school director arranged for several of his pupils aged twelve and over to obtain jobs as apprentices in workshops. These apprentices attended evening lessons at the school in French, arithmetic, Hebrew and religion. Those who concluded four years of apprenticeship received a certificate and a grant to buy tools. This method was employed up to the First World War and was fairly successful. In 1894, the charitable society *Gemilut Ḥasadim*—afterwards called *Maḥzikei 'Aniyim* ("maintainers of the poor")—founded in Izmir a similar apprenticeship project for the Talmud Torah pupils. These two projects came to an end in 1915, when the majority of the craftsmen were mobilized for the army so that there was nowhere to send the apprentices. In Izmir and Istanbul, dressmaking classes for girls were also opened.[66]

The *Alliance* also made an attempt to train youth for agricultural work. In 1890, they sent ten pupils to their agricultural school in Jaffa, and at the same time acquired land in the vicinity of Izmir on which six pupils worked in 1893. In 1904 this plot was sold and instead a piece of land of 28,000 dunams was bought in Akhisar, called *Or Yehuda*. This agricultural school, where the training period was five years and where languages were also taught, existed up to 1912–13, when several pupils emigrated with one of their teachers to Brazil, to settle on Jewish Colonization Association land there.[67] At the end of the last century, too, the *Alliance* sent a number of youths to Bordeaux, Vienna, Venice and Budapest, to learn trades unknown in Turkey.

Before the First World War *Alliance* schools in Istanbul also conducted evening classes for adults.[68]

On the outbreak of the First World War, all the *Alliance* activities in Turkey came to a standstill.

Jewish children wishing to continue their education in state schools were faced with a serious problem—they knew no Turkish. In 1840, the Chief Rabbi of Istanbul issued an appeal to the Jews to study Turkish, but it was only in the 'seventies that it began to be taught in Jewish schools. Some who knew Turkish founded, in 1900, a "society to spread the Turkish language" *(Ta'mīm-i-lisān-i-Othmānī)*,[69] which received a government licence, but whose endeavours did not achieve much.

Hence, until the end of the 19th century, Jewish young people could attend only the state schools where the instruction was not in Turkish, as, for instance, the Medical School founded in 1828 in Istanbul, the first Jew graduating from it in 1834. In 1848, the proselyte Moses Margoliouth found 24 Jewish students at that school whom the Sultan permitted to absent themselves on the Sabbath; in 1889, 25 students were attending it and another ten its preparatory school.[70] In 1867, members of the minorities were granted admittance to the *al-Rushdiya* secondary school, but Jews were reluctant to register there because it was a military school. But when the Government Lycée, a non-military secondary school, was opened in September 1868 in Galata Saray, in Istanbul, for non-Muslims as well, 34 Jews were among its 341 students.[71] Thereafter, an increasing number of Jews attended state secondary and higher education schools. In 1889 besides the 35 Jews in the Medical School and its preparatory school, there were also three in the Law Faculty.[72] Others studied at European universities. Before the end of the century, there were scores of Jewish university graduates; several of them received appointments as lecturers at Istanbul University.[73] Although the Turkish authorities did not prevent Jewish students from gaining admittance to its educational institutions, an attempt was made in 1870 to limit the number entering the Medical School to 15, but the Jewish community applied to the Ministry of Education on March 22,

1872 asking that 35 be admitted to that School, as had been the case previously.[74] And indeed, that many were studying there in 1889.

Despite the great educational progress made by the Turkish Jews, among the girls as well, during the sixty years preceding the First World War, there were still many illiterates, particularly in the Kurdistan region.[75]

MODERN EDUCATION SINCE 1914

On the outbreak of the First World War, most of the foreign schools were closed down, including those of the *Alliance*. They were reopened after the war had ended. In 1922, 10,340 pupils attended *Alliance* schools[76]; there had been 11,600 in 1913. But this beginning was nipped in the bud when the Turkish Republic came into existence in 1923. That year, the Ministry of Education issued instructions to the effect that all teachers of history, geography and the Turkish language in all educational institutions must be appointed by the Government. A more serious blow was inflicted on *Alliance* schools when a law was promulgated in 1926 providing that the language of instruction in all Turkish schools must be Turkish. (The Jewish schools were considered to be Turkish, since the Jews had renounced their minority rights.*) As a result, the majority of the *Alliance* institutions had to close down, and in 1928 all the rest were turned over to the local Jewish communities.

Most of the Jewish private schools were also among those shut down on the outbreak of the First World War. Gradually the number of children attending all Jewish schools dwindled. As against 5,700 pupils in 1913 in Istanbul and Adrianople, there were about 4,500 in 1925/26. In the whole of Turkey, only 5,746 attended Jewish schools in 1930/31,[77] and a mere 2,000 in 1950. These figures do not include Jewish pupils in state and foreign schools.

The evidence would seem to indicate that the growing number of Jewish pupils in state schools with the resulant decline in attendance at Jewish schools was mainly due to the Jews' eagerness to become integrated in the life of the country, after having resided for hundreds of years in Turkey as strangers. Moreover, in the days of the Republic, the Jewish schools hardly differed from state schools. The curriculum was that of the state schools, even Jewish history being taught as part of courses in general history. Hebrew was not taught at all.[78] The Ministry of Education re-enforced its supervision over the foreign schools, and in 1937 even appointed a special supervisor for them. Not until 1945 were the Jews permitted to teach Hebrew, and then only a few hours a week. In July 1949 the special supervision of Jewish schools was abolished but in the meantime, with the passage of

* See above, p. 20.

over twenty years, a new generation had arisen which, for the most part, had not studied Hebrew and knew very little about Judaism. Before 1945, some attempt had been made, quietly, to organize evening courses in Jewish history and the study of the Hebrew language, in the large cities and also in small towns like Bursa and Tekirdağ. The attendance could only be very small, even later, when the Government permitted the teaching of Hebrew in Jewish institutions.

Noteworthy attempts were made by the Jewish communities in Istanbul and Izmir to maintain Jewish secondary schools. In 1915, the Izmir Community founded a *gymnasium* (of three classes) which was co-educational and in which French was the language of instruction. On the termination of the Turkish War of Liberation in 1922, however, this institution became an elementary school and has remained such up to the present. Since then, Jews have received secondary school education in state schools in Izmir, while some travelled to Istanbul to study in the Jewish secondary school there. In 1958 a secondary school (three-year) in Izmir was planned and a permit received for the purpose from the Ministry of Education,[79] but nothing came of it.

In January 1915, a Jewish *gymnasium* was founded in Istanbul by Rabbi Dr. Marcus called *Midrashah Yavneh,* also known by the name of *Béné Bérith Lycée,* with 38 students. In 1924, the first *gymnasium* classes for girls were established, but closed down for lack of budget, the girls being transferred to the boys' school. Later the *Béné Bérith Lycée* became a co-educational secondary school.[80] At first, the teaching was in French, but with the rise of the Republic, French became a secondary language and all subjects were taught in Turkish. The curriculum was the same as that in all state schools, but the *gymnasium* was permitted to engage foreign teachers. There were 203 students (besides those in the elementary classes attached to the *gymnasium*) in 1930/31; the number had gone down to 127 in 1950.

These figures do not tell us how many Jewish children completed secondary school in Turkey. But from the data in the table at the beginning of this chapter, we see that the number of graduates was not small, for the median years of study of Turkish-born Jews in Israel was almost the same as those of the Egyptian- and Iraqi-born.

Some of the secondary school graduates also went on to higher education institutes in Turkey and abroad. In the 1920's a member of the Community Committee in Istanbul complained that Jews were not admitted to the Turkish universities. It is not known whether this complaint was justified or not, but in the 1940's, there were some scores of students in the Faculty of Medicine in Istanbul alone. It is difficult to ascertain the number of Jewish university graduates in Turkey, but it may be said that it is on the increase and that now girls, too, graduate. The fields specialized in have also multiplied, now including medicine, pharmacy, law, psychology, and engineering.

LITERATURE AND CULTURE

The decline of traditional education among Jews in Turkey left its mark most conspicuously on Jewish literature. Up to the end of the 19th century, Turkish Jews had among them Rabbis of stature, who wrote many books on religious subjects.[81] But after the First World War, very few such works appeared.

In the second half of the 19th century, there was an impressive development of the Jewish press, beyond that in any other Eastern Jewish community. The majority of the newspapers which appeared were written in Ladino. After the First World War, the number of Jewish newspapers decreased; most were then written in French, a few in Turkish, and, in the past two decades, also in Hebrew and in Ladino written in Latin characters.[82]

A similar process occurred in the sphere of secular literature. In the 19th century, there were Jewish authors writing mainly in Ladino or translating various works into that language. In the 1920's, Jewish writers and poets began to write in Turkish (among them one Jewess, Matilde Alçeh (1923–1967) a poet and a journalist) and French, although they were very few. Many more published works in history, medicine, law, economics and other subjects, mostly in French or Turkish.[83]

Before the First World War, some Jewish singers, players of various instruments and composers had become famous. There were also poets who wrote popular poems and songs, mainly in Ladino; but some used the Turkish language and became known among the non-Jewish population.[84] This does not mean that the Turkish Jews and other Turks had intermingled culturally. All the signs indicate that, particularly from the cultural aspect, Turkish Jews, up to 1923, were far from being integrated into Turkish society. The mother tongue of most was Ladino and only after the First World War did more Jews begin to learn Turkish. According to the population census taken in 1927, 84% of the Jews (68,900 out of 81,872) registered their mother-tongue as "Yahudice," i.e. Jewish (Ladino, and perhaps also Yiddish). In the 1935 census the percentage had dropped to 54% (42,607 out of 78,730), but it may be that because of the pressure put on the Jews to reveal more Turkish nationalism, less Jews gave their mother-tongue as "Jewish." And later, indeed, it was found that the percentage of those whose mother-tongue was "Jewish" had not declined that much. In the 1945 census, 66.3% declared their mother-tongue as "Jewish" (50,109 out of 76,965), and in 1955, 71.7% (32,975 out of 45,995), besides another 1,420 (or 3.1%) who declared that "Jewish" was their second language. In the 1960 census, however, it transpired that the percentage of those whose mother-tongue was "Jewish" had declined to 44.2%, and to 24 % in 1965.[85]

Syria and the Lebanon

There were demographic and economic differences between the Jews of Damascus and those of Aleppo and Beirut, and these were reflected in the educational structure as well. It has not always been possible to demonstrate these differences statistically, because of the internal migration among the Jews of these three cities. It is difficult to say, for example, whether the Jewish pupils and students who attended school in Beirut were from Aleppo, or Damascus, or were local residents. At the same time, it is evident that secular education had made more progress in the last hundred years in Beirut; that traditional education was widespread in Aleppo, although it declined later; and that both traditional and secular education were less advanced in Damascus.

THE LEBANON

Up to 1902 a Talmud Torah existed in Sidon, when about 100 children, aged two to eleven, were studying there. In 1902, a number of Jewish children also attended Christian schools in the city. In that year, the Talmud Torah was closed, and the *Alliance* founded a co-educational school, which was closed only in June 1965, despite the fact that the Jewish community in Sidon did not exceed a few scores.

In Beirut, although traditional education did not cease altogether, it did decline. In 1856, the Jewish traveller Ludwig August Frankl found 500 Jews in that city, with one Talmud Torah where a *Ḥakham* taught 70 boys to read and write. With the growth of the Jewish settlement there, a second Talmud Torah was opened. In 1923, the number of pupils had reached about 500. In 1926 another Talmud Torah was founded by Michael Ṭarrāb (a native of Damascus who became rich in Cuba), which bore his name, and which remained the only one in the city, 250 studying there in 1932, 290 in 1935, 250 in 1959, and 193 in 1962.[86] Up to 1930 the main subjects taught were Hebrew and the Bible, general subjects being introduced later. But even in 1950 its standard was considered low and its students were not qualified to take the Government and French elementary examinations. Since the parents who wanted their sons to learn more European languages sent them to secular schools, the children attending the Talmud Torah came from among the poor. Besides this institution, there was an *Oẓar Hatorah* school in the city, attended by about 100 children in 1959.[87] There were no Yeshivas in Beirut.

As early as 1875 *Ḥakham* Zaki Cohen understood the great desire of the Lebanese Jews to teach their sons foreign languages, when he founded a private school called *Tiferet Yisrael,* in which he taught eight languages. It was mainly children of the rich, from Damascus and Aleppo as well, who came to this school. For financial reasons it closed after about a year. It was reopened with a boarding-school in 1878, attended by pupils from Jaffa, Izmir and Istanbul, as well, 90 children studying there in 1879 and 82 in 1883. Now, only five languages were taught (Hebrew, Arabic, Turkish, French and German). After the director's death it was maintained by his sons; finally it closed down in 1904. This institution attracted many children because it taught languages and because it was headed by a Rabbi. In contrast, the director who arrived in Beirut in 1869 to open an *Alliance* school there was compelled to leave when only 19 children registered. In 1878, the *Alliance* opened a girls' school and, two years later, two boys' schools; it then discontinued the financial support it had been granting *Tiferet Yisrael.* Nevertheless, the latter school continued to compete with those of the *Alliance*, and only after Zaki Cohen's death did the number of pupils attending the *Alliance* schools increase. The subjects of instruction there were similar to those taught in other institutions in the Middle East. In 1883, three languages were already being studied in the first grade (Hebrew, Arabic and French) and Talmud. Physics, history and geography were added in the fourth and last grades. The girls learned the same subjects, except for Talmud, with the addition of the English language.[88]

The *Alliance* schools had competition not only from *Tiferet Yisrael,* but also from the Christian schools in the city. In 1865 the Scots opened a special school for Jews and in 1868 two additional ones especially for Jewish boys, which existed until the First World War. Despite the fact that in the Christian educational institutions the Jewish pupils had to pay fees, that they were compelled to desecrate the Sabbath and had to say Christian prayers, the rich parents preferred them to the *Alliance*, after the First World War as well,[89] because the latter were considered to be of a lower standard and because they lacked secondary school classes.

The *Alliance* attempted to correct this situation. At the end of the 1920's, girls who distinguished themselves in their schools in Beirut began to be prepared for the French *brevet* (intermediate) examinations and in each of the years 1929–1932, three girls passed these examinations successfully; in 1939, there were ten, and in 1945 eight.[90] On the other hand, the boys were not prepared for the *brevet* during this period, so that only a few pupils, who attended non-Jewish schools, sat for these examinations. In 1933, in all of the Lebanon, only three Jewish boys passed the French *brevet* examinations; in 1939, there were five; and in 1945, four.[91] Up to the 1940's there was no Jewish secondary school in Beirut; the attempts made by the *Béné Bérith* lodge to found one failed.[92] In the mid-'forties, however, the *Alliance* began to prepare a special co-educational class for the Lebanese Government *brevet* examinations. Thanks to that class, 46 Jews successfully passed these examinations in 1945, besides 12 who passed the French *brevet*. The figures for 1960 were 28 and 17 respectively.[93] These figures do not include those Jews who sat for the Government examinations not through the *Alliance* schools. Nevertheless, it cannot be assumed that the total number of those passing the intermediate examinations in 1945 exceeded 70–80 Jewish children, and in 1960 not more than 50.

From the small number of intermediate school graduates, we may imagine how few graduated from complete secondary schools or universities.

There is no doubt, however, that great progress was made in the last hundred years in the education of the Lebanese Jews, the girls included, and it appears that the problem of illiteracy practically disappeared among the young people in that country. This can be confirmed by the data on illiteracy among Israelis born in Syria and the Lebanon supplied by the 1961 census taken in Israel.

SYRIA

In Aleppo, Yeshivas had existed in the 11th and 12th centuries and were revived in the 16th century, when the Spanish exiles settled in the city, continuing to serve the Jewish Community there up to the end of the 19th century. In Damascus, however, the Yeshivas that had existed in the 16th and 17th centuries had practically disappeared. The traveller Yeḥiel Fischel Kastelman, who visited both cities in 1859, wrote that in Aleppo there were many Yeshivas, with many *Ḥakhams* (Rabbis), while in Damascus he could find but one Yeshiva. The traveller Wolff Schur (1875) also spoke about a large Yeshiva in Aleppo, with many groups studying Talmud and the *Posekim* (Rabbinical literature dealing with the legal side of Jewish tradition). Only in this city and in Baghdad, he reported, could "people be found who were erudite in Talmud and who could reach down to its depths and bring up its most precious pearls." Ephraim Neumark, who visited Aleppo in 1884, noted many Yeshivas, excelling even those of Baghdad, because they were maintained by rich Jews who themselves were taking part in the study of the Torah, the Talmud, and the *Shulḥan Aruch* (code of Jewish laws), and that they supported poor Yeshiva students. On the other hand, he found in Damascus only one Yeshiva, in which about ten *Ḥakhams* studied about two hours a day.[94]

At the start of the present century, the Yeshivas in Aleppo began to die out, only one or two remaining. Prior to the First World War, the *Reshit Ḥochma* Yeshiva was founded for the study of Talmud and foreign languages; it existed up to the outbreak of the war. Afterwards, the Institute for the Teaching of Talmud was established, attended by about 20 (in 1925) or 30 (in 1930) destitute pupils, who received a stipend from the community. Most of the time they studied Talmud, with a little Arabic and French.[95] In the 1940's Aleppo Jewry had no Yeshivas, although they were still able to train young people for Rabbinical posts.

With regard to *ḥeders* and Talmud Torahs, Aleppo could again boast of better institutions. Abraham Elmaleḥ, who was in Damascus in 1911, related that the *ḥeders* there were attended by about 400–500 children—about a quarter of all the Jewish children in the city, and that they were in very poor shape. The buildings were dark and damp and the children sat crowded together on worn-out mats in front of their old and miserable Rabbi. The Rabbi would read to them chapters of the Bible, the Zohar (the book of Jewish mysticism) and *'Ein Ya'akov* (collection of legends from the Talmud), without their understanding the contents. The pupils themselves were thin, weak and dirty.[96] According to the traveller Ludwig Frankl there were two Talmud Torahs in 1856, employing 15 teachers. But in the 1880's, only one was left (or perhaps the two merged), and because of its financial difficulties, the Jewish Community transferred it to the *Alliance* in 1895. The latter introduced into the curriculum a number of general subjects—arithmetic, geography, for example. About 450 pupils attended it in 1888, and 768 in 1910.[97] The *Alliance* directed the schools up to 1911, when the Community Committee contributed small sums for its maintenance. In 1911 the Jewish Community discontinued its support, and as a consequence the *Alliance* withdrew its management.[98]

In 1923 about 450 children were studying in two Talmud Torahs in Damascus, both of which were closed down in 1924, when some of the pupils transferred to the *Alliance* schools. After some time, a new Talmud Torah was opened, with about 300 children in 1938, but it, too, closed because of budgetary difficulties in 1939, and when reopened in 1941 was handed over to the *Alliance*.[99] It lasted until September 1945, when all the *Alliance* institutions in Syria were shut down, as shall be explained further on. Immediately a new institute named *Talmud Torah Ben-Maymon* was opened, the first to follow the Government curriculum: by July 1947, three of its pupils had successfully passed the Government elementary examinations.[100] Calling this institution a Talmud Torah was apparently a way of bypassing the prohibition against the *Alliance* activities, and it was closed down in 1947 when the *Alliance* was permitted to renew its activities.

Thus it can be seen that the traditional schools in Damascus were most unstable, ceasing to exist by 1941. It was revived only in 1950, when the *Oẓar Hatorah* Society of New York succeeded in establishing a religious school which, in 1959, was attended by 340 pupils.

On the other hand, the *ḥeders* and Talmud Torahs in Aleppo fared better. The traveller Wolff Schur wrote in 1875 that the *ḥeders* in Aleppo were not bad, compared with those elsewhere in Syria, and that in them the pupils learned to read and also to translate into Arabic.[101] In 1926, in the only Talmud Torah in the city, 245 boys were being taught.[102] There was a great demand for religious education in Aleppo, so that in 1925 a new Talmud Torah was founded, with 500 pupils.

It is interesting that the number of children in the two Talmud Torahs in Aleppo did not decrease during the years: in 1942, the first had an attendance of 250 and the second 600,[103] this despite the fact that up to 1939 the main subjects taught were

Hebrew and religion. At the end of that year, the Government curriculum was introduced. Even in this period however, some parents preferred Christian schools to Jewish. After the establishment of the State of Israel and the large Jewish emigration from the city, the one remaining Talmud Torah was transferred to the *Oẓar Hatorah* Society, which set up another school as well. In 1959, 426 children were studying in both institutions.

Thus traditional education in Aleppo, although on the decline, held out; unlike that in Damascus and Beirut, it did not disappear entirely. Modern education, too, did not follow the same lines in Damascus and Aleppo.

In 1883, 40 children were going to Christian schools in Damascus. Even after *Alliance* schools had been opened in Syria, many Jewish children continued to attend Christian schools in that city: in 1924, about 150, and in 1929, about 300.[104] Apparently the Jewish parents preferred them because of their higher standards. In Aleppo, too, even before the First World War, the rich Jews preferred to send their sons to Mission schools, although in view of the Aleppo Jews' piety, it is reasonable to assume that the number was smaller than that in Damascus. Jewish children in Aleppo and Damascus continued to attend Christian schools up to the 1940's.[105]

The *Alliance* schools developed slowly until the beginning of the present century. Their first school was founded in Damascus in 1864, but was closed down in December 1869 because of competition from the Christian schools, opposition of the *ḥeder* teachers and the rabbis to the *Alliance* activities, and because of the parents' reluctance to contribute to the costs of maintaining the institution. It was only in 1880, after the Turkish Governor of Damascus, Midḥat Pasha, had applied to the *Anglo Jewish Society,* that the *Alliance* reopened its school: in 1883, 114 boys were studying there, mainly Arabic, Hebrew, French and Turkish. That year a girls' school was opened, and the Talmud Torah was transferred to its management. In 1910, there were 1,129 pupils in *Alliance* schools in Damascus (including the Talmud Torah), in 1939, 1,073, and in 1962, 458.[106]

In Aleppo the local Jews had opened a modern school as early as 1869, a special teacher having been sent to them by the *Alliance.* In 1871, a girls' school was established, but it was closed immediately, since the number of girls attending it was small; those aged 7 to 12 were transferred to the boys' school. The girls had a school again only in 1894. The number of pupils attending the *Alliance* schools was small, because some parents objected to secular studies and the wealthy families preferred the Christian schools. It was not until the beginning of the 20th century that a more favourable attitude to the *Alliance* institutions was adopted, when two more *Alliance* schools were founded. Despite the constant decline in the city's Jewish population from the end of the 19th century, the number of children in the *Alliance* schools remained almost unchanged, until they were all closed down in 1945.

In October 1945, when Syria obtained its independence, the Government closed the foreign educational institutions, including those of the *Alliance*. Damascus children went about without any schooling, except for those who could be taken into the *Ben-Maymon Talmud Torah,* which, as indicated above, was opened that year. In Aleppo, the Government opened a special school for Jews with a Muslim principal. Many Jews abstained from registering their sons there, until the Government appointed a Jewish principal. In December 1946, the Government permitted the *Alliance* to renew the studies in their schools, on the condition that they would be called *"al-Ittiḥād Al-Isrā'īlī"* (Jewish Unity).[107]

With the large emigration from Syria in 1945 and the ensuing years, all the *Alliance* schools in the country ceased to function, except for one in Damascus. From an attendance of 2,173 in 1910 and 2,084 in 1939 in its schools in Syria, the number had declined to 458 in 1962.[108] Since only a few Jews were able to leave Syria since 1962, the number of *Alliance* pupils did not change. In 1970/71 480 students attended the *Alliance* school in Damascus.

A comparison between the number of pupils in the *Alliance* schools in Syria and those in the Lebanon shows that despite the fact that the Syrian Jewish community was four or five times larger than the Lebanese in the years prior to 1939, the number of children in the *Alliance* schools in Syria was only twice that in the Lebanon. The fact that the *Alliance* did not establish secondary schools in Syria as they had in the Lebanon may well account for the smaller proportion.

There are no data available on the number of Syrian and Lebanese Jews who attended higher schools of education in their countries or in Europe or America, although it is known that as far back as the 1870's the first Syrian Jews travelled to Europe to study medicine and pharmacy. Undoubtedly, the total number of Jewish university graduates in Syria and the Lebanon was small, despite the fact that universities of long standing were to be found in Beirut and Damascus. The few Jews who completed secondary school preferred, for the most part, to engage in commerce. Only in the last decade have more Syrian Jews been attending universities.

LITERATURE AND CULTURE

In religious creativity as well, there were outstanding differences between the Jews of Aleppo, Damascus and Beirut. Among the Jews of Aleppo there were many famous Rabbis who wrote and published religious works, especially before the First World War.[109] From that time, most of the Aleppo Jews' writings were published in Palestine. The Damascus Jews, on the other hand, produced few famous Rabbis writing religious books, because Damascus had no well-developed Hebrew printing press to publish such works, and mainly because there were no Yeshivas there worthy of the name.

A few journalists were active in Lebanon, such as Eliyahu Salīm Mann, editor of the only Jewish newspaper, which appeared in Beirut in the Arabic language,[110] and Tawfīq Mizraḥi, who published an economic paper in French. Among the few poets and writers worthy of note was the authoress, translator and journalist Mrs. Esther Azhari-Moyal, born in Beirut. Esther Lazar, whose name was distorted in Arabic to "Azhari" and who was married to Dr. Moyal, wrote a number of books, translated many more from French to Arabic, edited a number of newspapers, one of them with her husband, and was active in the women's organization in the Lebanon.[111] After she was widowed, she lived in Marseilles with her doctor daughters, and later moved to Jaffa, where she died on the eve of the establishment of the State of Israel. She and one Jewish authoress in Turkey and a journalist in Egypt were the only women writers to appear among Middle Eastern Jews of our days.

Iran

Up to the 1870's, there had not been any Jewish schools in Iran, and except for those few children who attended *ḥeder* for a short period, the Iranian Jews received no education at all. Tourists who reached this country in the 19th century reported very briefly on the educational situation of the Jews there, using the word "ignoramuses" over and over again. The convert Henry A. Stern, who visited Hamadhān and Kangavar in 1852, and Kastelman, who visited various places in Iran in 1861, told of the ignorance of the Jews in each place they visited.[112] Ephraim Neumark, who was in the country in 1884, reported that even the standard of studies in the *ḥeder* was very low and that it was a rarity "to find a Jew who knew Talmud and *Posekim*" (Rabbinical literature dealing with the legal side of Jewish tradition).[113] Although there were many Jewish *ḥakīms* (physicians) in Iran during this period and up to the end of the century, they had no higher education, and had acquired some knowledge of the profession from experience. Only in exceptional cases did Jews study in educational institutions in Baghdad.[114]

1875–1898. In 1873, during the visit to Europe of Nāṣir al-Dīn Shah, king of Iran, the *Alliance* asked his permission to establish a school for Jews in Teheran, which had a Jewish population of 1,800 at the time. The king agreed, and was even prepared to pay the salary of a teacher for the Persian language. Immediately, the enthusiasm of young Jews in the city was aroused and they founded a small school with 55 pupils, where Torah, Talmud(!), English, French, Persian, Turkish and Arabic were taught. They hoped that the *Alliance* would send them a director.[115]

The Society did not do so, and also did not reply to subsequent similar requests, made in 1876, in 1881, and in 1896.[116] Elken Adler, the son of the Chief Rabbi of

Britain, who visited Iran in 1896, mentioned the many requests of the Jews of Teheran and the small communities, such as those in Resht, Qazvīn, and Sicāl, that a school be established for them.[117] The Governor of Teheran, a relative of the Shah, even complained to Adler that the Jews of Europe had neglected their brethren in Iran, who were in need of modern education.[118] The *Alliance* claimed budgetary difficulties and the lack of suitable teachers, and, in 1889, apparently having despaired of the possibility of opening a school in Iran, asked the Shah, during his second visit to Europe, to permit the Iranian Jews to attend the State schools.[119] The Shah could not agree to this request, because of the Muslims' belief in the impurity of Jews, which would not permit Jewish children to sit alongside Muslim children. In 1896 or 1897, young Jews in Teheran again took the initiative, collected funds and founded a school in the city, in which several Mullas (Rabbi-teachers) taught a number of Jewish children. This institution served as the basis for the opening of the *Alliance* school in 1898.[120]

In the meantime, Christian missions had been making great efforts to draw Jewish children into their schools. In 1876, they opened a special school for Jewish boys in Teheran, in 1884 a similar one in Hamadhān, and in 1889, one in Iṣfahān. The latter two were closed after a few years. In 1894 two new Missionary schools for Jewish children were opened—one in Teheran for boys and the second, for girls, in Hamadhān. A considerable number of Jewish children attended these schools until those of the *Alliance* were opened.[121] Ephraim Neumark, on his visit to Iran in 1884, related that a Jewish Rabbi taught the Bible in the Mission school in Hamadhān, and a Christian taught the New Testament two hours a day. Neumark added, scornfully, that the parents, did not believe their children when they informed them that they were studying the New Testament, and even if they had, it was not important to them, for their sons were getting a free education. Neumark also pointed out, however, that the Missionary education had no negative results, and that no cases of conversion were known among the Jewish pupils. Out of concern for the future, he complained against the *Alliance* for not opening even one school in Iran, despite the Shah's approval in 1873.[122]

The Christian educational institutions existed only in a number of cities in Iran, and even where they did many parents were not prepared to send their children to them. The majority of the Iranian Jews, who, in those days were dispersed over many tens of cities, small towns and villages, received no modern education. As indicated, Jews were not admitted at that time to state educational institutions, so that it was only thanks to the Mission schools that a number of Jews were able, before the end of the century, to complete their higher education, studying mainly medicine in Beirut or Paris, partly at their own expense and partly with the assistance of the Missions.[123]

In this period, *ḥeders* and Talmud Torahs were to be found in Iran, not only in the large cities, but also in the small communities. The pupils—although their number is unknown—undoubtedly constituted only a small proportion of the Jewish children of school age, so that many, particularly in the Kurdistan region, did not attend any educational institution. Although the *ḥeders* were co-educational, there were very few girls among their pupils, most receiving no education at all. Above all, even the children who went to *ḥeder* learned very little. They were taught only Hebrew and this by antiquated methods. Ephraim Neumark related that "the children's education in Iran was the lowest of the low, about twenty sat together in front of the Mulla . . . after they managed to learn the form of the letters of the alphabet they were stuffed with the first two or three verses of the weekly portion of the Pentateuch . . . Thus passed the day, the morrow and the day after, and thus the order of the week ended. If the child was intelligent, he was able to read those three verses on Friday and if not . . . ? If not, he began a new portion the next week. It is easy to imagine the results of this kind of teaching." And Neumark added: "And so only a few could read correctly out of the Book in their tenth year, so as to be able to begin to learn the meaning of the words they had swallowed. And so, after much hard and tiring toil, a generation will be brought up which will be able to pray, and among them one from a city and two from a family who will be able to translate the Bible into Persian." [124]

1898–1925. In April 1898 the *Alliance* sent to Teheran a director for the school which had been established there two years previously by the local residents. He was greeted with great joy by the Jews, and the Shah showed his pleasure by ordering that the institution be given a grant of 200 *toman*.[125] The director organized the classes, introduced new methods of teaching and gradually also added lessons in general studies. In 1899 the *Alliance* also opened a girls' school in Teheran, followed by schools in Hamadhān and in Iṣfahān (1900), in Seneh (1903), in Shīrāz (1903), in Tūisīrkān (1903), in Kermanshāh (1904) and in Nahavand (1905). Those in Nahavand and Tūisīrkān were closed after a number of years. In each place where an *Alliance* director arrived to found a school, he was received with enthusiasm, not only by the Jews, but by the Government representatives as well; the Muslims and even their religious leaders also welcomed them. Within a brief period, the number of children attending the *Alliance* schools increased considerably, despite the interruptions caused by the First World War, as is shown in the table C-8.

The *Alliance* also conducted evening courses for adults in various places. Among the first was the course opened in Teheran for 150 people. In Iṣfahān, in 1910, attendance was 116, including 29 married people.[126] The *Alliance* directors were assisted by the French ambassador in Teheran until they were able to establish the status of their schools and even to impart a feeling of security to the Jews in the city.

Among the problems obstructing the development of the *Alliance* institutions

TABLE C-8: ALLIANCE SCHOOLS IN IRAN. 1900–1913[127]

City	1900		1905		1913	
	Boys	Girls	Boys	Girls	Boys	Girls
Teheran	422	—	445	170	466	172
Hamadhān	346	215	409	175	469	191
Iṣfahān	—	—	358	268	431	217
Seneh	—	—	185	90	225	54
Shīrāz	—	—	340	90	277	55
Kermanshāh	—	—	198	—	238	49
Tūisīrkān and Nahavand	—	—	122	—	—	—
Total	768	215	2,057	793	2,106	738

in this period was the competition presented by missionary educational institutions, whose practice of distributing money among the Jews helped them to attract Jewish pupils and remain in existence for a long time. Another problem facing the *Alliance* in Iran, perhaps more so than in any other Middle Eastern country, was the difficulty in finding competent personnel who would agree to go and teach there. The Society endeavoured, here too, to encourage local young people to train in teachers' institutes in Paris, and in 1903 it sent three young people from Hamadhān, and a few after that.[128] It appears that this problem persisted during the entire period under review. But the establishment of the *Alliance* institutions constituted an important turning point in the history of Jewish education in Iran.

Jewish children studied in *ḥeders* which had remained open in Iran. At the beginning of the century, there were in Seneh, for example, eight *ḥeder* teachers with 210 boys and 124 girls; in Urmiya 182 children were attending *ḥeder*. Such schools also existed in Burūjurd, Kāshān, Qaṣr-i-Shīrīn, Buzurkān[129] and elsewhere.

In view of their dispersal in all the cities and many smaller places in Iran, even in 1925, there were many children who did not manage to obtain a Jewish education. Moreover, in the cities where the *Alliance* maintained schools, most children were unable to complete their elementary education because of their poverty, and others who did so were compelled to transfer to a Christian secondary school, for the *Alliance* had no secondary schools. Despite the fact that the Iranian Jews were granted equal rights in 1906, few individuals could attend the state schools before 1925. Nevertheless, the period of 1898–1925—from the opening of the first *Alliance* school until the crowning of Riza Pahlavī as King of Iran—may be viewed as the beginning of an important change in the educational situation of the Jews of Iran.

1925–1971. When Riza Pahlavī was crowned King of Iran, a new period began in the history of the Jews of this country, not only from the demographic, economic and political aspects, but also in education. Jewish children could finally attend state schools together with Muslim children. The permission thus granted was of importance especially for the education of Jews who lived in towns without Jewish schools. Above all, Jews could now complete their secondary school studies in state schools, for up to 1930 there was no Jewish secondary school in Iran containing all the required classes. Graduates of a secondary school could now continue their studies at local universities without being compelled to go abroad.

Another change during this period was the expansion of the Jewish educational institutions. The *Alliance* founded complete secondary schools in Hamadhān and Teheran, and secondary school classes in other cities; and in 1928 a school in the city of Yazd. In 1930 a school called *Koresh* was set up in Teheran by the local Jews, which was transferred to the *Alliance* in 1946. In 1944, a network of the *Oẓar Hatorah* schools began to be established in Teheran, and in other cities which did not have *Alliance* schools, as in Rezaya (Urmiya), Kermām, Ārāk, Shīrāz and others. In 1950, the "Ort" Organization set up its first vocational schools in Iran. Although the attempts made by the *Alliance* at the beginning of the present century to spread vocational education had met with difficulties, Ort succeeded, in the few years of its existence, to found many such schools. In 1957 Ort had 23 vocational schools in Iran, and workshops in Teheran, Isfahān and Shīrāz, attended by 732 pupils. It may be that the Iranian Jews' change of attitude, having their children learn a trade, was due not only to Ort's educational methods, but also to the desire of the young people intending to emigrate to Israel to acquire vocational training so as to facilitate their absorption there.

From the following table it will be seen that the number of pupils increased substantially up to 1950 as a result, of course, of the additional Jewish schools opened in that period, fell after 1950, when many Jews left for Israel (49,000 in the years 1948–1965) but rose again with the expansion of the *Oẓar Hatorah* network and the appearance of Ort on the scene. The children who had not attended school before 1948 for lack of space in the existing schools could now take the place of the children who left for Israel. Moreover, an increasing number of non-Jewish pupils attended the *Alliance* institutions. In 1962/63, for instance, about 600 (or 10% of all the pupils) were non-Jewish.[130]

TABLE C-9: PUPILS IN JEWISH SCHOOLS IN IRAN, 1922–1971

Year	*Alliance* and *Koresh*	*Oẓar Hatorah*	Ort	Total
1922	3,064	—	—	3,064
1935	5,273	—	—	5,273
1950	8,259	—	198	8,457
1953	7,580	—	—	7,580
1957	7,848	5,296	732	13,876
1961	6,049	5,543	1,238	12,830
1965	4,400	3,915	1,982	10,297
1971	4,033			

Since 1925, more and more Jewish children completed elementary and secondary school. From the *Alliance* schools alone 539 succeeded in passing the Persian elementary examinations in 1956, and in 1964, 534; those who passed the intermediate examinations rose from 20 in 1950 to 54 in 1956 and to 242 in 1971. Eighteen graduated from complete secondary school in 1956, 37 in 1964 and 41 in 1971.[131] In addition, some completed foreign and state schools.

Some Jewish graduates of secondary schools in Iran went on to universities in Iran. Of the 30 *Alliance* graduates in 1961, ten were admitted to Iranian universities. In that year it is estimated that about 350 Jewish students were attending Iranian universities: about 50 in Iṣfahān and 300 in Teheran. In 1964, the number of Jewish students in Iranian universities was estimated to be about 300.[132] In that year 62 Israeli youth born in Iran were studying in Israeli universities (besides the non-Israeli Iranian-born Jewish students), as well as about 50 whose fathers had been born in Iran. The number of Iranian Jewish students studying at American and European universities is unknown. Most of those students attending universities outside Iran establish families and settle down in foreign countries, few returning to Iran.

Until a few years ago some Jewish children attended no school at all. According to a 1949 estimate, there were 16,400 Jewish children in educational institutions in all Iran, while other 8,000–9,000 children of school age, mostly girls, were not studying at all.[133] After the large emigration to Israel and the development of educational institutions in Iran, it may be assumed that the majority of children of school age do attend school today, with a resulting decrease in the percentage of illiterate Jews, particularly among the young people. One can perhaps still find a small number of young girls who did not attend school, but the majority of illiterates today consist of people of advanced age.

Contrary to the decline in traditional Jewish education in other Middle Eastern countries, in Iran both modern and traditional education made rapid progress. Up to the end of the Second World War the process had indeed been parallel to that in Iraq, Egypt, Syria and the Lebanon, for the *Alliance* schools had reduced the number of hours devoted to Hebrew and religion while increasing those for the study of the Persian language. A Government law of 1926 obliged all schools to follow the Government curriculum, with Persian as the language of instruction, and French studied as a foreign language—five hours a week in the elementary school classes and seven hours in the secondary. In the 1940's traditional education was improved when the *Oẓar Hatorah* schools introduced more intensive study of religious subjects. The *Oẓar Hatorah* instructors even undertook to teach these subjects in the *Alliance* schools as well.[134] In the last decade the *Alliance* schools have been teaching their pupils Hebrew during the summer holidays too, and have also begun to try out new educational methods, such as audio-visual techniques, with the assistance of experts of the American Technical Assistance Programme (in accordance with section 4). Every summer since 1957, a six-week pedagogical course for veteran teachers has been conducted.[135]

In 1947, the American Joint Distribution Committee began to operate in Iran. This body supports educational institutions by giving medical care and social welfare aid to pupils. In 1957, 10,500 Jewish pupils in Iran received assistance from this committee.[136]

Although much progress has been achieved by Iranian Jews since the 1870's, few intellectuals emerged who made some contribution in the fields of literature, science or religion. Among those worthy of note are Rabbi Menaḥem Levy, born in Hamadhān, and the blind teacher Mulla Ḥayyim, who published pamphlets and books on the history of the Jewish people and related subjects. Dr. Ḥabīb Levy, a dental surgeon, published a work in three volumes on the history of the Jews of Iran, in the Persian language.

There was some Jewish journalism. The first Jewish newspaper in Iran, *Shalom,* appeared in 1914–1916; it was followed by *Hageulah* (1920–1921) and *Heḥayyim* (1922–1925). All three were published in Persian in Hebrew characters. In the 1940's, newspapers in the Hebrew language and others in Persian, now written in Arabic-Persian characters, appeared, such as *'Alam-i-Yahūd, Israel, Rāhna'-i-Yahūd, Majalla Sina,* and others. The change from Hebrew characters to Arabic-Persian is indicative of the change that took place in the education of the Iranian Jews in the last generation.

The Jews of Iran were not well-known in other fields of creative work, such as handicrafts, but they were outstanding as dancers and singers. They appeared mainly before Muslim audiences, even in the period when the Muslims considered Jews impure.

The Yemen and Aden

The Jews of Yemen did not send their children to school to obtain an education for its own sake, but to train them to pray, to read the Torah and to observe the religious rules and duties. The traveller Jacob Sapir stressed this in 1859. He wrote: "All know well the reading of the Torah, with its movements, tunes, and its grammar. For here prevails the ancient custom—according to the correct rule, each one who goes up to the Torah, reads the portion himself, not the *ḥazzan* [cantor], and whoever cannot read by himself, will not be called to the Torah. Therefore, they teach them from their early childhood, from their first studies, to be able to read the entire Torah completely by heart."[137] In this regard, no change occurred up to our times. Since the purpose of study was praying and reading the Torah, it is obvious why the Yemenite Jews did not teach their daughters, and why they were not interested in modern education, and even why writing was not considered essential. Because the Jewish communities in the Yemen were small and half of their members—the women—did not study, and because their economic circumstances were so bad, they could not even found Talmud Torahs or Yeshivas, so that the Jewish children who did any studying in the Yemen did so in private *ḥeders.*

There were no kindergartens. On reaching the age of two or three a child was taught some of the blessings by his father and was taken to the synagogue on the Sabbath. From this day the synagogue became part of the child's life. The synagogue generally also served as the *ḥeder*—very seldom was there another place for it. They even called the *ḥeder "kenees"* (synagogue); in order to distinguish between it and the synagogue they referred to it as the "*kenees* of the children" or "the little *kenees.*"[138] At the age of three the child was brought to the *ḥeder.*

The *ḥeder* was generally small and unfurnished. Yomtov Sémach, while in the Yemen in 1910, described his visit to the *ḥeders* in San'a: "I first went to the '*kenees*' of the *melameds,* and I returned disappointed and bitter. The method of teaching there is stupid and backward, the hygienic conditions grievous . . . Enter for a moment to visit this *ḥeder* of infants. A courtyard of some square metres and a small door to the right. I push it, and what do I see? How monstrous! Inside a lower room there sits a group of shadows from whom a rancid smell fills the air and chokes the breath . . . and since I came from outside, from the light of the sun, it seems to me that the darkness of Egypt prevails within . . . the length of this cellar is three metres, its width two and a half and its height two. Forty-eight children, aged three to eleven, sit on the ground, on torn and worn-out mats. Miserable infants."

In another *ḥeder*, 2.32 by 3.35 metres, without windows, he found 63 pupils. This *ḥeder* was, according to him, like a dirty stable, for it had not been swept for many weeks. The mats on the dirt floor were nothing more than pieces of palm leaves, so that the children were actually sitting on dung. Besides the two *ḥeders* referred to, there were six others in San'a in which 152 children studied, on an average of 25 in each, so that not all were as crowded as these two. Altogether, 263 children attended the 8 *ḥeders,* and another 20 the *maktab* (on which see below) in all of San'a, according to Sémach—all without any furniture, except for small stools which served as tables.[139]

The *melamed's* work began early in the morning. Before breakfast the little children had already arrived at the *ḥeder* (the older ones went to the synagogue) and the teacher said prayers with them. After breakfast, the older and younger children returned to the *ḥeder.* There was another interruption at noon to permit the children to go home for lunch. The studies continued until sundown, when they said the evening prayers. After that, only the older children remained to be prepared for the

Sabbath service, or to be given a lesson in the *Mishne Torah* of the Rambam, if the *melamed* himself knew it.[140]

The children studied from the age of three to about 12 years, although many left before that. Up to the age of six or seven they learned reading of the Torah and prayers; then the Onkelos (Aramaic) version of the Bible; at the age of eight, translation of the week's portion with the *Haftarah* (a chapter from the Prophets read in the synagogue after the portion from the Pentateuch); at nine to ten years, Sa'adia Gaon's translation of the Torah. At the age of 12, the child could already read a portion from the Pentateuch with two translations, the Onkelos and Rabbi Sa'adia Gaon's. At this age he left the *ḥeder*.[141]

Since children of various ages sat in the same *ḥeder*, each child could be called up to the teacher only once or twice a day. Sometimes the children were taught in two or three groups, according to their age and level of knowledge, with the son of the teacher or one of the older children supervising or teaching the younger. Yomtov Sémach relates that in the *ḥeder* of the *melamed* Josef Dahbānī, who was then considered the best among the teachers in San'a and who taught the children of the Community's notables, found "forty-eight pupils divided into ten groups, and studying together in this one particular room. Some are studying the first part of the alphabet, others the last part, some the syllables and some the words, and others the Parasha [the weekly portion of the Pentateuch], the translation [Onkelos] and the *Haftarah*. Here, there is tumult and confusion which cannot be described in words. This is a grating on the ears which actually deafens one. The little ones, of course, compete with each other. Each tries to shout louder than his fellow pupil sitting alongside him and to compete with him in shrieking . . . the *melamed* goes from group to group, trying to guide the backward pupils and to bring them back to the straight path.Towards evening, the pupils and their teacher leave this hell, tired out, broken, depressed and weak."[142]

The curriculum lacked, of course, songs and games, let alone secular subjects such as Arabic, history and geography. Religious commands were also not taught, and almost no writing. To be more exact, in the first year the child was taught to write the alphabet as a means of recognizing the characters, and when he had learned that, there was no more writing. Only those children who remained to an older age were trained to write, with a view to becoming scribes of religious works. The Yemenites explain that since they were not merchants they did not need to know how to write—only merchants required such knowledge.[143]

The teaching method in the *ḥeder* was that of repetition. The child was made to repeat over and over again the letters of the alphabet or the sentence or whatever he was learning until he could say it all by heart. This method was used with the little children and the older ones, including those who studied texts requiring more understanding, such as Sa'adia Gaon's translation and *Hayyad Haḥazakah.*

The result was that the children studying these books could actually read them, but seldom understood them, since the teacher himself was not able to explain what he read with them.[144] Yomtov Sémach has given a vivid description of the teaching method in the *ḥeder*. He relates that in one of the best ones he wished to test the pupils and a child of three was brought up to him. "I was at once introduced to the most wonderful, the most amusing and the most foolish pedagogy. This little one of three years is taught the alphabet by heart—this is a monotonous amusing song, which is engraved on his heart. Afterwards the child is handed the alphabet in writing and he must make his delightful song heard while pointing with his finger to the tiny letters written on the paper in front of him." Then the child learns the vowels. "At the end of four years, when he is handed the Bible, he succeeds in reading, almost without mistakes, the week's portion, since he already knows the characters and the vowels and complete paragraphs by heart . . . as soon as the little boy recognizes the first word at the beginning of the verse he reads the entire verse or passage. The Yemenites excel in an amazing memory. They remember the sounds, and the forms, and they have perceptiveness." Sémach then tested a child of seven. "He reads the portion with fluency, only the parts learned by heart, of course. In other parts, he does not even succeed in pronouncing the word by its letters, and that is the case also with the Onkelos translation of the Bible and the *Tafsīr*. The child indeed learned three languages at one time: Hebrew—the language of the Bible, the Onkelos translation and the *Tafsīr,* which is Sa'adia Gaon's translation of the Bible in literary Arabic written in Hebrew characters, and he does not understand even one of them." It seems that Sémach exaggerated here, for in any event, according to his own evidence, "almost all the adult Jews speak Hebrew, not fluently, it is true, but correctly. When did they learn Hebrew? Surely while reading in the synagogue."[145]

To speed up the studies, the *melamed* would hit the children without cruelty; the parents saw nothing wrong in that, for they believed that in each child there is an evil spirit which can be driven out by the stick and the strap. The children could expect punishment particularly on Wednesdays, which they called the black day or the cursed day, for that was the day of the weekly test and they received blows for every mistake.[146]

The relation between teacher and child was that of a master to his servant, and this was even expressed in the terms used. The teacher was called *mari,* the Aramaic for master. This master, however, was a miserable creature, whose salary was paid him as charity and such he considered it. His wage was one loaf of bread from each child each day, which the child brought with him when returning from lunch. The bread was made of wheat, barley or millet, or something else, according to what was used in the child's home. The *melamed* brought back to his home some of the loaves and sold the rest. In addition to the bread, he received a weekly wage which he had to collect himself from the parents' homes every Friday. Generally, even the poor paid him their pittances, and there were *melameds* who would not waive this payment. Since all the payments they received, in kind or in money, were very small, some *melameds* were compelled to seek assistance from the Community's fund, and most had to take on additional work, such as, for example, weaving during teaching hours. Yomtov Sémach told about a teacher who used to spin during instruction time "and the noise of the spindle wheel accompanies the music of the translation of the week's portion. In another place, the teacher is sewing glittering pieces of brass on a farmer's wife's dress, one of the pupils holding for him the box of brass pieces. A second is threading a needle, and the teacher and his pupils are reciting by heart the week's portion."[147]

Since the work of teaching was confined to repeating texts, there was no need for any great knowledge to be a teacher. Persons who did not succeed in their occupations turned to teaching. Sometimes it was possible to find children aged 9–10, who had generally been *melameds'* assistants at a still younger age, serving as teachers. The job was given to such children who, for the most part, were orphans and who were prepared to travel even to the smallest villages to teach there. Among the *melameds* were also old men who were not able to do any other work. Hence, teaching standards could only be very low indeed, especially in the villages. There were, of course, very few professional educators among them: before the mass exodus to Israel, there were about twenty in San'a, the capital, and three to six in the other cities of the Yemen.[148]

Unlike other Eastern countries, several teachers were never brought together to teach in a single institution. It was only in 1939 or 1940 that three teachers and their three classes were housed in one airy and well-lit building, but the method of instruction was like that in the *ḥeders*, and this innovation lasted only until about 1945, when this school was closed down.[149]

In addition to these appalling shortcomings, the children lacked books, for there were no printing-houses and books were usually handwritten. Though copying was cheap, the majority of the children could not afford to acquire a book. At times, therefore, six to eight children read from one book, which they placed in the centre of the group, with the children sitting around it, so that they learned to read the characters straight, upside down or sideways.

Despite all these difficulties, most of the Yemenite Jewish men learned to read, for they felt that it was a religious duty. Some parents in the villages sent their children to the nearest city, if they had relatives there, so that they could obtain an education. Pressure was put on parents who neglected to send their children to *ḥeder*—for example, the ritual slaughterer refused to slaughter for them, so that the family was deprived of meat. Sometimes the father was also not permitted to take part in public prayers. Nevertheless, there were some children who did not study at all[150] or who studied for only a year or less.[151]

The parents were interested in bringing their children speedily to the stage where they would leave their childhood behind, and the child for his part tried to resemble a grown-up by learning to sit quietly, without moving. He was taken into the society of adults in the synagogue and at celebrations, and by imitating them he learned to behave like an adult.[152] The kind of education that the Jewish child received, added to the influence on him of the Muslims' suppression, undoubtedly had an effect on the formation of his character, and he generally grew up an obedient individual.

Yeshivas. There was no higher institution of Torah education in the Yemen than the *ḥeder.* It is true that, in 1911, Shmuel Yavnieli found in San'a a number of Yeshivas,[153] but those attending them were not true Yeshiva students whose only business it was to study; they worked during the day and devoted the early hours of the morning, before daybreak, to study. Two Yeshivas of this kind, in which several hours a day were devoted to study, were also to be found in San'a in the 1930's.

Modern education. In 1903, the *Alliance Israélite Universelle* sent the director of its Cairo school, Somekh, to the Yemen to investigate the possibility of establishing a school in San'a, but the authorities did not permit him to enter the country, imprisoned him in Ḥudayda for several days and then deported him. In a second attempt made by the *Alliance,* however, its representative, Yomtov Sémach, who was the director of its Beirut school, succeeded in reaching San'a in February 1910. He informed the *Alliance* Central Committee that he had acquired some land, with an area of 30,000 square metres, for the establishment of a school and a public park. But apparently the deal was not completed. Several years later the Chief Rabbi of Turkey, Rabbi Ḥayyim Naḥum, applied to the Imam Yahya asking him to extend his patronage to the educational institutions of the *Alliance.* Yahya replied on January 19, 1914 that he did not oppose the establishment of a school in San'a, on the condition that its founders would not interfere in matters not permitted them by the law; but he added that, so as not to arouse the anger of the population against them, it was desirable to leave the education as it had been up to then. In any event, the *Alliance* appointed a director to set up a school in San'a but when he was about to leave to take up his post, the First World War broke out, and the whole idea of an *Alliance* school in San'a was, therefore, abandoned, never to be implemented.

Nevertheless, an attempt was made to set up a school different from the *ḥeders* in the Yemen. At the end of 1909, the Turkish authorities in San'a opened a *maktab* (school) which was handed over to Rabbi Yahya al-Kāfiḥ for him to direct. The institution was housed in a building of two rooms in the Jewish quarter which had been rented by the authorities and was supported by them with a sum of 100 francs a month. But the Jews were not inclined to send their children to it, notwithstanding the fact that the studies were free. Only after much effort was it possible to gather together about fifty boys. The Jewish parents feared that the Turkish authorities were interested in educating the Jews in this institution so as to hand them over later to military service. Moreover, most of the Jews were opponents of Rabbi Kāfiḥ, the director. It was as a result of the disputes between his few followers and his many opponents that the school was closed in 1913.

Rabbi Kāfiḥ headed a group of Jews known as *Dar-Da'*. This name was given them because they stood for knowledge and rejected Kabbalah (Jewish mysticism), and the Zohar (the book of Kabbalah)—and were content with the study of the Torah, the books of the Rambam as well as the Talmud. The opponents of this group, who represented the majority and were headed by the Chief Rabbi, Yahya Isaac, were called the *Eqshim* (stubborn ones).

The Dar-Da' followers claim that the closing of the institution by the Imam Yahya in 1913 was the result of the slander against Rabbi Kāfiḥ accusing him of being pro-British and negotiating with the French and British governments. Rabbi Kāfiḥ and some of his followers were also arrested on this charge.[154]

Despite the fact that the school was closed after about four years, it is worth describing it, since it was the only attempt made to introduce a different kind of education to the Yemenite Jews.

Yomtov Sémach, who visited this institution a few months after its opening wrote that "here, too, a storm of voices is raging. The shouts can deafen the ears of even the deaf and dumb. The pedagogy here does not differ in the least from the pedagogy in *kenees* [i.e., the *ḥeder*]—the same customs and the same methods. But the small courtyard here is very clean. Three steps to the right there is a class, and five steps to the left—another class. At this moment, all the children are gathered into the first room to study the lesson in Hebrew . . . all the fifty pupils are sitting in groups on the floor, on worn-out mats, bits of black carpets and small mattresses around low stools and old empty oil cans. The teacher is sitting with his back leaning against a cushion, and his assistant is standing and waving a small whip . . . these little ones are now giving preference to the study of Arabic and Turkish over the reading of the Bible . . . they are beginning to write Arabic and prattling several words in the language of the lords of the land, that is, Turkish. And also this they do not learn with any greater success than the study of Hebrew. The Turkish instructor is teaching his pupils to read, and is forcing them to learn by heart a very long list of words." Sémach adds that "the *maktab* in comparison to *kenees* is vast progress. But, despite the good intentions of the officialdom which is striving to help our brethren, and despite the great efforts of the pupils and their teachers—this school is unable to improve the condition of the Jewish community. Through this school, the little children will know less Hebrew and more Arabic and Turkish than their parents, but their intellectual and moral situation will not change. Here a modern school is necessary." Sémach, who considered this school to be a failure, proposed setting up an *Alliance* institution, in which Hebrew, Arabic and Turkish would be taught, and, in the higher classes, also French. Rabbi 'Amram Koraḥ, too, regarded the failure of Kāfiḥ's school to be due to the rote methods employed there.[155]

On the other hand, Rabbi Kāfiḥ's followers claim that the school was housed in a pleasant, bright and airy flat, that the pupils sat on clean mats, and that Rabbi Kāfiḥ did not accept pupils under the age of six; also, that Hebrew, Mishnah, the Rambam, grammar and the meaning of words were taught, and that, at the end of the year, the pupils were examined in Turkish by officials of the Ottoman regime and that they were successful.

Even if we assume that Sémach exaggerated in describing the bad points of this institution, so as to justify the establishment of an *Alliance* school, we may doubt the extent of success attained by Kāfiḥ's institution in the brief period of its existence, especially as its few teachers had no pedagogical training and no experience. Rabbi Kāfiḥ was satisfied with his school, so much so that he asked the Chief Rabbi of Istanbul to clarify whether the Turkish authorities were prepared to found a secondary school for Jews.[156] But a few months later, in 1913, Kāfiḥ's school was closed and there was no further attempt to change the educational method and the curriculum in the Yemenite *ḥeders*.

The Yemenite Jews were thus left without any modern education. Jews were not permitted to study in the state schools for Muslims either, but it is doubtful whether any would have been willing to attend them, because of their extreme piety.

EDUCATION IN ADEN

There are no details available regarding education among the dozens of small Jewish communities in the Republic of Southern Yemen (the Protectorate of Aden), but it may be assumed that there was not much difference between them and the Yemenite Jews in this respect.

In the city of Aden, however, where the Jewish population was constantly on the increase since the British occupation in 1839, there was some change at least, in that modern schools were founded there, including a school for girls. Several Jews also completed state secondary school, and a few went on to higher studies in Europe.

As early as 1872 a number of Jews in the Colony of Aden began to study in non-Jewish schools in the city, although they dropped out after a short while because the language of instruction was Hindustani. The authorities placed no restrictions on Jews in state schools, and eight of them were already attending these in 1875. Shmuel Yavnieli, who reached Aden in 1910, found a few Jewish children attending the state schools and twenty boys and girls in the Jesuit Mission school.[157] It is reasonable to assume that most of them were the children of Jews from Turkey or of *Béné Israel*, who had come from India and settled in Aden.

Yomtov Sémach relates that in 1910 there were already three Jewish educational institutions in Aden: two of them he described as good, and the third, a Talmud Torah, as weak, with an unsuccessful teacher. About two hundred children were attending them at the time. All the pupils, and especially those at the Talmud Torah, studied mainly prayers and the Bible. Sémach proposed setting up an *Alliance* school there, but this was not done because of the opposition of a rich local Jew, who promised to establish a Jewish school himself;[158] after the First World War, a Jewish boys' school was indeed opened, with the Aden Government participating in its budget from 1939. In December 1947, this school was burned down in the anti-Jewish riots; it was then housed in separate rooms in the city, with fewer pupils attending. As a result, the number of those sitting for the Government examinations fell to three or four in 1948/49. The school was not reopened until 1951. In 1951/52 it was attended by 140 boys, and in 1955/56 by 160 boys and girls. The teachers—four in 1952—all came from Europe. Because of the school's high standards, all the pupils in the top class—15 in 1958/59 and a similar number in 1959/60—were able to pass the Government examinations and thus to gain admittance to the secondary school.[159] This institution was closed in 1967, when a Jewish community no longer existed in Aden.

Besides this institution Jewish boys studied in *ḥeders*, most of them conducted by teachers from the Yemen. In the 1930's, a girls' school was opened by Miriam Ben-Yehuda: here the girls studied up to the age of twelve, when they completed the fifth elementary class. About 200 girls attended this school and the Community's schools in 1947. In December 1947, the Community's girls' school was burned down and was not reopened. Mrs. Ben-Yehuda's school was also closed in 1954, when the boys' school became coeducational and the only school remaining for the Jews of Aden. It was in use until 1967. The fact that a coeducational school existed in Aden is in itself a sign of progress in Jewish education in that city.

LITERATURE AND CULTURE

Although there were no Yeshivas in the Yemen or in Aden, there was no lack of Rabbis, several of whom produced books on religious subjects, generally not published. The few works that did appear in print were those which reached Palestine, or were written by Yemenite Jews after their arrival in Israel. There were also a number of historians, but few of their works were saved from destruction. The absence of a Hebrew printing press in the Yemen, and, frequently, the writers' modesty, prevented them from perpetuating their works. Moreover, the lack of appreciation of non-religious writings undoubtedly led to the loss of many folk songs and stories. Only a small part of the religious songs and a few secular ones have been published recently.

It is doubtful whether any thought was ever given to the publication of newspapers in the Yemen. On the other hand, the Yemenite Jews were famous for their singing, music and fine handicrafts; they put all their creative spirit into these arts.

Chapter Five
SOCIAL CHANGES

Along with the changes in their political, economic and educational situation, important social changes took place in all the Jewish communities in the Middle East, excluding the Yemen.

Out of the complex of these changes worthy of note, we shall deal in this chapter with the attitude to religion and the status of women, although because of the lack of material, these problems cannot be examined exhaustively; brief mention will be made of offences and crimes committed by Jews in the Middle East.

Changes in relation to religion were expressed in young people breaking away from the tradition of their fathers, the secular education they received having shaken their faith. In Turkey, there was an additional factor—state propaganda to abandon the observance of religious rules and duties of all faiths. Despite the move away from religion in all the Eastern countries, however, there were not many cases of conversion, since for the most part, no pressure was exerted on the Jews in the last hundred years by the State or the population to change their religion, and often, we are told, no material or other advantage was gained by becoming a Muslim.

Changes in the status of women came about when they began to acquire an education and general knowledge, which led to changes in their occupations, their clothes and their marriage age. There was less change, however, in the extent of freedom girls and women enjoyed in their contacts with the opposite sex, for despite the weakening of religious tendencies in the past generation, traditional conservatism was not affected to any considerable extent.

Offences and Crimes

None of the states of the region published statistics on offenses and crimes committed in their respective countries according to the religion of the offenders. From scrutiny of local newspapers, however, and with the assistance of the comments of travellers and tourists who put their impressions in writing, it is certain that the Jews in all the countries of the regions were, for the most part, guilty of only minor offences, only infrequently committing offences of a more serious nature, and it may be assumed from the evidence available that the number of offenders among them was small. There were Jewish thieves, but they were involved in petty thefts rather than burglary. It may well be that, here and there, there were Jews who joined groups of Muslim thieves and with them broke into places, but there is no proof of this. There were few, if any, cases of financial embezzlement; in general, Jewish clerks were considered loyal and honest by Muslim merchants. Cases of drunkenness and unruly behaviour were rare: Jews did perpetrate murder, although very infrequently, sometimes in a burst of anger, and sometimes when family honour was involved, such as a brother killing a sister who had become pregnant out of wedlock. But these cases were rare in Middle Eastern Jewish society. A murderer was sentenced to death, but in all the countries of the region there was an unwritten law obliging the ruler, immediately on the publication of the sentences, to grant amnesty to the murderer and to reduce his punishment to a number of years of imprisonment.

The fact that only a few Jews were criminals may be accounted for by their having grown up with the fear of God, the head of the family, whose authority was strong, and fear of prison, since Muslim prisoners usually maltreated a Jewish prisoner.

It was difficult to interview Jews from the Eastern lands regarding the prevalence of prostitution. It is evident that it existed, although, here again, on a small scale. On the basis of various sources of evidence, it may be said that at the beginning of the present century there were Jewish girls in Turkey who had been made pregnant by non-Jews,[1] and even in the Yemen, in the middle of the last century, there were girls who engaged in prostitution. There were also cases in various periods of girls in the Yemen who had been seduced by Muslims.[2] Jewish prostitutes, as well as owners of houses of ill-fame, were to be found in Iraq too, and several there were sentenced to imprisonment.[3] But it would seem that, with the exception of the city of Damascus, where prostitution was more serious, these were rare phenomena among Jews in the Middle East. As far back as the end of the 19th century, E. N. Adler had reported that in Aleppo, Jewish prostitutes were to be found who had come from Damascus; in Damascus itself the number of Jewish prostitutes was proportionally large, and the Chief Rabbi of the city, Rabbi Shlomo Alfandari (1826–1930), demanded that women be prohibited from sitting in cafés in the company of men and from playing the violin or other instruments. The Chief Rabbi who followed him, Rabbi Jacob Dannon (1910–1923), applied shortly after his appointment, to the Chief Rabbi of Istanbul, Rabbi Ḥayyim Naḥum, asking him to issue an order compelling the Jewish singers, i.e., prostitutes, to leave the Jewish quarter. Such an order was indeed obtained, but the Governor of Damascus was not prepared to implement it, explaining that these girls exercised great influence: even the Muslims and Christians applied to them to arrange matters for them with the authorities. Abraham Elmaleḥ, who was in Damascus in 1911 and asked the Governor of the city to drive out the prostitutes from the Jewish quarter, was told that meeting this request meant expelling all the Jewesses from the quarter. This gives the impression—no doubt a wrong one—that many Jewesses engaged in this occupation. Rabbi Dannon, determined to fight prostitution, imposed a ban on the girls and on their families, since, in some cases, their brothers or fathers served as their procurers. Rabbi Dannon forbade the girls' families to pray in the synagogue, and prohibited the burial of their dead in a Jewish cemetery, the circumcision of their sons and the sale of kosher meat to them. The girls who agreed to give up prostitution were obliged to leave a sum of money in the office of the Rabbinate. Due to Rabbi Dannon's efforts, the Jewish quarter was almost entirely cleansed of prostitution, but only for a short period. According to reports by some Damascus Jews, it still exists.[4] A proposal made to set up a society to assist poor girls to marry was put into practice in March 1941; in its first year the society assisted nine girls in this way,[5] but discontinued its activities before prostitution had been stopped.

Special research would be required to reveal the reasons for prostitution among Jewish women; the poverty, the ignorance of religious matters and the lack of young Jewish men in Damascus (as a result of continuous emigration) are not sufficient to explain it. It seems likely that its proportions have been inflated because it is so rare among the Jews of the Middle East.

Attitudes to Religion

IRAQ

Until the beginning of the present century, the majority of Iraqi Jews strictly observed the Jewish religious rules and duties: they went to the synagogue on Sabbaths, Holydays and festivals, and, for the greater part, also on week-days; they did not light a fire or smoke on the Sabbath; they fasted on the Day of Atonement; they did not work on the Holydays and Sabbaths; and they kept the dietary laws, at home and outside it. They did not marry members of other religions, except for isolated cases who converted so as to marry Muslims. Practically every Jewish child in Babylonian Iraq—but fewer in Kurdistani Iraq—went to a *ḥeder* or a Talmud Torah, if only for a short time, where he learned at least the Hebrew alphabet. At the same time, there is no doubt that many, especially in the Kurdistan mountains, had no fundamental understanding of the religious duties and observed them because of what they had seen in their parents' homes, out of obedience to their parents, and because Muslim society, too, was generally conservative. Since the Iraqi Jews were practically cut off from the outside world, and secular education was not widespread among them, there was no background for breaking with tradition until the beginning of the 20th century.

The year 1908, when the Young Turks came to power in Turkey, can be viewed as the beginning of the break with tradition—at first secretly and then openly—by Jews in Iraq, especially in Baghdad and Basra. The first to break away were those who had received a modern education in Jewish and state schools, particularly those who travelled to Europe and Turkey to receive a higher education. Before the First World War, Jews were already to be found—although these were few—who smoked and lit a fire on the Sabbath, ate non-kosher food and were lax about observing other religious duties.[6] With the British occupation of Iraq, many Jews began to work as civil servants, among them some who worked on the Sabbath. In the course of the years, the majority of the Jewish civil servants worked on the Sabbath and even on the Holydays. Since the 'twenties, some parents permitted their sons to study in state schools, which were open on the Sabbath as well, when there was no Jewish elementary or secondary school in the city, or if their sons wished to attend an institute of higher education in Iraq or abroad. Thus, a not inconsiderable percentage of young Jews in the provinces, and a larger percentage in Baghdad and Basra, having received all their education in a non-Jewish school, did not adhere to religious observance, and there were some who did not recognize a word of Hebrew. Nevertheless, even in recent years the Iraqi Jews have been strict about fasting on the Day of Atonement and on maintaining a dietary kitchen at home, and practically no self-employed open their businesses on the Sabbath. The rule concerning circumcision, marriage and burial according to religious laws have been observed faithfully. The other religious duties were considered by the young people as marginal, which need not be strictly kept if they interfered with getting an education and earning a living. The Jewish intellectual, in recent decades, even if he grew up in a traditional home, regarded the religious duties as outdated customs. Most of the Jews who observed them did so automatically, without understanding why they did so. In the mid-1900's there were only a few who were religious out of conviction.

Because the observant parents were not extremists in their religious beliefs and the sons did not go too far in their disregard of them, at least not in the presence of their parents, no tension was created between fathers and sons on this score.

Since the mass emigration to Israel, there has been some further change among the small number of Jews remaining in Iraq: there are now families who do not observe the dietary laws even in their homes and do not adhere to many of the Jewish religious rules, not even the fast on the Day of Atonement.

Despite the young people's weakened inclination to religious observance, there were practically no cases of conversion, no more than there had been in previous centuries. The regime did not force Islam on the people under its aegis, and since there had been no persecution of the Iraqi Jews, they saw no need to change their religion. The few cases of conversion to Islam—there were scarcely any cases of conversion to Christianity—were the result of family disputes. Jewish girls, and a lesser number of married women, generally adopted the Muslim religion if they had been seduced before marriage or had betrayed their husbands. If a man converted, he did so because he did not succeed in obtaining a divorce from his wife. But certainly there must also have been individual cases of conversion out of hope of material benefit—money, a job, or the like.[7]

There were no cases of mixed marriages. Muslim religious law forbade a Muslim girl to marry a Jew, but permitted a Muslim man to marry a Jewess. In the latter case a Jewess converted to Islam before her marriage to a Muslim, for such a marriage meant her excommunication from Jewish society and as a Jewess she was not accepted among the Muslims. Mixed marriages between Jews and Christians did not occur for, according to the Iraqi law, a couple could marry only according to the marriage laws of the man's faith. But a Jew who fell in love with a Christian woman could not expect a Rabbi to marry them. In such cases they lived together without marrying.

The Iraqi Jews were not drawn to other religious beliefs, which were at times considered "progressive". The Bahai faith, which many Jews in Iran accepted in the second half of the 19th century, for political and economic reasons, hardly attracted Jews or Muslims in Iraq. The Theosophist faith—which transformed a mixture of various Indian philosophies into a new faith—attracted a few Jews in Basra, who had close contact with India, where the world spiritual centre of Theosophy was located.[8]

IRAN

Iran was the scene of something which had not occurred in the past hundred years in any other Jewish community in the East—conversion on a large scale. This was the result of the persecution and humiliation which were the lot of the Jews in this country, and also of their being cut off from World Jewry, geographically and linguistically, which made them ignorant in matters of religious duties.

Up to the middle of the 19th century, many cases of forced conversion were known among the Iranian Jews, at times on a mass scale. The most outstanding of these cases was that which occurred in Meshed in 1839. This was not the only case; the details of this particular case have been retained because the Jews there continued to observe the religion of their ancestors in secrecy, although outwardly they, their children and their grandchildren lived as Muslims. Evidence of many conversions in the past may be found in various regions of Iran, where Muslims observe Jewish religious rules and duties, no doubt passed on to them by their Jewish ancestors, although not all are aware of the origin of their customs.[9] There were, indeed, and still are, cases of Jews becoming Muslims of their own free will, and not always to escape from humiliation, but these were relatively few.

As to adoption of Christianity by Jews, it is known that in the year 1825 the convert Josef Wolff came from Europe with the purpose of proselytizing the Jews in Iran, but he failed in his task. In 1847, the London Society for the Spread of Christianity sent the convert Henry (Aharon) Stern, and after him Straus, to spread Christianity among the Jews. In a book on his work in Iran and on some of his successes in converting Jews, H. A. Stern admitted indirectly that he had failed, blaming Islam for preventing the spread of Christianity among the Jews.[10] A short time later, American missionaries arrived: they opened hospitals, prayer-houses and schools in Teheran, Hamadhān, Iṣfahān and Kermanshāh, and distributed aid among the needy. Not many Jews adopted Christianity and those who did so were enticed by the money which the missionaries distributed, or wished to escape from their life of humiliation, and hoped that the diplomatic representatives in Iran would protect them as Christians. When persecution by the Muslims weakened at the beginning of the 20th century and the first *Alliance* schools were established, there were very few cases of conversion to Christianity among the Iranian Jews.[11]

On the other hand, many Jews were attracted by the Bahai religion, a new faith which arose in Iran. In 1844, an Iranian Muslim by the name of Mirza 'Ali Muhammad, who called himself Baha'ullah (the honour of the Lord) or Bab (gate) to God, claimed that he had been sent from heaven and he preached the love of all creation in His image and sublime morality—honesty, mercy and modesty. The Bahai religion includes few practical religious duties, no prohibitions against certain foods and no rules regarding purity and impurity. The Bahais believe that Baha'ullah unites all faiths: in other words, all religions are true ones, but from the hour that the Baha'ullah appeared all religions must unite into one religion—the Bahai.

The simplicity of this religion's principles drew into its ranks large numbers of Muslims in Iran and not a few Jews. Neumark related, in 1884, that then it already had two million followers, among them many Jews. Dr. A. J. Brawer, too, who was in Iran fifty years after Neumark, reported that there were hundreds of thousands of believers in this faith, including thousands, and perhaps ten thousand of Jews.[12] The Bahai success among the Jews, despite its persecution by the authorities (while the central authorities did not persecute the Jews in this period), may be attributed to a number of reasons, the main ones being:

a. The Bahai religion does not deny Moses and his Torah;
b. There was no need for a formal act of conversion to become a Bahai;
c. Many Muslims were attracted by this new religion, and the Jews saw in its spread a hope of improving their situation;
d. The hope that Muslim Bahais would furnish protection against persecution by

the Muslims, at a time when the authorities' protection was not sufficient, particularly outside of Teheran.

Other explanations have been offered, namely, that the Iranian Jews were drawn to the Bahai religion because of their ignorance in matters of religion, lack of Rabbis of stature, their indifference to apostasy, and the financial assistance given by the Bahais to their followers.[13] These explanations might account for only a few Jews having been attracted to the Bahai religion.

It is not known just how many Jews converted to this religion, since the act of conversion did not require any ceremony and since its followers were often not inclined to reveal their belief in it, for it was a religion persecuted by the authorities. Moreover, the children, and especially the grandchildren, of the first converts broke off almost all contact with Judaism. It is certain, however, that after the First World War fewer Jews adopted the Bahai religion, mainly because there was then no need to run away from the Jewish religion, which ceased to be one of persecution and humiliation. There were even cases of Bahais returning to the Jewish religion. But even today a few Jews convert to the Bahai religion.[14]

The surprising thing about conversion among the Iranian Jews was their attitude towards their converted relatives and friends, whether they were Muslims, Christians or Bahais. A Jewish father would sit at one table with a son who had converted to Islam, a second son who had adopted Christianity, and a third who had become a Bahai.[15] It is doubtful whether this lack of hostility towards the converts—completely contrary to the Jews' negative attitude towards apostates in the other lands of the East—can be explained by the Jews in Iran being less religious. The fact that conversion was a frequent phenomenon made it difficult for the Jewish community to impose a ban on the converts or to fight it by other means.

Although the many cases of conversion cannot be attributed to ignorance of religious law and rules, it is a fact that there was much ignorance. During the past hundred years, no great Torah scholars appeared in Iran, nor were there any important Torah educational institutions. Education was confined to a few years of study in the *ḥeder* with the *mulla* (teacher, Rabbi), whose knowledge was often very slight. Many did not even learn to read Hebrew, and others could not say their prayers, let alone have a profound knowledge of the religious precepts. All they knew of the Jewish religion was what they saw of it in their parents' homes and they did as their parents did. Because of the persecutions—in various places and in various periods—they could not observe important commands, such as donning of phylacteries *(tefillin)*,[16] and the boys often did not know about them. Thus they were forgotten, or at least considered unimportant. As a result of the absence of higher Torah institutions, the Rabbis were poorly educated, most of the *mullas* knowing only some of the rules about ritual slaughter and circumcision. The lack of a common language between them and the majority of the other Eastern Jews cut them off from the yeshivas which arose in the last hundred years in Turkey, Syria, and even in nearby Baghdad.

Despite their ignorance of religious duties the Jews of Iran should not be considered as irreligious. The fact is that they were religious to such an extent that they practised even superstitions without knowing that doing so was heretical. The young generation, however, is not as ignorant of the religious duties as its elders were. Thanks to the *Alliance Israélite Universelle* schools and in the past thirty years thanks also to the local Jewish schools and those of *Oẓar Hatorah*—knowledge of Hebrew, the Torah and something of the religious rules began to spread. But this education was not sufficient to stop the general trend of secularization which had become prevalent among Jews all over the world, including Iran. From the impressions gained by visitors and immigrants, the indications are that today Iranian Jewry is less religious in its consciousness, although not in its knowledge, than it was at the beginning of the century. A large proportion of the Iranian Jews today do not observe the *mitzvot*. Keeping the Sabbath is limited to a few circles; the majority go to school or to work on Saturdays, and even open their shops and businesses. Smoking and travelling—including to the synagogue—on the Sabbath are not considered as opposed to religion. Eating non-kosher food outside the home is quite usual among the young people, although in their homes they observe the dietary laws to the extent that they understand them, that is, they eat beef which they believe to be kosher, although it is not always so, since not all slaughterers know all the rules of ritual slaughtering. Donning of *tefillin* is practised by very few. Going about bareheaded—and often in the synagogue—is not considered a religious sin, for the synagogue is regarded as a place of gathering in which prayers are held at certain hours. In some synagogues in Teheran, contributions for being called up to the Torah are paid on the Sabbath, in cash,[17] which is strictly opposed by the religious commands.

Apparently this process of secularization is not so widespread among the Jews living in the Jewish quarter, for which the *Oẓar Hatorah* and the *Heḥaluẓ Hadati* (Religious Pioneers) established in Iran in recent years by emissaries from Israel may claim credit.

The situation differed somewhat from the above in three areas of Iran; namely, in Kurdistan, Yazd and Meshed.

In the Kurdistan region, there was much ignorance regarding religious matters, but since persecution of the Jews was not as severe there as in the other parts of the country, there were fewer cases of conversion,[18] and secularization did not affect the last generation, for scarcely any modern schools had been established there. There is no indication of any change in the Kurdistan Jews' strong leaning to religion; for the greater part, however, they performed their religious duties without understanding, and often without any knowledge of all of them.

In Yazd, on the other hand, various travellers who were there in the years 1884–1935 pointed out that the majority of the Jews in the city were very pious. Among them were to be found men with beards and sidelocks, and some who studied the Talmud, which was a "precious revelation in Persia", according to Ephraim Neumark. But A. J. Brawer said in 1935 that in recent years a process of weakening was felt in regard to religion after the establishment in the city of an *Alliance* school, and that this school was mainly to blame for it.[19]

The situation was entirely different among the Marrano Jews in Meshed, who, since the time they were forced to convert in 1839, were known as *Islām-i-Jedid* (new Muslims). Since then, they and their descendants observed the Muslim religious rules outwardly, but did all in their power to retain their Jewishness. They went to the mosque, and in secrecy prayed in their homes as Jews; they fasted during the month of Ramaḍān and on the Day of Atonement; they bore Muslim names, and also Hebrew ones; they circumcized their sons (the Muslims also do so), were married by the Qāḍī, but also before a Rabbi of their own according to Jewish law; they had two marriage certificates, one Muslim written in Persian and the other Jewish, written in Aramaic; they observed the dietary laws, as far as they possibly could, sometimes buying meat from a Muslim butcher but not eating it; they ate *maẓẓot* on the Passover, but bought bread and distributed it among poor Muslims, to demonstrate their loyalty to Islam; they opened their shops on the Sabbath, but tried not to sell by demanding exaggerated prices or by placing a child in the shop who replied to customers that he could not sell and his father had not yet arrived. Above all, they married only among themselves. So as not to have their daughters marry Muslims they betrothed them while they were infants to Marranos, and when a daughter grew up and a Muslim asked for her hand, they replied that she was already engaged and showed them the document testifying to this. They also strictly kept the burial rules, with one of them saying the prescribed prayer over the dead later in the evening, after a Muslim prayer had been said by the Imām at the time of burial. Some of them even made the pilgrimage to Mecca.[20] This double life in a fanatically Muslim environment involved much strength and not a little danger.

From the end of the 19th century, some descendants of the Marranos began to move to Teheran, and a few emigrated to Jerusalem and to England. Some of those who left Iran returned openly to Judaism. But those who remained in Meshed do not dare to do so; they still live as Muslims outwardly and as Jews in their homes. Even in 1954, when Yani Avidov, an emissary from Israel, visited the city, he was not invited by the Meshed Jews, and in the street he was asked not to walk alongside them. Only when he arrived at the synagogue (which apparently belongs to Jews who had settled in the city after the mass conversion) was he received with enthusiasm. It must be remembered that despite their efforts to conceal their Jewishness, they are still suspected by the population of lack of loyalty to Islam. They are still hated, so much so that in April 1946, immediately after the departure of the Russians from Meshed, the Muslims rioted against them.[21]

In the last generation, the Marranos have become somewhat less observant. Some of the young people have begun to disregard the traditions of their fathers, to marry Muslim girls and to reveal a strong tendency to assimilation.

How the Meshed Jews succeeded in retaining their Jewishness for such a long period, while other Marranos in both Europe and the East failed to do so, is a question which requires separate research.

EGYPT, TURKEY, SYRIA AND THE LEBANON

As far back as the end of the 19th century, some young Jews in Turkey and Egypt broke away from religion and ceased to observe some of its commands. The Jewish communities in these two countries were the first in the Middle East to do so. Most probably, they had been influenced by the European Jews who had emigrated to these lands. After the establishment of the Turkish Republic, this process was intensified, as a result of the propaganda against religion, including the Muslim religion, which the State conducted, and the prohibition against giving lessons in religion in state and private schools. In Egypt there was no such pressure on religion, but a similar process occurred. This went on in Turkey and in Egypt until in the middle of this century most Jewish youth often lacked even an elementary knowledge of their religion, they were not strict about observing the Sabbath and eating kosher food, and seldom went to synagogue. In these two countries, Jews could be found after the First World War who worked on Holydays and the Sabbath, not only those who were clerks or other employees, but also merchants, shopkeepers and owners of their own workshops. In the 19th century the majority of the Jews in Turkey and in Egypt—even the intellectual youth—had been observant. At that time, observance of the religious commands was mainly a matter of family tradition and custom. Keeping the religious rules was not always accompanied by enthusiasm or spiritual exaltation. The fathers who saw their sons turning away from the observance of religious duties did not insist on their retaining their faith, did not ban them from home and did not punish them. David Yellin, who, at the end of the 19th century, wrote about the young Jews of Izmir breaking with religion, remarked that this was not accompanied by the appearance of assimilation. He explained it thus: "They were assisted in this by the Sephardic trait of being far from 'fanatics'. The pious father and the son who spurns the traditions are not enemies. The father says: 'What shall we do? The times have changed and this is the custom of this generation', and accepts the situation with love. And the son understands his father as a man who did not have 'civilization' and does not rebel against him. Therefore there is no fanaticism, not as regards faith and not as regards education, and the sons do not 'depart from their fathers' households' and find their place among their people."[22]

This was true of the majority of the Egyptian Jews, as of the Jews in most of the Middle East countries.

Conversion was not a frequent occurrence. Some cases were known in Turkey in the 19th century and prior to that, of Jews who adopted Islam; the majority, being girls and women who had to work outside their homes, were seduced by Muslims and married them.[23] A few Jewish girls were baptized, having been influenced by the teachers of the missionary schools which they attended.[24]

In Egypt, too, cases of conversion to Islam were rare, since there was less contact between Jews and Muslims there, and, to a certain extent, because the Jews scorned the Muslims. But there were cases of girls who married Christians and adopted Christianity, not for economic reasons but because they had fallen in love with Christians or, in some cases, because they had been educated in missionary schools. There were also cases of mixed marriages between Jews and Christians. Out of 622 Jewish men who married in 1945, seven married Christian women. There were also nine Jewesses who married Christians in that year.[25]

A number of mixed marriages occurred in Turkey as well. According to the Turkish law pertaining to civil marriage, in force since the 'twenties, any man could marry a woman in a civil ceremony without consideration of differences in religion.

In Syria and the Lebanon, the Jews were, generally speaking, conservative, adhering strictly to the observance of the religious commands; this was true particularly of the Aleppo Jews. They did not suffer from forced or voluntary conversion, and there was no danger to their existence as a national minority. Despite the fact that the Jews had been attending Christian schools for decades, there were not many cases of conversion. In recent years, however, religion has weakened in certain circles, especially among the Jews of Beirut, and cases of conversion to Christianity of Jewish men and women have been registered.

THE YEMEN

In contrast to all the other Middle Eastern Jewries, the Jews of the Yemen, until their mass immigration to Israel, adhered to Jewish tradition, without being fanatical. They raised their children according to the Torah; at the age of two the child went to synagogue regularly, and at the age of three or four he attended *ḥeder,* where he learned practically nothing else but Torah. Religion became an organic part of his life. Since the Yemenite Jews had no modern schools and they were not permitted to attend Muslim state schools, and since the Muslim environment was religious and western culture scarcely penetrated the State, there was nothing to encourage impiety or breaking away from religion. In addition, the closed life in a special quarter, where the actions of each member of the community were known to all the others, made it difficult for anyone attempting to break away. The environmental factor was of decisive influence, for some of the young Yemenite Jews were religious out of fear of their parents. Among the young people who moved to Aden, where they were not known and there was no one to supervise them, were some who were not strict about observing the religious duties as they had been in their homes. When they reached Palestine, they became even less observant.

The Yemenite Jews were not very learned in religious matters. Only in San'a and Shar'ab were there learned Jews. San'a was the spiritual centre to which Jews from all over the Yemen turned.[26] A few of the Yemenite Jews were ascetics, devoting themselves to mysticism, and viewing this world as a path to the world to come.[27]

Because of their great dispersal, their poverty and their unfortunate political circumstances, they could not maintain Yeshivas, and their Rabbis could not earn a livelihood without engaging in some occupation, many being silver- and goldsmiths. This was an additional reason why only a few were able to delve deeply into the study of religious rules and traditional literature.

Despite their poverty and oppression, very few Yemenite Jews chose the road to conversion. Shmuel Yavnieli told of a number of such cases, among them the conversion to Islam of a young girl who had gone astray, a woman who had betrayed her husband, and a woman whose husband refused to give her a divorce. All of these converted of their own will, but many more Jews were forced to convert. Ladislas Farago, who visited the Yemen in 1937, reported that Jewish girls were compelled to adopt Islam and marry Muslims if a Muslim proposed marriage to them—they could not refuse to do so.[28]

Moreover, orphans were compelled to adopt Islam, if they had not managed to get married early. Parents therefore tried to marry off their children at an early age, from fear of their becoming orphaned before establishing a family. Sometimes relatives and friends attempted to hide an orphan, despite the danger involved, and sometimes they smuggled him out of the country. There is no information on how many orphans were forced to adopt Islam.[29]

With regard to conversion to Christianity, since there were no Christians in the Yemen during the last hundred years, the claim of the convert Joseph Wolff that at the time of his visit to San'a in 1832 he converted a number of Jews, whose names he attached, can be regarded with scepticism.[30]

The piety of the Yemenite Jews guarded them not only against conversion and assimilation, but also ensured their existence as Jews. The Torah was their strength, and their hardships and sufferings appeared to them as a decree from heaven.

Changes in the Status of Women

IRAQ

In most of the Eastern lands, in the past and in recent years as well, the birth of a daughter, in families of all religions, was not considered desirable. And so it was with Jewish families in Iraq.[31] Even the congratulations conveyed to parents after a daughter was born were different from those bestowed on them after the birth of a son. When a son was born, the well-wishers said *besiman tov* (good luck) and *tesewihum sab'a* (may there be seven!), while if the newborn was a girl, they merely said *mazal tov* (good luck!) sometimes adding what were in effect words of sympathy: *al-ḥamd lilah 'ala salāmitha* (thank God the mother is well), or *'ala rāsha libnin* (may boys follows her!). Only if there were already three or four sons, was the family not saddened by the birth of a girl, some even rejoicing, having feared that the evil eye might harm a family which had the good luck to bring only sons into the world.

Up to the beginning of the present century, parents sometimes sent their daughters to *ḥeder* with the boys when they reached the age of three or four, to study the Hebrew alphabet for a year or two. In the 'thirties and 'forties, girls were sent to Jewish or state kindergartens in Baghdad, and later in the southern cities as well. In rare cases, a Jewish girl in Kurdistan was sent to *ḥeder* or kindergarten.

After kindergarten, the girl went on to school, generally with the boys, up to the age of nine or ten. At that age they were separated, some of the girls finishing their schooling then if there was no Jewish, state or other school in the city, for girls only. From the mid-1930's a number of girls aged 15–18 were permitted to study in the two higher classes of the Jewish secondary school Shammash in Baghdad. This was the only institution in Iraq which allowed coeducational classes at this age. At the end of the 'thirties, Jewish, as well as Muslim and Christian girls, began to be accepted in the institutes of higher education in Iraq—in the Faculties of Law, Medicine, Pharmacy and Economics—together with the boys, of course. But even in 1950 only a few dozen Jewish girls graduated.

MARRIAGE

Young Jewish girls, with the exception of those few who studied with boys, had little opportunity to meet young men. From the 1930's, some had the possibility of doing so in the Jewish family clubs which were opened in Baghdad and Basra, or at work, when the girls began to work outside the home. But most girls did not have this opportunity. If a girl had no cousin to marry, her family usually used the services of a professional matchmaker or a relative to find her a husband.

Until the end of the 19th century, girls were married at the age of 12 or 13, and sometimes even at 11. Benjamin ben Joseph, who visited Baghdad in 1848, related that they had been accustomed to marry at the age of 8, but a few years before his arrival in the city, a government order was issued stipulating that rich girls could not marry before the age of 10, daughters of families of moderate means not before 11, and poor girls not before they reached the age of 12. Since then, the customary marriage age was 12 to 14. On the eve of the First World War, the age was raised to 15,[32] few girls marrying at 12 or 13. In the 'forties, there were only rare cases of Jewish girls living in central and southern Iraq who married at the age of 14 or under: most did so at 16 to 18, and sometimes even older.

The young Jewish girl in Kurdistan was married off, in recent years as well, at an early age—12 to 14. When a girl began to menstruate, her relatives said to her *lakhmat betit bābūk—ḥiremli elek* (the bread of your father's house is forbidden you), and she was married off that same year, even if she became orphaned of both her parents that year.[33]

Since the marriage age was so low and since the girl had little opportunity to become acquainted with boys herself, her parents' consent was essential. The Babylonian father had to agree to the amount of the dowry to be given his daughter, and the Kurdish father to the amount that the groom would pay as *neqda* (the payment for a bride to buy herself jewellery). For the daughter, and more so for her father, it was important that the boy came from a well-known family, that he was a good person who did not indulge in drink or wild behaviour, that he had a trade or profession from which he earned a living or was the son of a rich man, and that he asked for a small dowry. For the Kurdish fathers, it was important that the young man pay more *neqda*. The young man, on the other hand, sought a beautiful and well-born girl, with a big dowry (or, if he were a Kurd, a low *neqda* to be paid). The question of character and of whether the two young people were compatible was not taken into account, and the two people concerned were not even given the opportunity to become acquainted before their marriage.

Among the Babylonian Jews the size of the dowry was decisive: it was fixed after negotiations between the matchmaker and the father of the bride-to-be. Not infrequently marriage proposals were cancelled because the bargaining did not result in agreement. In rare cases the young man waived the dowry. Up to the First World War, the amount of the dowry reached some hundreds of rupees (a rupee equals one and a half English shillings), but when the Iraqi Jews became rich during the War, the sum was raised to some thousands of rupees, until a group of young Jews appeared who tried to put an end to this custom. This group broke up after a short time. In 1924, a group of young intellectuals demanded that the custom of dowries be abolished entirely: they demanded that the furnishing of the couple's home be financed by the man, as was the custom among the Muslims. A Government committee of experts was about to propose a law to this effect, to be submitted to the Government for its approval. The judge Reuben Baṭṭāṭ, who was among those supporting the abolition of dowries, basing himself on what was customary in Egypt, demanded that the Rabbinate in Baghdad take such a decision. The then Chief Rabbi, Rabbi Ezra Dangoor, explained that Rabbi Joseph Ḥayyim (died 1909), who knew what was customary in Egypt, had refused to put it into practice in Iraq. After lengthy discussions by Jewish jurists and intellectuals with the members of the Baghdad Jewish Community Committee, no decision was taken in the matter and dowries remained the practice.[34] During the Second World War, the dowry was even raised, and in some cases rich families paid as much as twenty thousand pounds sterling.

When the question of dowry was settled, an engagement was arranged, in accordance with religious law. Before the First World War, even an engaged couple was not permitted to meet or see each other. It was not until the 'forties that engaged couples were allowed to meet in a home, or even to go out walking together; in most cases, conservatism demanded that a child accompany them as an escort.[35]

Before the First World War the engagement period used to last a number of years, because the girl was engaged at a very early age and married only when she matured. But there were cases where the boy or the girl refused to marry his or her fiancé(e). Since the engagement had been conducted with a religious ceremony *(kiddushin)*, such refusal meant divorce. To avoid having many divorced single girls, the Baghdad Rabbis, in the 18th century, established a new regulation *(takana)* where by *kiddushin* would not be conducted at the time of the engagement, but instead at a time close to the wedding ceremony. This agreement was not sufficient to break a tradition of hundreds of years, and the Rabbis retracted it in 1812.[36] Iraqi Jews continued to have their sons and daughters engaged with *kiddushin*. In 1890 the Rabbis considered another way to prevent divorces of couples before their marriage. In a *takana* issued that year they laid down that the party retracting was obliged to pay the other party a third of the amount of the dowry. Even this regulation did not change the custom of *kiddushin* at the time of engagement. Sometimes the parents of the girl were prepared to cancel the engagement against payment of a third of the dowry, but the young man did not always agree to this.[37]

In 1926, the struggle against *kiddushin* at the time of engagement was renewed, and this time by intellectual young men, among them the lawyer Salmān Shīna, who published articles on the subject in his newspaper *al-Miṣbāḥ-Hamenorah*,[38] but these efforts also failed. The conservatism of the Babylonian Jews in this matter made it impossible to effect a change in the custom until the mass exodus to Israel, although the problem was already less grave by then, since the engagement age had risen and the couple married a short time after their engagement.

Among the Jews of Kurdistan, it was the man who paid money to the girl. In the villages he was often obliged to pay the girl's father for bringing her up. The Kurdish young man, therefore, had to work to collect the *neqda* money if he did not have a rich father. The amount of the *neqda* was small in accordance with the low standard of living, and when it rose, the 'Amādiya Rabbis laid down, in 1890, that it was forbidden for it to exceed 130 qran (about 6.5 pounds sterling). Following the inflation after the First World War, the *neqda* price rose to about 20 pounds sterling.

Preventing the young Jewish girl from meeting boys and marrying her off at an early age were due, in the main, to the fear that she might be seduced before her marriage, for the Babylonian and Kurdish Jews held that a girl must prove her virginity on the wedding night, and the groom's relatives must be shown the sheet. The Iraqi Jews, even the intellectuals among them, adhered to this custom until the time of emigration. For that reason, a girl who had been seduced had little possibility of marrying a Jew. She therefore adopted Islam and married a Muslim, for fear that her relatives would kill her. Such cases, about which the Iraqi Jews do not like to speak, were rare, although it may be that there were relatively more among the Jews in the Kurdish villages.

THE MARRIED WOMAN

Until the beginning of this century, the status of the woman in her husband's home was generally that of an inferior person, with her husband ruling over her. The young couple usually lived in the house of the husband's father. In this patriarchal home, the husband's mother was the first lady of the house, her daughters-in-law and her single daughters helping her to do the housekeeping. Each daughter-in-law, with her husband and sons, had one room; only when the house became too small to contain all the married sons and their families, or when the married son was compelled to move to another city to earn his living, did he leave his parents' home with his wife and children. Until that time, the daughter-in-law learned to conduct a household in the possibility that she might leave the enlarged family house for one of her own. Above all, she learned to honour and obey her husband and his mother. It was only in the last generation that it became customary among the Babylonian Jews for a married son not to live in his parents' house.

The woman's task was to conduct her household and to bear children. She never even thought of rebelling against this form of life. In the 19th century she also served her husband at meals, not eating at the same table with him, but in the kitchen. Gradually this custom was abolished, but even in the 1940's, the women of the older generation continued the practice.

The position of the Jewish woman in Kurdistan was even worse, for she was her husband's possession—he had bought her. She, too, served her husband, but in addition, she was compelled to work to add to the family income. She sometimes received blows from her husband, even in the presence of strangers. On the other hand, she was less closed up in the house than the Babylonian Jewess; she sometimes danced with Jewish men on joyful occasions and on the festivals, as did the Muslim Kurdish women at Muslim festivities. A few cases of married women betraying their husbands occurred. When this happened, the woman had to run away with her lover, who was generally a Muslim.

POLYGAMY AND DIVORCE

If a woman bore no child after ten years of marriage, or bore only daughters, her husband considered it his right to marry a second woman, either to acquire a son who would be his heir and say *kaddish* (liturgical doxology) for him after his death, or because his family urged him to do so. Divorcing the first wife was not customary, for the woman herself preferred to live with her rival wife than to be divorced. A Babylonian Jewish divorcee had slight possibilities of remarrying; one in Kurdistan had greater chances, for the fact that there a man had to pay a low price for a divorced woman was an inducement to the prospective husband. Among the Babylonians, to marry a divorcee was considered undesirable. The Rabbis also made divorce difficult; they instead facilitated the marriage of a man to a second woman, to enable him to acquire a son and to prevent divorces, naturally after they had ascertained that a number of years had passed since the first marriage. Despite this, there were cases of a man marrying a second wife before two witnesses, sometimes without the knowledge of his first wife and even if she had born him sons. Such cases led to tragedies and trials before the Rabbinical Court. In some cases when the first wife learned that her husband had married a second wife, she adopted Islam.[39]

To prevent bigamy, the Baghdad Jewish Community Committee issued an instruction, in November 1925, providing that those intending marriage had to register before the ceremony in the office of the Chief Rabbinate, and the Rabbinate could instruct the person who was to perform the marriage not to do so.[40] However, since this instruction did not have the validity of a ban and since, in any event, it did not apply to Jews outside Baghdad, marriages that were not registered in the Baghdad Chief Rabbinate office were also valid from the point of view of Jewish religious law.

Despite the lack of statistical data on polygamous marriages among the Iraqi Jews, it seems that they were not a widespread phenomenon. They were more usual among the few Kurdish Jews of means. The data on immigration to Israel reveal that in 1950–51, 20,337 married men and 20,986 married women had come from

Iraq.[41] The fact that there were 649 more married women must be attributed, in part, to the immigration in those years of families before the husbands, and, in part, to the polygamous marriages among the Kurdish Jews, and to a lesser extent among the Babylonians.

Divorce was apparently rare among the Iraqi Jews. Of 27,042 women who reached Israel in 1950-1951 and who were married or had been married, only 226 or 0.8% were divorcees.[42] One of the reasons for this was that only a Jewish religious court could grant a divorce, and it was not inclined to do so. In the event of infertility of the woman, the husband was permitted to take another wife; if there were disputes between the husband and wife granting of the divorce was delayed. Usually, the woman did not want a divorce, for, as explained above, her possibilities of marrying again were few. Incompatibility did not constitute a reason for divorce, particularly before the First World War, when a woman married at an early age and it was considered easy for her to adapt herself to her husband's ways. It was only in Kurdistan that it was easy to arrange a divorce, for the husband who had paid money for his wife considered it his right to waive his money and send his wife home to her parents.

WIDOWS AND INHERITANCE

When her husband died, a Jewish woman was not allotted any of his possessions, in accordance with Jewish religious law. Usually the eldest son inherited it all, and he filled the place of his father. If the sons were already married when the father died, they divided the inheritance among them according to the Law of the Torah, the daughters not receiving any part of it. In such a case, the brothers considered themselves obliged to pay dowries for their single sisters when they married later on. In 1924, a number of young people, among them the jurist Reuben Baṭṭāṭ, submitted a proposal to the Baghdad Jewish Community Committee to the effect that it be set down explicitly that the daughter would receive half the son's inheritance,[43] as stipulated in Muslim religious law. But it appears that his suggestion did not even merit discussion and it was the Rabbinical law which determined the rules of inheritance until the mass exodus to Israel.

EMPLOYMENT AND ATTIRE OF WOMEN

Jewish women in central Iraq, in the south and in the Kurdistan region generally, did not work. A needy family, a widow or a divorcee, if compelled to do so, preferred to take on work at home, such as sewing and weaving, against payment. Poor girls in need of an income sometimes did housework, generally in Jewish homes.

In the last generation a few educated girls began to work in teaching, and even in clerical work and in the liberal professions, as nurses, pharmacists, etc. The total number of working women was small. Out of 35,000 aged 15 and over who came to Israel in 1950–1951 only 2,300, or 6.5%, had worked (78% among the men). Of those, 60% had worked in dressmaking and clothing, 8% as teachers, 8% as doctors, midwives, nurses and pharmacists, 4% as clerks, 12.5% in personal services, 2.2% in commerce, 1.8% in farming, and the rest (3.5%) in various trades or professions. The fact that 20% of the Jewish women breadwinners had been engaged in clerical work, teaching and medicine is important evidence of the change which occurred in the status of the Jewish woman, socially and educationally, since the First World War.

Until 1951, no change occurred in the legal position of the Jewish woman in Iraq. The State did not grant women the right to vote for, or be elected to, parliament or the district and municipal councils; nor did the Jews permit women to vote or be elected to the Jewish Community institutions. Nevertheless, in practice women began to be appointed members of educational committees of the Jewish School Committee and to other institutions. A considerable advance was also made in the attire of the Jewish woman in the last generation. In the 'forties she no longer wore the long robe nor covered her face on going out in the street, an obligation which Arab tradition had imposed on her mother and her grandmother before her. It is true that earlier, on the eve of the First World War, some Jewish girls in Baghdad began to use a thin face covering,[44] but later on most Iraqi Jewish and Christian women removed the robe and the veil. The removal of these articles of clothing, or any other reform in the life of the Iraqi Jewess, was not the result of a law or compulsion.

EGYPT AND THE OTHER MIDDLE EAST COUNTRIES

In the 1840's the Jewish woman in Egypt was degraded and uneducated, and in this respect she resembled her sister in Yemen.[45] But since then a great change occurred in the status of the Jewess in Egypt and, to a lesser extent in Turkey. This is most conspicuous with regard to the education of the Egyptian Jewess, which exceeded that of her sisters in all of the Middle Eastern countries, and in her employment. According to the Egyptian population census of 1937, about 9% of all Jewish women were employed (against 4% in Iraq and about 1% in the Yemen and Aden), and a considerable number of them were engaged in commerce (33.8%); next came industry and building (28.9%) and general administration and public services, such as clerical work, medicine, etc. (16.4%). In Turkey, in 1960, 48.2% of the women employed were engaged in clerical work and the liberal professions, and only 9.9% in commerce and salesmanship; 24.9% were engaged in handicrafts and 17% in services. There is no doubt that the fact that about half of the Jewish women working in Turkey were engaged in clerical work, medicine, pharmacy and so on, was one of the most important revolutionary changes in the history of the Jews in this State.

According to the 1937 census in Egypt there were 11,881 married women, against 11,770 married men—that is 111 more married women. It may be that some of the husbands of the 111 married women were not in Egypt on the day the census was taken. In any case, there is no doubt that there were only a few cases of polygamy among Jews in Egypt in 1937. On the other hand, there were 282 divorced Jewish women in Egypt out of 15,842 women who had been married at any time (1.8%), on the day of the 1937 census. The percentage of such women among the immigrants to Israel from Iraq was 0.8%, and among those from the Yemen and Aden—1%. Despite the larger proportion of divorced women in Egypt, it may be said that divorce was not a usual phenomenon in that country, or in any other of the Middle East countries.

In Egypt, in Turkey, in the Lebanon and in Aleppo[46] in Syria, as far back as the 19th century, Jewish women did not go about with veiled faces and did not wear the robe. In Damascus, Syria, and Iran, however, they left off the robe only in the last generation.

The marriage age of Jewish girls in Turkey, Egypt, Syria and the Lebanon was low, but it has been on the rise in the past few decades. In the Yemen, however, it may be assumed that there has been no improvement in this respect. As in education and in economic circumstances, so too, with regard to the status of the Jewish woman, no change has occurred in the Yemen during the past hundred years.

Epilogue

During the 1860's there were outstanding differences in the political, economic and social situations of the Jews who lived in Turkey, Syria, the Lebanon, Egypt and Iraq, in comparison with the conditions under which the Yemenite, Kurdish and Iranian Jews lived, but after that time, changes occurred in all of these communities. The political situation improved, although it deteriorated again after the 1930's in Iraq and Syria, and after 1947 in Egypt, owing to the Palestine problem. The political situation of the Yemenite Jews neither improved nor deteriorated in the last hundred years of their exile.

There was a second turning point in the demographic situation of the Jews of the Middle East when they began to move from the small towns and villages to the big cities. Although Jews lived in the big cities in the 1850's, the proportion of those who remained in villages and small towns a hundred years later was still smaller, with the exception of the Yemen. In Iran, it was only in the last thirty years that Jews began to concentrate in Teheran, so that the economic, educational, and social improvements in Iran are still in their early beginnings. In general, during the last fifty years the Jewish communities in the Middle East, excluding the Yemen, changed from a poor, mostly illiterate society to a much richer and better educated one.

The most important change in the history of the Jews of the Middle East came about in the last two decades, when most of them emigrated to the State of Israel: out of the approximately 275,000 Jews who in 1947 lived in Iraq, Egypt, the Yemen, Aden and Syria, only about 5,000 remain there at present. The number of Jews in Turkey, Iran and the Lebanon decreased from 185,000 to about 100,000. Even before the establishment of the State of Israel there was a large immigration from Middle Eastern countries to Palestine—larger in proportion to the number of Jews in the Diaspora, than from any other country in the world. A third of the Yemenite Jews came to Israel in the years 1919–1948, about 20–25% of the Turkish, Syrian and Lebanese Jews, about an eighth of the Jewish population of Kurdistan and about 4–6% of the Jews of Iran, Egypt, and Babylonian Iraq. The main emigration took place in periods of economic crisis, and especially following pressure and persecution on the part of the authorities and the Muslims, when the Arab nationalist movement began to develop, and began to view the Jews as a national-Zionist minority which, like all national minorities, was not tolerated in the Arab countries, whatever the religious faith. The Kurdish Muslims in Iraq, in Iran and in Turkey, the Assyrian Christians in Iraq, and the Copts in Egypt likewise often suffered severe persecutions.

Immigration to Palestine, both before and after the establishment of the State of Israel, was in some cases for religious and Zionist reasons. But, these reasons would not have led to a mass exodus, if there had not been political or economic pressure. The situation in the Middle Eastern countries was no different. When pogroms against the Jewish communities in the Arab countries started in the 1940's, many of the Jews there were ready to leave to the only country which opened its gates to them—the State of Israel.[1]

Many factors had an impact on their absorption in Israel, but it would appear that their economic and educational level upon arrival was of preponderant importance. In other words, the economic and educational changes which took place in their countries of origin in the last hundred years had far-reaching effects on the possibilities of their absorption in Israel.[2]

NOTES TO THE INTRODUCTION

(Complete bibliographic references are given in the Bibliography, on p. 199ff.)

1. Benjamin of Tudela, pp. 48–55.
2. Ratzaby, Musa', pp. 337–395.
3. The most concise source on this period is Ratzaby's *Yemenite Jews.*
4. *AJA* 1873/74, p. 31.
5. Ḥabshush, *Massa'ot,* pp. 48–52.
6. Some Yemenite Jews in San'a wrote, in 1880, to the *Alliance Israélite Universelle* in Paris that Jews used to live among the Shī'ite-Zaydīs in the inland towns of the Yemen, since the latter treated the Jews well, while no Jews lived in the coastal towns among the fanatic Sunnis (*Bulletin,* 1881, 1er sem., p. 63). Nevertheless, it may be that Jews preferred inland towns for other reasons.
7. cf. Yavnieli, p. 46; Yesha'yāhū, p. 22. Mr. Somekh, director of the *Alliance* school in Cairo who visited the Yemen in 1903, also found physiological differences among the Jews in Yemen. He described the Jewish farmers as tall and strong, and the town-dwellers as short people (Somekh 1905, p. 93).
8. Gamlieli, p. 167.
9. Wellsted, II, pp. 158–159. Wellsted visited Aden in 1834.
10. Goldziher, pp. 237–238 (Heb. p. 171).
11. Louria, 1907, pp. 68–72; Levy, III, p. 1017.
12. Fischel, *Kurdistan,* pp. 223–225; Galanté (Marranes, pp. 102–114) provides a French translation of an Armenian book describing the persecutions of Jews in Tabrīz.
13. Fischel, *Kurdistan,* p. 225.
14. Benjamin II, pp. 209, 214 (Heb. pp. 93, 95).
15. Galanté, *Istanbul,* II, pp. 3–10.
16. ibid, p. 26. Although in some cases minorities suffered even in Syria in the middle of the 19th century (Maoz, pp. 158–166).
17. Heyd, pp. 135–149.
18. At the beginning of the 18th century three Jews were executed in Turkey as the result of a blood libel (Rosanes, IV, p. 188). A number of Jews died after being tortured during the investigation following the blood libel of Damascus in 1840.
19. Galanté, *Istanbul,* I, pp. 11–28.
20. Longrigg, *Four Centuries,* pp. 195, 219, 263.
21. Fargeon, pp. 157, 305.
22. Jabartī, III, p. 32, 42.
23. Jabartī, III, pp. 132, 190, 194; IV, p. 205.

24. Benjamin II, pp. 237–238 (Heb., pp. 105–106); Lane, p. 558; Clot Bey, I, p. 243; II, pp. 140–141; Dodwell, p. 240.
25. Ben Jacob, *Somekh*, pp. 9–10; Ben Jacob, *Kurdistan*, p. 38.
26. Ben Jacob, *Kurdistan*, p. 78; Fischel, *Kurdistan*, p. 214; Rivlin, *Shirat*, pp. 15–16; Brauer, *Kurdistan*, pp. 49–52.
27. Wolff, J., *Researches*.
28. Fischel, *Kurdistan*, p. 212.
29. Wellsted, I, p. 276.
30. Benjamin II, p. 109 (Heb. pp. 44, 46).
31. Kastelman, p. 52.
32. Longrigg, *Four Centuries*, p. 263.
33. In 1848 Benjamin II found (p. 118; Heb. pp. 42–45, 48) that trade with India was completely in the hands of the Jews of Baghdad.
34. Such as Rabbi Sason Mordekhai (1747–1830); Rabbi Moshe Ḥayyim (d. 1837); Rabbi Jacob, son of Rabbi Joseph Harofeh (d. 1851); Rabbi Abdalla Somekh (1813–1889) and others.
35. Benjamin II, p. 112 (Heb. p. 46).
36. Fischel, *Kurdistan*, p. 212; Longrigg, *Four Centuries*, pp. 195, 219.
37. According to Benjamin II (p. 137; Heb. p. 58), some 50 Jewish families lived in Basra. Twelve years later Kastelman (p. 57) found only about 40 families there.
38. In the 12th century several Jewish communities existed in central and southern Iraq. The main ones were those in Baghdad (40,000 Jews), Ḥilla (10,000) and Basra (10,000) (Cf. Benjamin of Tudela, pp. 60–73).
39. For amplification see my book, *Zionist*, pp. 11–17.
40. Rivlin, Dammesek, pp. 4–5, 28, 31; Lutzki, pp. 46–79; Adler, p. 165.
41. Benjamin II, p. 48 (Heb. p. 15). In 1884 Neumark (pp. 53–54) found only one Jewish family in Aleppo who spoke Ladino.
42. Elmaleḥ, p. 18.
43. Lutzki, pp. 46–79.
44. Brawer, Ḥomer, p. 268; Sémach, Avril 1931, p. 7.
45. In 1826 there were, according to David d'Beth Hillel, 15 Jewish families in Beirut, 15 in Tripoli and 25 in Sidon (Ya'ari, d'Beth Hillel, pp. 48–50).

NOTES TO CHAPTER ONE

1. For texts of the decrees cf. Hurewitz, I, pp. 113–116, 149–153.
2. Galanté, *Turcs*, pp. 112–115; Franco, p. 258.
3. Galanté, *Turcs*, pp. 122–126; Galanté, *Izmir*, pp. 168–172; Franco, pp. 239–242.
4. *AJA* 1876/77, p. 98.
5. In 1872 the Chief Rabbinate in Istanbul demanded that a Jewish representative be appointed in the municipality of Diarbakir (Galanté, *Sixième*, p. 22), and it is known that one was acting in 1875. (*Bulletin*, 1875, 2e sem., p. 13.)
6. In 1847 the Sultan Abd al-Ḥamid ordered that a Jewish cook be employed at the School of Medicine in Istanbul and that Jewish students there be permitted to absent themselves on Saturdays (Margoliouth, II, p. 141; Franco, pp. 156, 241). In 1889 there was also a Jewish cook at the Istakhané school (school of arts) in Izmir (Galanté, *Izmir*, pp. 127.)
7. Galanté, *Izmir*, p. 147.
8. Galanté, *Encore*, pp. 26–27.
9. Galanté, *Turcs*, p. 15.
10. Galanté, *Turcs*, pp. 18–21; *Bulletin*, 1893, pp. 38–39.
11. In 1881, for example, part of the Jewish cemetery in Izmir was confiscated (*AJA*, 1881/82, p. 28).
12. *AJA*, 1888/89, p. 58.
13. *AJA*, 1891/92, p. 18; *Bulletin*, 1892, pp. 47–48; Galanté, *Turcs*, pp. 31–37; Galanté, *Cinquième*, pp. 4–8.
14. Franco, pp. 210–211; *Bulletin*, 1873, 1er sem., pp. 61–62; 1875, 1er sem., pp. 66–67; *AJA*, 1876/77, p. 43; 1888/89, p. 24.
15. Galanté, *Izmir*, pp. 183–199; *Franco*, pp. 221–232; *Bulletin*, 1901, pp. 85–88, 1896, p. 70.
16. Blood-libels were spread in Istanbul in the years 1863, 1866, 1868, 1870, 1874, 1876, 1884 and 1887 (Galanté, *Istanbul*, II, pp. 125–137; Franco, pp. 221–231).
17. *Bulletin*, 1874, 1er sem., pp. 87–88; Franco, pp. 223–224.
18. *Bulletin*, 1896, p. 70.
19. *Bulletin*, 1893, pp. 57–58.
20. *Bulletin*, 1892, p. 68.
21. *Bulletin*, 1899, pp. 101–103.
22. Galanté, *Turcs*, pp. 16–22.

23. Franco, p. 222.
24. *Bulletin,* 1908, pp. 73–75.
25. Galanté, *Turcs,* pp. 86–92.
26. The Law of August 7th, 1909 in French translation in Galanté, *Documents,* pp. 31–32.
27. Galanté, *Turcs,* pp. 41–57; Galanté, *Anatolie,* II, *passim.*
28. *AJA,* 1901/02, p. 51; 1902/03, p. 34.
29. *AJA,* 1899/1900, pp. 21, 25; Galanté, *Izmir,* p. 13.
30. Hurewitz, II, pp. 122–123.
31. *Hamenora,* Fév.-Mars 1926, pp. 80–84; *Paix et Droit,* Juin 1926, p. 11.
32. Galanté, *Turcs,* pp. 57–60.
33. Thomas, p. 113.
34. *Paix et Droit,* Mai 1928, p. 2; Mars 1937, p. 12.
35. *Paix et Droit,* Oct. 1923, p. 11; Mai 1928, pp. 1–2; *All. Rev.,* Nov.-Dec. 1949, p. 5.
36. Galanté, *Anatolie,* II, pp. 254–258; *Hamenora,* Juin-Sept. 1934, pp. 151–156; *Paix et Droit,* Sept. 1934, pp. 15–16.
37. Galanté, *Istanbul,* I, pp. 39–40.
38. *Jerusalem Post,* August 3rd, 1959.
39. *Hed Hammizrah,* 30.6.1944, p. 5.
40. *Hed Hammizrah,* 29.9.1942, p. 4; Galanté, *Istanbul,* I, pp. 228–229.
41. Lewis, pp. 103–105.
42. *Hed Hammizrah,* 5.10.1945, p. 9.
43. Bell, *Amurath,* p. 187, *AJYB,* 1912/13, p. 184; 1913/14, p. 345.
44. Albala, Mésopotamie, p. 262; *Yeshurun,* 15 Keslev, 5681 (1920), p. 1.
45. Ben Jacob, *Somekh; AJA,* 1889/90, pp. 18–24; Somekh, 1889, pp. 37–48.
46. Benjamin, II, 96–103 (Heb. pp. 38–41); Ben Jacob, *Kurdistan; Bulletin,* 1895, pp. 64–65; 1896, pp. 52–55; 1889, pp. 48–49; *AJA,* 1876/77, p. 95; Niego, p. 102.
47. Ghanīmah, p. 180; 'Azzāwī, VIII, p. 164.
48. On this period cf. 'Azzāwī, VIII, 249–250, 270–299; Ghanīmah, pp. 181–182; Coke, *Baghdad,* p. 287.
49. Sassoon, *Baghdad,* p. 178, 213.
50. Wilson, II, 334–335; Ireland, pp. 170–171; Bell, *Review,* pp. 126–127; Al Far'ūn, I, pp. 108, 123–124.
51. Ḥasanī, II, pp. 50–51; Cohen, *Zionist,* pp. 41–45.
52. Khadduri, pp. 69–234.
53. Ḥasanī, IV, pp. 7–8.
54. *AJYB,* 1937/38, pp. 490–491; Letter from Baghdad dated November 1936 in Central Zionist Archives, Jerusalem File No. S 25/3528.
55. *AJYB,* 1938/39, p. 334; 1939/40, p. 373; and letters from Baghdad dated August to November 1938 in the file mentioned in the previous note.
56. Cohen, *Farhūd,* pp. 2–18.
57. Aghasi, *20 Shanah.*
58. Longrigg, *Iraq,* p. 350; Asa, *Mibifnim,* pp. 636–641.
59. Asa, *Mibifnim,* p. 646.

60. Asa, *Mibifnim*, p. 642.
61. Shinah, pp. 138–140; *Yalkut*, Feb. 1949, p. 22; May 1949, p. 15; Longrigg, *Iraq*, pp. 353ff.
61a. Cf. Cohen in *AJYB*.
62. Coke, *Heart*, p. 203. See also Albala, Mésopotamie, p. 247.
63. According to *AJA*, 1876/77, p. 97 blood libels were spread by the Nestorians against the Jews in Kurdistan, but no details were given.
64. Somekh, 1884, pp. 56–57.
65. *AJYB*, 1911/1912, p. 187; *AI*, 12.2.1925, p. 3.
66. Galanté, *Documents*, pp. 214–223; Franco, pp. 130–132; Brawer, He'arot, pp. 294–297; Brawer, Ḥomer, pp. 360–402.
67. Elmaleḥ, pp. 45–46.
68. Elmaleḥ, pp. 42–43.
69. *AI*, 12.2.1925, p. 3; 12.3.1925, p. 2.
70. *AI*, 10.2.1927, p. 4; 20.10.1944, p. 11; 9.2.1945, p. 9.
71. *Ḥayāt*, 2–3.11.1957.
72. Shoshkes, p. 222.
73. *AI*, 31.7.1939; 11.8.1939, p. 26; Schechtman, pp. 170–175; *Alliance Review*, June 1951, p. 1; *Cahiers*, Mai 1963, p. 65.
74. Farhi, Aperçu, p. 226; Silver, p. 12; Elmaleḥ, p. 48.
75. *Paix et Droit*, Dec. 1923, p. 9.
76. *Hamenora*, Jan. 1926, pp. 24–28; Oct. 1926, pp. 276–277; *Paix et Droit*, Nov. 1925, pp. 8–10; Dec. 1925, p. 10; Mars 1926, p. 9; Mai 1926, p. 11.
77. *AI*, 4.6., 25.7., 11.8., 15.9., 25.9.1938.
78. *AI*, 15.4., 25.7.1938.
79. *AI*, 14.1.1944; 31.5.1945; 15.6.1945.
80. *AI*, 26.10.1945; 25.3.1946.
81. *Salām*, 16.1.1948, pp. 6, 9.
82. *AI*, 26.10; 9.11.1945; 1.2.1946.
83. *AI*, 15.2., 8.3., 25.3., 12.4.1946; *Salām*, 10.2.1947.
84. *AI*, 21.5.1946; *Salām*, 1.7.1946.
85. *Salām*, 16.1., 6.2.1948.
86. Schechtman, pp. 22, 154–158, 164–165.
87. *Cahiers*, Fév.–Mars 1951, p. 15.
87a. On this period cf. Cohen in *AJYB*.
88. *AJA*, 1882/83, p. 14; *Bulletin*, 1897, p. 88–89.
89. Cf. Gendzier, *The Practical Visions*.
90. Landau, *Parliaments*, p. 101.
91. *Bulletin*, 1892, pp. 67–68; 1900, pp. 91–92; 1903, pp. 157–164; Fargeon, pp. 232, 250, 263; *AI*, 27.3.1930, p. 2; Landau, 'Alilot, pp. 415–460.
92. *AI*, 31.7.1939, p. 9.
93. Schechtman, p. 187.
94. Landshut, p. 33.
95. Schechtman, pp. 188–191.

96. Landshut, pp. 36–38.
97. Schechtman, pp. 190–191.
98. Schechtman, pp. 192–194.
99. Moch, pp. 14–18.
100. Schechtman, pp. 194–201; On this period cf. also Yahudiya Masriya, pp. 61–62.
101. Schechtman, pp. 203–205; *Muṣawwar,* 6.9.1957.
102. On persecution of Jews after the war of June 1967 see Miloslavsky and Cohen in *AJYB.*
103. Tādrūs, pp. 21–24.
104. *Mishlowaḥ manot el benei Yisrael me'ereẓ Paras me'et haḥevrah hanoda'at beshem Kol Yisrael Ḥaverim* (A sending of (Purim) gifts to the Jews in Persia from the Society known as *Alliance Israélite Universelle*), Paris 1874.
105. *Mishlowaḥ,* p. 12.
106. *Mishlowaḥ,* pp. 14, 27.
107. Neumark, p. 77.
108. *AJA,* 1875/76, pp. 23–29; 1876/77, pp. 62–63, 92.
109. *Bulletin,* 1879, pp. 20, 63–64; *AJA,* 1881/82, pp. 32–33; Confino, *L'action,* pp. 38–39.
110. Neumark, p. 76.
111. Neumark, pp. 75–78.
112. Confino, *L'action,* p. 45; Neumark, p. 85.
113. Confino, *L'action,* pp. 76–78; *AJA,* 1889/90, pp. 28–30; *Bulletin,* 1889, pp. 50–51; 1890, p. 33.
114. Cohen, Morris, 1888/89, p. 43.
115. *AJA,* 1888/89, pp. 26–28.
116. *Bulletin,* 1889, p. 64.
117. *Bulletin,* 1892, pp. 49–54; 1893, pp. 45–47; *AJA,* 1892/3, pp. 19–24, 57–63; 1893/94, p. 18; 1894/95, pp. 13–14; 1895/96, pp. 23–24; Confino, *L'action,* pp. 110–116.
118. *Bulletin,* 1897, pp. 75–81; 1898, pp. 63–71; *AJA,* 1896/97, pp. 14–15; Confino, *L'action,* pp. 49–52.
119. *Bulletin,* 1902, pp. 59–77; 1904, pp. 67–80; 1905, pp. 78–86; Confino, *L'action,* pp. 151–152.
120. Levy, III, pp. 847–848.
121. Levy, III, p. 854.
122. *Bulletin,* 1906, pp. 67–68, 80–84; 1908, pp. 88–99; 1909, pp. 70–85; 1910, pp. 179–195; *AJA,* 1910/11, pp. 17–18.
123. *Paix et Droit,* Sept. 1925, p. 11.
124. Schechtman, pp. 237–238; Haas, p. 72; Brawer, Meparashat, II, p. 240, III, p. 85.
125. Avidov, pp. 30–31, 37–38, 78.
126. Brawer, Meparashat, II, p. 245, III, p. 82; Yishai, pp. 196, 292; Schechtman, pp. 249–250; Spicehandler.
127. *Bulletin,* 1873, 1er sem., pp. 93–95; *AJA,* 1875/76, pp. 53–54; Schechtman, p. 38.
128. *Bulletin,* 1876, 1er sem., pp. 8–11, *AJA,* 1875/76, pp. 53–54; Franco, pp. 217–218.
129. Kāfiḥ, Meẓokot, pp. 407–408.
130. *Bulletin,* 1905, pp. 88–89; Sémach, Une mission, pp. 113–135.
131. Ḥabshush, *Ashkolot,* pp. 26–27. Translated from Arabic following Prof. S. D. Goitein's translation into Hebrew.

132. In 1937 the minimum poll-tax was three riyāls (Farago, p. 274).
133. Nevertheless, there were 3 or 4 storey houses in the Jewish quarter of San'a (cf. pictures of such houses in Rathjens).
134. Bury, p. 16.
135. *Paix et Droit,* Avr. 1923, p. 13; Oct. 1929, p. 12; Barer, p. 126.
136. *Paix et Droit,* Mai 1924, p. 10.
137. Ratzaby, *Yemenite Jews,* pp. 72–73.
138. Sémach, Une mission, p. 127.
139. Sémach, Une mission, pp. 169–170; Rihani, pp. 181–188; Kāfiḥ, *Halikhot,* pp. 290–292.
140. Morag, pp. 37–40.
141. Yavnieli, pp. 29, 32–33, 37, 84–85, 88, 124, 131, 211.
142. Qubain, p. 274. More about that incident can be found in letters from Jews of Bahrein to Jerusalem, in file S25/5291 of the Central Zionist Archives.
143. Ẓadok, pp. 132–133, 176–192.
144. *AJA,* 1932, p. 11; Ẓror Egrot, p. 7.
145. Colonial Office, Aden, p. 30.
146. Sicron, II, p. 22.

NOTES TO CHAPTER TWO

1. Egypt, *Census 1907, 1917, 1937, 1947, 1960.*
2. Benas, p. 69; Levi, Dec. 1956, p. 7.
3. Adams, p. 41.
4. *Bulletin,* 1904, pp. 165–167; Wilson, I, p. 236; *Statesman's Yearbook 1935,* p. 1033, Iraq, *Census 1947.*
5. *Bulletin,* 1910, p. 224; 1913, p. 133.
6. The city of 'Amāra was established in 1861 ('Azzāwī, VIII, p. 13), and in 1870 Jews had already started to settle there. In 1881, the first synagogue was built. Jewish migration to 'Amāra continued, making a second synagogue necessary, which was built in 1896. In the years 1910–1913 the Jewish population in the city was estimated at between 1400 and 1500. (Sassoon, *Massa',* p. 116; *Bulletin,* 1910, p. 222; 1913, p. 131). Jews started to settle in Qal'at Ṣāliḥ in the 1860's, and in 1884 they built a synagogue there. In Musayyab the first synagogue was built in 1878 (Sassoon, *Massa',* pp. 116, 173). The number of Ḥilla Jews was estimated in 1826 to be 25 families (Fischel, *Massa',* p. 246), and in 1848, 50 families (Benjamin, II, pp. 122–123); in 1904 official estimates put their numbers as 1500. (*Bulletin,* 1904, p. 166).
7. Benjamin II, p. 109 (Heb. p. 46); *Bulletin,* 1890–1900.
8. Wilson, I, p. 236; Iraq, *Census 1947.*
9. *Bulletin,* 1909, p. 367; Niego, p. 97; Benjamin II, p. 86 (Heb. 34).
10. Sicron, II, pp. 36, 50.
11. *Bulletin,* 1904, pp. 165–166.
12. Loupo, p. 112; *Bulletin,* 1904, p. 165.
13. Galanté, *Anatolie,* II.
14. Galanté, *Izmir,* pp. 14–15.
15. *Paix et Droit,* Jan. 1931, p. 12.
16. Galanté, *Istanbul,* I, p. 70.
17. *Bulletin,* 1904, p. 166; Galanté population, pp. 246–248; Turkey, *Census 1960, Census 1965.*
18. Turkey, *Census 1960, 1965;* Turquie, *Annuaire 1959,* p. 83.
19. Galanté, population, pp. 246–248.
20. Farhi, Aperçu, p. 225.
21. *Hamenora,* Jan. 1926, p. 28; Oct. 1926, p. 275.
22. *Bulletin,* 1904, p. 167; 1913, pp. 129, 139.

23. Silver, p. 10.
24. Hourani, p. 121.
25. Ya'ari, d'Beth Hillel, pp. 48–50.
26. *Bulletin,* 1904, p. 167; 1913, pp. 133, 151.
27. Hourani, pp. 121, 386; Libanaire, *Statistiques 1947–48,* pp. 22.
28. Iran, *Census 1956;* Spicehandler, p. 32.
29. According to an 1826 estimate, some 100 Jewish families lived in Teheran (Fischel, Massa', p. 254) and in 1848, there were 300 families (Stern, p. 196). In 1884, the estimate was raised to 1,000 families (Neumark, p. 83) and in 1889–1913 to 6,000 souls (*Bulletin,* 1899, p. 129; 1913, p. 155).
30. Brawer, Meparashat, II, p. 249.
31. The number of Jews in Iran according to the 1966 census was 60,684, of whom 39,716 lived in Teheran, 6,268 in Shīrāz, 2,507 in Işfahān, 821 in Hamadhān, 657 in Yazd and 762 in Abadān.
32. Sicron, II, p. 50; Iran, *Census 1956* and *Census 1966.*
33. *Bulletin,* 1904, 1er sem., pp. 167–168.
34. Sémach, Une mission, pp. 103, 205; Yavnieli, pp. 13, 77, 213.
35. Sicron, II, p. 22.
36. Somekh, 1907, p. 102.
37. Sémach, Une mission, p. 103; Schechtman, p. 74; Colonial Office, Aden, p. 30.
38. Schechtman, p. 80.
39. Qubain, p. 274; Bahrein, *Census 1959.*
40. Sémach, Une mission, pp. 209–214.
41. Yavnieli, p. 213.
42. Goitein, p. 112.
43. Sicron, II, p. 63.
44. Yavnieli, p. 213.

NOTES TO CHAPTER THREE

1. Benjamin II, p. 238; Landau, *Jews*, pp. 9–12; Lane, pp. 558–562; Clot Bey, II, p. 142; Benas, p. 68.
2. Landau, *Jews*, pp. 13–15.
Egypt, *Census 1937* and *Census 1947*.
4. Albala, 1907, p. 97; *Handbook*, I, p. 97; II, p. 381.
5. Albala, 1913, pp. 109–111; Schur, p. 56.
6. Sidi, pp. 248, 261. Cf. also Niego, pp. 101–102.
7. *Bulletin*, 1880, 2^{er}sem., pp. 21–28; 1884, 1^{er}sem., p. 58.
8. Cohen Morris, 1883/84, pp. 48–53; Albala, Mésopotamie, pp. 254–256.
9. Sicron, pp. 74–75.
10. Fischel, Anosim, pp. 71–72; Brawer, Meparashat, III, p. 76; Brawer, Avak, II, p. 208.
11. Fischel, Kurdistan, pp. 213–215; Fischel, Massa', pp. 235–242; *AJA*, 1876/77, p. 95.
12. Brawer, *Avak*, II, pp. 118–121.
13. *AJA*, 1888/89, p. 44; Fischel, Massa', p. 244.
14. Bassan, 1903, pp. 137–138; Asa, *Yalkut*, p. 120.
15. *Cahiers* Juin-Juillet 1947, pp. 11–13.
16. Kastelman, p. 71; Neumark, pp. 81, 93–94; Cohen Morris, 1888/89, p. 44.
17. *AJA*, 1876/77, p. 93; *Mishlowaḥ*, p. 18.
18. Kastelman, pp. 69–70; Neumark, p. 84; *AJA*, 1876/77, p. 92; Adler, p. 48; Curzon, I, p. 333.
19. Brawer, *Avak*, II, pp. 171–172; Yishai, pp. 52–55, 196–197, 223–224.
20. Rosen, 1957, p. 13.
21. Wolff, *Travels*, p. 216; Confino 1903, pp. 122–123; Louria, 1907, pp. 77–79; Yishai, p. 308; Asa, *Yalkut*, p. 119.
22. Lariedo, pp. 9–11; Yishai, p. 199; Kastelman, p. 62; Brawer, Meparashat, III, p. 76; Fischel, Anosim, p. 72.
23. Confino, *L'action*, p. 78; Kastelman, pp. 62–66; Brawer, *Avak*, II, pp. 275–276; Brawer, Meparashet, III, pp. 81–82; Yishai, pp. 313–314; *AJA*, 1876/77, p. 78.
24. Kastelman, p. 69; Brawer, *Avak*, II, p. 281.
25. Ort 1957, p. 18.
26. Sicron, II, pp. 74–75.
27. Brawer, Meparashat, II, p. 4.
28. Fischel, Massa', p. 239–240; Schur, pp. 14–17, 26; Benjamin II, p. 57; Niego, pp. 87–88, 95–97.

29. *AJA*, 1886/87, p. 24; 1887/88, p. 35; 1894/95, p. 20; Pariente, 1893/94, p. 64.
30. *AJA*, 1880/81, p. 77; 1901/02, p. 22; *Bulletin*, 1897, p. 83; Loewy, p. 60; Galanté, *Istanbul*, II, pp. 73–85.
31. Galanté, *Izmir*, pp. 130–148; Samuel, p. 166.
32. Lewis, pp. 117–119; Schechtman, pp. 218–222.
32a. Turkey, *Census of Population, 1960.*
33. Lutzki, pp. 64, 69.
34. Benjamin II, p. 48 (Heb. p. 15); Schur, p. 9; Neumark, p. 66.
35. *AI*, 20.11.1942, p. 10.
36. Rivlin, Dammesek, pp. 8–11.
37. Margoliouth, II, pp. 243–247.
38. Neumark, pp. 50–52, 66.
39. Astroc, p. 66.
40. Elmaleḥ, pp. 21–22.
41. These data were collected by the Béné Bérith Lodge in Damascus in April 1926 (*Hamenora*, Oct. 1926, p. 275).
42. Sémach, Dec. 1930, p. 11.
43. *AI*, 14.1.1944; 29.6.1945; Schechtman, pp. 161–162.
44. Samuel, p. 6.
45. Bury, p. 74; Rihani, p. 184; Helfritz, p. 248.
46. Sémach, Une mission, pp. 176–183; Yavnieli, pp. 14, 43.
47. Sémach, Une mission, p. 182; Somekh 1905, p. 93; Brauer, Haḥaklaot, pp. 75–77.
48. Sémach, Une mission, p. 104.
49. Sémach, Une mission, pp. 209–214.
50. Sicron, II, pp. 73–74.

NOTES TO CHAPTER FOUR

1. Israel, *Census 1961*, no. 30, tables 2, 18.
2. Fargeon, p. 258.
3. Taragan, p. 135.
4. Taragan (Heb.) pp. 185–186.
5. Aghion, p. 24.
6. Fargeon, p. 258; Taragan, pp. 41–42.
7. *Bulletin*, 1900, p. 135, 138; 1905, p. 119; 1910, p. 214; 1913, pp. 130–155; *Paix et Droit*, Oct. 1922, p. 16; Juin 1936, p. 16; *Cahiers*, Jan. 1950; Nov. 1956, p. 34.
8. Egypt, *Statistiques 1913*, p. 97; 1931/1932, p. 141; 1945/1946 et 1946/1947, p. 215.
9. Egypt, *Census, 1907, 1927, 1937, 1947.*
10. Egypt, *Census, 1947.*
11. On Sanu' and his publications cf. Gendzier.
12. Author of *La communauté juive d'Alexandrie de l'antiquité à nos jours*, Alexandrie 1946. 31p.
13. Author of *Le règne de Mohamed Aly d'après les archives russes en Egypte*, 3 vols. Caire 1931–1936.
14. Author of *Contribution a l'étude de là procédure judicaire dans l'ancien empire égyptienne*, 65 p.
15. Author of *Coup d'oeil sur la chronologie de la nation égyptienne*. Paris 1931. 447 p.
16. Fargeon, p. 237.
17. Cohen Morris, 1879/1880, pp. 93–94; Abrevaya, p. 87; Ben Jacob, Haḥeder.
18. Cohen Morris, 1879/1880, pp. 94–95; Baghdad, Comité des écoles; Baghdad, Lajnat al-Madāris.
19. Cohen Morris, 1879/1880, pp. 94–95; Baghdad, Comité des écoles; Baghdad, Lajnat al-Madāris, p. 20 and appendices.
20. Baghdad, Lajnat al-Madāris, pp. 11–12.
21. Benjamin II, p. 112 (Heb. p. 64); Cohen Morris, 1879/1880, p. 96.
22. *al-Miṣbāḥ*, 4.9.1924, pp. 1–2.
23. *Bulletin*, 1867, 2e sem., pp. 19–20.
24. Louria, 1886, p. 57.
25. *Bulletin*, 1880, 1er sem., p. 56; 1900, p. 136; 1913, pp. 130–148; *Paix et Droit*, Oct. 1922, p. 16; Mars 1939, p. 12; *Cahiers*, Dec. 1947–Jan. 1948, p. 11.
26. Baghdad, Comité des écoles.

27. *Bulletin*, 1873, 2e sem., pp. 9, 54.
28. Cohen Morris, 1879/1880, p. 93; *Alliance Review*, Winter 1962, pp. 28–29.
29. Albala, 1910, p. 37.
30. Baghdad, Comité des écoles.
31. Baghdad, Lajnat al-Madāris, pp. 24–25, 50–51, 63.
32. For titles of books published see Ya'ari, *Hadfus*, II, pp. 144–146.
33. Baghdad, Lajnat al-Madāris, p. 36.
34. do., pp. 39–40, 59, 61; Baghdad, Comité des écoles.
35. Coeducation was not customary in Iraqi schools, but in the Jewish schools it existed up to the third class. In 1935, the Shammash school was the only one to allow a limited number of girls to study together with the boys in the secondary school classes. This was the only school in Iraq to have coeducational classes at this age. But even in this school, the number of girls was small and they had a special rest-room where they spent the intermission periods.
36. Baghdad, Lajnat al-Madāris, pp. 8–9.
37. Baghdad, Lajnat al-Madāris, pp. 56, 60–65.
38. do., p. 61; Baghdad, Comité des écoles; *Iraq Directory*, pp. 461–462.
39. Lajnat al-Madāris, pp. 45–49, 52.
40. See my article on the subject in *Jewish Journal of Sociology*, June 1969.
41. For list of titles of books written by Rabbis in Iraq cf. Ben Jacob, *Bavel*, pp. 190–208, 302–303.
42. Author of *al-Ḥisād al-Awwal* (The first harvest) Baghdad 1930; *Hamasāt al-Zaman* (The Whisper of Time) Baghdad 1956; *Fī Ziḥām al-Madīnah* (In the Turmoil of the city), Baghdad 1955; *Qiṣaṣ min al-Gharb* (Stories from the West) Baghdad 1937; Anwar Shaul translated also Sheridan's *William Tell* (Baghdad, 1931). Cf. also Marmorstein.
43. Author of *Mabāḥith fī al-Iqtiṣād al-'Iraqī* (Essays on the Economy of Iraq) Baghdad 1948; *Rijāl wa-Ḍilāl* (Men and Shadows), Baghdad 1955; *Nufūs Ḍāmiʿa* (Thirsty Spirits), Baghdad 1966, and *Aghānī al-Ḥubb* (Poems of Love).
44. Author of *Murūj wa-Ṣaḥāra* (Pastures and Deserts), Baghdad 1931. His other poems had been published in periodicals.
45. Author of *al-Jamrah al-Aūla* (The First Burning Coal), Baghdad 1938. His other poems, which appeared in Iraqi daily newspapers in 1941, were collected and typed in a few copies under the name *Majmū'a min al-Shi'r al-Ramzī* (A Collection of Symbolic Poems), Jerusalem 1964.
46. Author of *Aḥrār wa-'abīd* (Free People and Slaves), Baghdad 1941; *Ba'ḍ al-Nās* (Some People), Baghdad 1948. On Darwish see also Marmorstein.
47. Author of *Wābil wa-Ṭal* (Shower and Dew), Baghdad 1949; *Khafaqāt Qalb* (Pulses of a Heart), Baghdad 1945; *Fī Sukūn al-Layl* (In the Silence of the Night), Baghdad 1947; *Zahra Fī Kharīf* (A Flower in Autumn), Baghdad.
48. Author of *Mawākib al-Ḥirmān* (The Processions of Want), Beirut 1949; *Washwashāt al-Fajr* (The Whispers of Dawn), Tel Aviv 1958.
49. Ben Jacob, *Bavel*, pp. 201–203.

50. For biographies of some of the Jewish musicians cf. Rajab.
51. Franco, pp. 261–262; Cazes 1875, pp. 142–143; Pariente, 1884, pp. 51–53.
52. Loewy, pp. 62–63.
53. *AJA*, 1879/1880, p. 89; 1896/97, p. 27; 1902/03, p. 34; *Messeret*, 22, 28.1., 3.2., 10.2.1914.
54. *AJA*, 1901/1902, p. 27; 1902/03, p. 34; 1905/06, p. 17; *Bulletin*, 1906, p. 111.
55. *AJA*, 1873/74, p. 44; Loewy, p. 63; Franco, p. 261, Galanté, *Izmir*, p. 108.
56. *Bulletin*, 1892, pp. 77–79; 1894, p. 70; 1896, p. 81; 1898, p. 95; 1903, p. 176; 1910, p. 211.
57. *AJA*, 1903/04, p. 25; *Bulletin*, 1904, pp. 97–98; Galanté, *Istanbul*, I, p. 196.
58. *Hed Hamizrah*, June 8, 1945.
59. Loewy, p. 68; Pariente, 1879/80, p. 90; *AJA*, 1895/96, p. 33; 1905/06, p. 27; Galanté, *Izmir*, pp. 116–117.
60. Galanté, *Istanbul*, I, pp. 31, 183–184; Franco, pp. 155, 164–166.
61. Loewy, p. 65.
62. *AJA*, 1871/72, pp. 32–34; 1873/74, p. 39; Galanté, *Izmir*, pp. 109–115.
63. *Bulletin*, 1875, 2ᵉ sem., pp. 32–34; 1900, pp. 135–150; 1910, pp. 211–213; 1913, pp. 123–125.
64. *AJA*, 1882/83, p. 53; 1898/99, pp. 87–88.
65. Lewis, p. 159.
66. *AJA*, 1879/80, pp. 87–92; 1882/83, p. 56; 1893/94, pp. 61, 64; Galanté, *Izmir*, pp. 134–136.
67. *AJA*, 1893/94, pp. 65; Galanté, *Izmir*, p. 136; Galanté, *Anatolie*, II, pp. 117–119; *Messeret*, 1.12.1913, p. 2.
68. *AJA*, 1888/1889, p. 34; 1901/02, p. 22; *Bulletin*, 1897, pp. 94–97.
69. Galanté, *Istanbul*, I, pp. 222–223.
70. Galanté, 1925, p. 118; Franco, pp. 156, 241; Margoliouth, II, p. 141; Loewy, 1889/90, pp. 66–68.
71. Galanté, *Turcs*, pp. 141–142; Galanté, *Sixième*, p. 19.
72. Loewy, 1888/89, pp. 66–68.
73. Franco, p. 258; Galanté, *Istanbul*, II, pp. 111–115; Galanté, *Izmir*, pp. 173–176; Galanté, *Turcs*, pp. 118–119.
74. Galanté, *Cinquième*, pp. 31–32.
75. Niego, pp. 88, 91.
76. *Paix et Droit*, Oct. 1922, p. 16.
77. Turquie, *Annuaire 1931/32*, p. 156.
78. *Paix et Droit*, Oct. 1932, pp. 11–12.
79. *Cahiers*, Sept.–Oct. 1958, p. 110.
80. Galanté, 1925, p. 118; Galanté, *Istanbul*, I, p. 199; *Hamenora*, Jan. 1924, p. 15.
81. Franco, pp. 266–269; Galanté, *Izmir*, pp. 57–76; Ya'ari, *Kushta*.
82. Galanté, *Izmir*, pp. 118–122; Galanté, *Istanbul*, II, pp. 91–97; Galanté, *Turcs*, pp. 129–131; Gaon, *Ha'itonot be-Ladino;* Franco, pp. 277–283.
83. Franco, p. 288; Galanté, *Izmir*, p. 122; Galanté, *Istanbul*, II, pp. 97–109; Galanté, *Turcs*, pp. 126–129.
84. Galanté, *Istanbul*, II, pp. 103–111; Galanté, *Izmir*, pp. 163–167.
85. Lestschinky, p. 10; Lewis, pp. 156–157; Turkey, *Census 1955, 1960* and *1965*.

86. *AI,* 5.7.1923, p. 2; 26.8.1926, p. 3; 12.9.1932, p. 3; *Paix et Droit,* Juin 1935, p. 12; *Cahiers,* Fev. 1962, p. 7; Schechtman, p. 182.
87. Schechtman, p. 182.
88. Goldsmid, pp. 41–43; Bāz in *AI,* 29.9.1943, p. 8.
89. *AI,* 19.10.1922, pp. 1–2. In the *Alliance* schools in the Lebanon there were 25 pupils in 1880, 516 in 1910, 1135 in 1939 and 1301 in 1962. The number decreased to 409 in the year 1970/71.
90. *AI,* 4.7.1929; 3.7.1930; 20.6.1932; 30.6.1939; 13.7.1945, p. 7.
91. *AI,* 10.7.1933, p. 3; 30.6.1939, p. 13; 13.7.1945, p. 7.
92. *Hamenora,* Dec. 1930, pp. 390–391.
93. *Cahiers,* Oct.–Nov. 1960, p. 7; Dec. 1964, p. 11.
94. Kastelman, pp. 13–14, 35; Schur, p. 11; Neumark, pp. 52, 68–69.
95. *AI,* 20.8.1925, p. 2; 21.5.1925, p. 5; 19.9.1930, p. 2.
96. Elmaleḥ, pp. 29, 36.
97. *AJA,* 1888/89, p. 29; *Bulletin,* 1910, p. 213.
98. *AJA,* 1895/96, p. 31; Elmaleḥ, p. 35.
99. *AI,* 20.12.1923, p. 6; 9.2.1938, pp. 21–22; 16.1.1940, p. 13; Farḥi, 1925, p. 54.
100. *AI,* 5.10.1945, p. 9; *Salām,* 28.7.1947, p. 10.
101. Schur, p. 10.
102. *AI,* 12.8.1926, p. 2.
103. *AI,* 20.8.1925, p. 2; 18.10.1928, p. 3; 18.8.1942, p. 9.
104. Farḥi, Aperçu, p. 226; Sémach, Dec. 1930, p. 11.
105. *Hed Hammiraḥ,* 12.3.1943, p. 13.
106. *Bulletin,* 1910, p. 213; *Paix et Droit.* Mars 1939, p. 12; *Cahiers.* Juillet 1962, p. 50.
107. *AI,* 30.11.1945, p. 11; *Salām,* 17.12.1946, p. 8.
108. See note 106.
109. For incomplete list of their publication cf. Ya'ari, *Hadfus,* I, pp. 31–52.
110. In the years 1921–1934 and 1938–1946 he published the weekly *al-'Ālam al-Isra'īlī,* which in 1946 changed its name to *al-Salām.* It was closed down in April 1948.
111. *AI,* 12.4.1946, p. 10.
112. Kastelman, p. 69; Stern, pp. 244, 293.
113. Neumark, pp. 72–73, 94–97.
114. *AJA,* 1876/77, p. 99.
115. *Bulletin,* 1875, 1er sem., pp. 60–61.
116. *AJA,* 1876/77, p. 92; 1881/82, p. 35; *Bulletin,* 1896, pp. 68–69.
117. Adler, pp. 190–194.
118. *AJA,* 1896/97, pp. 47–48.
119. *AJA,* 1875/76, p. 29; 1881/82, p. 35; 1882/83, pp. 24–25; 1889/90, p. 28.
120. *Bulletin,* 1898, p. 69; Confino, *L'action,* pp. 60, 63.
121. Confino, 1901, pp. 57–62; Louria, 1907, pp. 82–83.
122. Neumark, pp. 80–81.
123. *Bulletin,* 1906, pp. 73–74.
124. Neumark, p. 94.

125. *Bulletin,* 1898, p. 69; Confino, *L'action,* pp. 60–63.
126. Levy, III, p. 789; *Bulletin Mensuel,* Jan.–Mars 1910, pp. 36–37.
127. *Bulletin,* 1900, pp. 143–149; 1905, p. 120; 1913, pp. 136–155.
128. Levy, III, p. 811; *Bulletin,* 1904, p. 23.
129. Levy, III, pp. 1022, 1028; *Bulletin,* 1901, p. 65; 1902, p. 81; 1903, p. 130; 1907, pp. 79–80.
130. *Cahiers,* Oct. 1962, p. 16.
131. *Cahiers,* Nov. 1956, p. 20; Dec. 1964, p. 11.
132. *Cahiers,* Oct. 1962, p. 16; *All. Review,* Winter 1964, p. 34.
133. *Yalkut,* June 1949, p. 13.
134. Rosen, 1959, p. 27.
135. *Cahiers,* Mai 1953, p. 72; Dec. 1957, pp. 19–24; Oct. 1962, p. 15; Fev. 1964, p. 39.
136. Schechtman, pp. 246–247.
137. Sapir, p. 66.
138. Goitein, pp. 117, 135.
139. Sémach, Une mission, pp. 148–154. See also Goitein, p. 135.
140. Sémach, Une mission, pp. 148–149. See also Goitein, p. 137.
141. Goitein, pp. 139–140.
142. Sémach, Une mission, p. 149. See also Goitein, p. 137; Koraḥ, pp. 109–110.
143. Goitein, pp. 139–140.
144. Goitein, p. 119.
145. Sémach, Une mission, pp. 149–150.
146. Goitein, pp. 114, 139.
147. Goitein, pp. 131, 136; Sémach, Une mission, pp. 150–151.
148. Goitein, pp. 132–137.
149. *'Am va-sefer,* Aug. 1940, p. 57; Aug. 1944, p. 65.
150. In the Israel population census of 1961, it was found that 40% and over of the men born in the Yemen who were 60 years old and over were illiterates (see Table C-1), but it may be that they were defined as such when some of them could read but could not write.
151. Goitein, pp. 116, 134.
152. Goitein, p. 114.
153. Yavnieli, p. 56.
154. More details on the Dar-da' see several articles in Yesha'yāhū and Ẓadok, especially pages 166–231. See also Moshe Ẓadok, pp. 123–128; 134–137.
155. Sémach, Une mission, pp. 151–153; Koraḥ, p. 70.
156. See a letter from Yahya al-Kāfiḥ from San'a to Chief Rabbi Ḥayyim Naḥum in Istanbul dated end of 1912 or the beginning of 1913, translated into Hebrew in Yesha'yāhū and Ẓadok, p. 229.
157. *AJA,* 1875/76, pp. 52–55; Yavnieli, p. 77.
158. Yavnieli, p. 77; Sémach, Une mission, p. 105.
159. *AJA,* 1951/52, pp. 20–21; 1955/56; p. 29; 1958/59, p. 26; 1959/60, p. 30.

NOTES TO CHAPTER FIVE

1. Messeret, 30.10.1903, p. 3.
2. The traveller Ḥayyim Ḥabshush found a Jewish family in Najrān, who intended to kill their daughter because she had become pregnant. The mother told Ḥabshush that there were similar cases in the families of three of her relatives (Ḥabshush, Mass'ot, pp. 147, 156). Ḥabshush also met Jewish prostitutes in al-Madīd in the Yemen (Ḥabshush, p. 50). In 1874 the Ottoman Governor of San'a drew the attention of the Chief Rabbi of San'a, Yizḥak Shaul, to the incidence of prostitution among Jews there (Franco, p. 218). In 1905, Imam Yahya demanded that Jewish women who sinned with Turkish soldiers be removed (Ḥabshush, *Ashkolot*, p. 23). A. Rihani who visited San'a in 1922, knew of prostitution among Jewish women there (Rihani, p. 182).
3. *Istiqlāl*, 17.7.1935.
4. Elmaleḥ, pp. 27–28; A. Ben Jacob, *Hed Hammizrah*, 22 June 1945, p. 7; *Ha'aretz*, 14.8.1964.
5. *AI*, 8.4.1941, pp. 11–12; 3.7.1942, p. 10.
6. In Basra such cases were found as early as 1910 (Sassoon, *Massa'*, p. 27), and in Baghdad in 1913 (Shim'on Aghasi, *Drashah* (Sermon), pp. 35–39).
7. Two Iraqi Jews who converted to Islam published books to explain why they did so. Moshe Menashe, who converted in 1933 and was thereafter called Mūsa ben Nuṣayr, wrote in his book *Shdhūdh wa-ma'āsī fī al-ṭā'īfah al-Isrā'īliyah* (Arabic), Baghdad 1352 (1933), that he converted to Islam because the Jewish religious court in Baghdad permitted his brother-in-law to marry a second wife, without divorcing the first, who was Nuṣayr's sister. The second convert, Dr. Nissim Sūsa, became a Muslim in 1936, after which he was called Dr. Ahmad Nissim Sūsa. In his book *Fī Ṭarīqī ilā al-Islām* (On my Way to Islam) part I, Cairo 1936; part II, Najaf 1938, he stated that he had written a seminar paper for a university in the U.S.A. on the Muslim religion. His research led him to the conclusion that Islam was a more moral religion than Judaism or Christianity. Nevertheless it is not certain that Dr. Sūsa had not converted for other reasons.
8. Cohen, Theosophists, pp. 401–407.
9. Brawer, Meparashat, III, p. 78; Stern, p. 128.
10. Stern, pp. 86–87, 164.
11. Fischel, Persia, pp. 146–150; Schechtman, p. 234.
12. Neumark, p. 80; Brawer, *Avak*, II, pp. 146–153.
13. Brawer, Meparashat, II, p. 248.

14. Brawer, *Avak*, II, pp. 146–153, 281; Sémach, Mai 1930, p. 11; *Cahiers*, Dec. 1948–Jan. 1949, p. 12; Fischel, Bahai, pp. 47–55; Spicehandler, pp. 43–44.
15. Brawer, *Avak*, II, p. 153; Brawer, Meparashet, II, pp. 247, 430.
16. Brawer, Meparashet, II, p. 246.
17. Brawer, Meparashat, II, p. 241, 246–247; III, 82–84.
18. It seems that up to the beginning of this century conversions to Islam among Kurdish Jews in Iran were frequent to such an extent that Rabbi Joseph Ḥayyim of Baghdad suggested in 1907 to the Jews of Seneh that they add in their marriage contracts *(ketuba)* one more article to the effect that the marriage will be null and void if the husband converts (Brawer, Meparashet, II, pp. 432–433).
19. Fischel, Anosim, p. 77; Neumark, p. 86; Brawer, *Avak*, II, p. 281; Brawer, Meparashat, III, p. 84; Lariedo, p. 9; *Paix et Droit*, Mars 1931, p. 6.
20. Fischel, Secret, pp. 28–33; Fischel, Anosim, pp. 49–74; Brawer, Meparashet, III, p. 82–83; Ben Zvi, pp. 250–257. This community before they were forced to convert is described by Wolff, *Researches*, pp. 125–151.
21. Avidov, pp. 30–31; Muradi, pp. 129–131.
22. Loewy, p. 31, See also Yelin, pp. 464–465.
23. *AJA*, 1883/84, p. 32; Galanté, *Izmir*, pp. 102, 171.
24. *AJA*, 1882/83, p. 34; 1889/90, p. 68.
25. Egypte, *statistiques, 1945/46 and 1946/47*, p. 67.
26. Mahalal Ha'adani, pp. 7–8; Yavnieli, pp. 125, 211, 222; Ḥabshush, *Massa'ot*, p. 66.
27. Mahalal Ha'adani, p. 98; Yavnieli, pp. 53; Yesha'yāhū, pp. 23–27.
28. Yavnieli, pp. 50, 223, 228; Farago, p. 272.
29. Farago (pp. 272–273) speaks of Marranos in the Yemen who were Jewish orphans converted to Islam, and who did not forget their Judaism.
30. Wolff, *Travels*, II, p. 303.
31. Benjamin II, p. 114.
32. Cohen Morris, 1879/1880, p. 97; Benjamin II, p. 114; Albala, Mésopotamie, p. 247.
33. On Kurdish women cf. Brauer, *Kurdistan*, pp. 90–91, 123, 150–156.
34. *Miṣbāḥ*, 14.8.1924, p. 19; 21.8.1924, pp. 7–8; 11.9.1924, p. 1; 18.9.1924, p. 7; 2.10.1924, p. 6; 5.3.1925, p. 1; 10.9.1925, p. 1.
35. Albala, Mésopotamie, p. 260; Shinah, p. 107.
36. Sassoon, *Massa'*, pp. 200–201.
37. *Yeshurun*, Keslev 22nd, 5681 (1920), p. 2.
38. *Miṣbāḥ*, 13.5.1926; 27.5.1926; 10.6.1926.
39. *Yeshurun*, Keslev 22nd, 5681 (1920), p. 2; Sidi, p. 257.
40. *Miṣbāḥ*, 3.12.1925, p. 7.
41. Sicron, II, p. 50.
42. *ibid.*
43. *Miṣbāḥ*, 11.9.1924, p. 1.
44. Aghasi, *Drashah*, p. 49; Albala, 1913, p. 112.
45. Cremieux, p. 35–36.
46. Schur, pp. 18, 85.

NOTES TO THE EPILOGUE

1. Cf. also Cohen, Aliya.
2. Many books and articles have been published on this topic. The best are those by Shumsky and Weingrod. See also my articles in *The Wiener Library Bulletin,* 1972, vol. XXV, nos. 3/4, pp. 3–12, and in *Molad,* Sept. 1966.

BIBLIOGRAPHY

Abrevaya, Écoles primaires. *Bulletin de l'A.I.U.*, 1912, pp. 86–90.

Adams, D. *Iraq's People and Resources.* Los Angeles 1958.

Adler, E.A. *Jews in Many Lands.* London 1905.

Aghasi, Eliahu. *20 Shanah lefra'ot Baghdad* (20 years after the pogroms in Baghdad). Tel Aviv 1961.

Aghasi, Shim'on. *Drashah me'et Harrab Hagga'on . . . Shim'on Aghasi* (Sermon given by Rabbi Shim'on Aghasi in 1913 in Baghdad). Jerusalem 1964.

Aghion, V. Schools in the East: Alexandria. *AJA*, 1883/84, pp. 23–24.

AI, al-'Ālam al-Isrāʿīlī (The Jewish World). Weekly in Arabic. Beirut 1929–1934, 1938–1946.

AJA. Anglo Jewish Association Report. Annually, London. 1872–1962.

AJYB. American Jewish Yearbook. Annually, New York. 1899–1971.

Albala, Nissim (1907). Écoles primaires. *Bulletin de l'AIU*, 1907, pp. 95–100.

Albala (1910). Écoles primaires: Baghdad. *Bulletin Mensuel de l'AIU*, Jan.–Mars 1910, pp. 37–42.

Albala (1913). Écoles primaires. *Bulletin de l'AIU*, 1913, pp. 109–115.

Albala (1925). Le Judaïsme actuel en Mésopotamie. *Hamenora*, Oct. 1925, pp. 245–262.

Āl Far'ūn, Farīq al-Maẓhar. *al-Ḥaqāiq al-nāṣi'a fī al-thawra al-'Irāqīya sanat 1920* (The glowing truth about the Iraqi revolt of the year 1920, and its results). Baghdad 1952.

Alliance Review. Monthly, New York, 1946–1965.

'Am Vasefer. Monthly in Hebrew. Jerusalem 1936–1966.

Asa, Yeraḥmiel. Be'aḥat megaloyot Yisrael (In an Israeli diaspora). *Mibifnim*, April 1949, pp. 632–650.

Asa (Yalkut). Meppi shliḥim (Letters from emissaries). *Yalkut Hammizraḥ Hattikhon*, July–August 1950, pp. 118–122.

Astroc. Écoles des garçons de Damas. *Bulletin de l'AIU*, 1886, 2 sem., pp. 63–66.

Avidov, Yani, *'Alilot Iraq* (Adventures in Iraq). Tel Aviv 1959.

ʾAzzāwī al-, Abbas. *Ta'rīkh al-'Iraq bayn iḥtilālayn* (History of Iraq between two occupations). 8 vols. Baghdad 1935–1956.

Bagdad, Comité des écoles israélites. *Rapport du comité des écoles israélites sur les écoles israélites de Bagdad.* (Bagdad 1930).

Baghdad, Lajnat al-madāris. *Taqrīr 'an al-Madāris al-Isrā'īliyah* (Schools Committee. Report on Jewish schools). Baghdad 1950.

Bahrein, *The Third Population Census of Bahrain. May 1959.* Beirut 1961.
Barer, Shlomo. *The Magic Carpet.* New York 1952.
Bassan, I. Israélites de Perse. *Bulletin de l'AIU,* 1903, pp. 115–140.
Bell, Gertrude. *Amurath to Amurath.* London 1924.
[Bell, G.] *Review of Civil Administration of Mesopotamia 1920.* London 1920.
Benas, B.L. Report on B.L. Benas' Travels in the East. *AJA,* 1884/1885, pp. 66–77.
Ben Jacob, Abraham. Haḥeder habavli beyamenu (The contemporary ḥeder in Babylon). *Hed Hamizraḥ* (Jerusalem), Ab 1st, 5695 (1935), pp. 87–92; Kislev 1st 5696 (1936), pp. 22–25, 40.
—. *Toldot Harrab Abdalla Somekh* (Biography of Rabbi Abdalla Somekh). Jerusalem 1949.
—. *Kehillot Yehudei Kurdistan.* Jerusalem 1959.
—. *Yehudei Bavel messof tekufat haggeonim 'ad yamenu* (A history of the Jews in Iraq, from the end of the Gaonic Period (1038 C.E.) to the present time). Jerusalem 1965.
Benjamin (II), Israel Joseph. *Eight Years in Asia and Africa from 1846 to 1855.* Hanover 1859, in Hebrew; *Massa'ei Israel.* Leik 1859.
The Itinerary of Benjamin of Tudela, critical text, translation and commentary by Marcus Nathan Adler, New York.
Ben Zvi, I. Middevrei yemei anosei Meshed (History of the Marranos in Meshed). *Ẓiyon,* 1939, pp. 250–257.
Brauer, Erich. Haḥaklaot vehamlakhah eẓel yehudei Teyman (Agriculture and crafts among Yemenite Jews) in: Yesha'yahu and Ẓadok (eds.) *Shvut Teyman.* Tel Aviv 1945, pp. 75–91.
—. The Yemenite Jewish Women. *Jewish Review,* April–June 1933, pp. 35–47.
—. *Yehudei Kurdistan* (The Jews of Kurdistan). Tel Aviv 1947.
Brawer, Abraham J. Meparashat massa'otay be-Sūriya, Bavel ve-Ashur (A chapter from my journey in Syria, Babylonia and Kurdistan) in *Menḥa Le-David* a Jubilee Book presented to R. David Yellin. Jerusalem 1935, pp. 238–251.
—. Ḥomer ḥadash leyedi'at 'alilat Dammesek (New material on the Damascus blood-libel), in: *Sefer Hayyovel* (Jubilee Book of) *Prof. Samuel Kraus.* Jerusalem 1937, pp. 260–302.
—. Meparashat massa'otay be-Paras (A chapter from my journey in Iran). *Sinai,* vol. II, 1938, pp. 238–250, 430–438; vol. III, 1938/39, pp. 72–87.
—. He'arot le'alilat Dammesek (Notes on the Damascus blood-libel). *Ẓiyon,* V, 1940, pp. 294–297.
—. *Avak drakhim* (Dust of roads), 2 vols. Tel Aviv 1944–1946.
Bulletin de l'Alliance Israélite Universelle. Paris 1862–1913.
Bury, Wyman. *Arabia Infelix.* London 1915.
Les Cahiers de l'Alliance Israélite Universelle. Paris 1946–1971.
Cazes, Une communauté juive en Turquie. *Bulletin de l'AIU,* 1875, 2er sem., pp. 16–19.
Clot-Bey, A.B. *Aperçu sur l'Egypte.* 2 vols. London 1840.
Cohen, Hayyim J. Teosofim Yehudim Be-Basra (Jewish Theosophists in Basra). *Hamizraḥ Heḥadash* (Jerusalem) 1965, pp. 401–407.
—. Mabbat sheni 'al ḥinnokh bnei 'edot Hamizraḥ (Further aspects on the education of the Oriental Jews). *Molad.,* Sept. 1966, pp. 556–562.

—. The anti-Jewish *Farhūd* in Baghdad. *Middle Eastern Studies,* Oct. 1966, pp. 2–18.
—. University Education Among Iraqi-Born Jews. *The Jewish Journal of Sociology,* XI, 1, June 1969, pp. 59–66.
—. *Hap'ilot Hazziyonit be-'Iraq* (Zionist activity in Iraq). Jerusalem 1969.
—. Integrating Israel's Underprivileged Immigrants. *The Wiener Library Bulletin,* XXV (1971/72), nos. 3/4, pp. 3–12.
—. *20th Century Aliya from Asia and Africa* (Hebrew). Jerusalem 1968.
—. Jews in Arab and Moslem Countries. *American Jewish Year Book 1971.* New York 1971, pp. 443–449.
Cohen, Morris (1879/1880). On the condition of the Jews in Baghdad. *AJA,* 1879/80, pp. 92–98.
—. (1883/84). How the Jews obtain their livelihood at Baghdad. *AJA,* 1883/84, pp. 48–53.
—. (1888/89). On the Jews in Persian and Turkish Kurdistan. *AJA,* 1888/89, pp. 42–45.
Coke, Richard. *The Heart of the Middle East.* London 1925.
—. *Baghdad, The City of Peace.* London 1927.
Colonial Office. *Report of the Commission of Inquiry into Disturbances in Aden in December 1947.* London 1948. (Colonial no. 232).
Confino, A. (1903). Israélites de Perse. *Bulletin de l'AIU,* 1903, pp. 115–128.
—. *L'Action de l'Alliance Israélite en Perse.* Alger (1950?).
Cremieux, A. (Adresse du président a l'assemblée générale de l'A.I.U. du 29 Nov. 1866). *Bulletin,* 2ᵉ sem., 1866, pp. 35–36.
Curzon, G.N. *Persia and the Persian Question.* London 1892.
Dodwell, H. *The Founder of Modern Egypt.* Cambridge 1931.
Egypt, Ministry of Finance. *The Census of Egypt Taken in 1907,* Cairo 1909.
—. *The Census of Egypt taken in 1917,* Cairo 1920.
—. *Population Census of Egypt, 1927,* Cairo 1931.
—. *Population Census of Egypt, 1937,* Cairo 1942.
—. *Population Census of Egypt, 1947 (Arabic) Alexandria district,* Cairo 1952.
—. . . . *Cairo district,* Cairo 1952.
—. *General Census of Population . . . 1960* (Arabic). Cairo 1964.
Egypte. *Annuaire statistique de l'Egypte 1913,* Le Caire.
—. *Annuaire . . . 1931/32.* Le Caire 1933.
—. *Annuaire . . . 1945/46 et 1946/47.* Le Caire 1951.
Elmaleḥ, Abraham. *Hayyehudim be Dammesek* (The Jews in Damascus). Jaffa 1912.
Farago, Ladislas. *The Riddle of Arabia.* London 1939.
Fargeon, M. *Les juifs en Egypte depuis les origines jusqu'à ce jour.* Le Caire 1938.
Farhi, J. Aperçu général sur la communauté de Damas. *Hamenora,* Juillet–Août 1924, pp. 225–226.
—. (1925). Activité de la loge Adolphe Cremieux, Damas. *Hamenora.* Fev. 1925, p. 54.
Fischel, W.J. The Bahai movement and Persian Jewry. *The Jewish Review.* March 1934, pp. 47–55.
—. Kehillat Ha'anosim be-Paras (Marranoes community in Persia). *Ẓiyon,* I, 1936, pp. 49–74.

—. Massa' le-Kurdistan, Paras u-Bavel (A journey to Kurdistan, Persia and Babylon, from the book of the travels of Rabbi David d'Beth Hillel). *Sinai,* V, 1939/1940, pp. 218–254.
—. The Jews of Kurdistan a Hundred Years Ago. *Jewish Social Studies,* July 1944, pp. 195–226.
—. Secret Jews of Persia. *Commentary.* January 1949, pp. 28–33.
—. The Jews of Persia, 1795–1940. *The Jewish Journal of Sociology,* April 1950, pp. 119–160.
Franco, Maurice. *Essai sur l'histoire des Israélites de l'Empire Ottoman.* Paris 1897.
Frankl, August Ludwig. *Nach Jerusalem.* Berlin 1935.
Galanté, Abraham (1925). L'état intellectuel des juifs de Turquie. *Hamenora,* Avril 1925, pp. 117–119.
—. *Turcs et Juifs.* Stamboul 1932.
—. La population juive de Turquie. *Hamenora,* Juillet 1930, pp. 246–248.
—. Marranes Iraniens. *Hamenora,* Mai–Juin 1935, pp. 102–115.
—. *Histoire des Juifs d'Anatolie,* 1er vol.: *Les juifs d'Izmir (Smyrne).* Istanbul 1937.
—. *Histoire des juifs d'Anatolie,* 2e vol. Istanbul 1939.
—. *Histoire des juifs d'Istanbul.* 2 vols. Istanbul 1941–42.
—. *Documents officiels turcs concernant des juifs de Turquie.* Istanbul 1931.
—. *Encore un nouveau recueil de documents concernant l'histoire des juifs de Turquie.* Galata 1953.
—. *Cinquième recueil de documents concernant les juifs de Turquie.* Istanbul 1955.
—. *Sixième recueil de documents concernant les juifs de Turquie.* Istanbul 1956.
Gamlieli, Benjamin. *Teyman u-maḥanei Geullah* (The Yemen and the Hashed camp). Tel Aviv 1960.
Gaon, M.D. *Ha'itonot be-Ladino* (Newspapers in Ladino). Jerusalem 1965.
Gendzier, I.L. *The Practical Visions of Ya'qub Sanu'.* Cambridge 1966.
Ghanīmah, Yūsuf. *Nuzhat al-mushtāq fī ta'rīkh yahūd al-'Irāq* (History of the Jews of Iraq). Baghdad 1924.
Goitein, S.D. Jewish Education in Yemen as an Archetype of Traditional Jewish Education: in: C. Frankenstein (ed.), *Between Past and Future.* Jerusalem 1953, pp. 109–146.
—. *Jews and Arabs Through the Ages.* New York 1955.
—. Portrait of a Yemenite Weavers' Village. *Jewish Social Studies.* January 1955, pp. 3–26.
Gridy, Sh. (ed.), *Me-Teyman leẒiyyon* (From Yemen to Zion). Tel Aviv 1938.
Goldsmid, A.E.W. Report on Jewish Schools in Palestine. *AJA,* 1882/83, pp. 41–44.
Goldziher, Ignaz. *Volesungen über den Islam.* Heidelberg 1925. *Harzaot 'al ha-Islam* (Hebrew translation by J.J. Rivlin). Jerusalem 1951.
Haas, W.S. *Iran.* New York 1946.
Ḥabshush, Ḥayyim. *Massa'ot Ḥabshush* (The travels of Ḥabshush) translated from the Arabic into Hebrew, with notes and introduction by S.D. Goitein. Tel Aviv 1939.
Ḥabshush, Shalom. *Ashkolot Merorot* (Bunch of bitters) with notes by S. D. Goitein. Jerusalem 1938.
Hamenora. Organ périodique des Béné Bérith du District d'Orient. Istanbul 1923–1937.
A Handbook of Mesopotamia. Admirality War Staff. Intelligence Division. 4 vols. London 1916–1917.

Ḥasani al-, 'Abd a-Razzāq. *Ta'rīkh al-Wizārāt al-'Irāqīa* (History of Iraqi governments). 4 vols. Sidon 1933–1955.
Ḥayāt, al-. Daily in Arabic. Beirut.
Hed Hammizraḥ. Weekly in Hebrew. Jerusalem 1942–1951.
Helfritz, M. *Lands Without Shade*. London 1935.
Heyd, U. 'Alilot-dam be-Turkya bammeot XV and XVI (Ritual murder accusations in 15th and 16th century Turkey), in: *Sefunot*, V, Jerusalem 1961, pp. 135–150.
Hourani, A.H. *Syria and Lebanon*. London 1954.
Hurewitz, J.C. *Diplomacy in the Near and Middle East*. 2vols. Princeton 1956.
Iran. *District Statistics of the First National Census of Iran*. Aban 1335 (Nov. 1956). Teheran.
Iran. *National Census of Population and Housing, 1966*. Teheran 1967–1968.
Iraq. *Census of Population in 1947*. Baghdad 1954.
Iraq. *Collection of Statistics from the Population Census 1957*. Baghdad 1964.
Iraq Directory, The. 1936. Baghdad 1937.
Ireland, Ph. *Iraq, A Study in Political Development*. London 1937.
Israel, Central Bureau of Statistics. *Population and Housing Census 1961, publication no. 30*. Jerusalem 1966.
Istiqlāl, al-. Daily in Arabic. Baghdad.
Jabartī, al-Abd al-Raḥmān. *'Ajā'ib al-Āthār fī al-tarājim wa-al-akhbār* (History of Egypt). 4 vols. Bulaq 1297 (1880).
Jerusalem Post. Daily, Jerusalem.
Kāfiḥ, Joseph. Meẓokot Teyman (Tribulations of Yemen) in: *Sefunot*, V, Jerusalem 1961, pp. 397–413.
—. *Halikhot Teyman* (Yemenite manners). Jerusalem 1961.
Kastelman, Yeḥiel Fischel. *Massa'ot shaliyaḥ Ẓfat learẓot hammizraḥ* (Travels of Safad emissary to oriental countries), published by A. Ya'ari. Jerusalem 1942.
Khadduri, Majid. *Independent Iraq*. London 1960.
Koraḥ, 'Amram. *Sa'arat Teyman* (Yemenite storm). Jerusalem 1954.
Landau, Jacob M. *Parliaments and Parties in Egypt*. Tel Aviv 1953.
—. 'Alilot-dam werdifot yehudim be-Miẓrayim besof hammeah hatesha'-'esreh (Ritual murder accusations and persecutions of Jews in the 19th century Egypt), in: *Sefunot*, V, Jerusalem 1961, pp. 415–460.
—. *Jews in Nineteenth-Century Egypt*. New York, London 1969.
Landshut, S. *Jewish Communities in the Muslim Countries of the Middle East*. London 1950.
Lane, E.W. *The Manners and Customs of the Modern Egyptians*. London 1954.
Lariedo. Les juifs du Yezd. *Paix et Droit*, Oct. 1926, pp. 9–11.
Lestschinsky, J. *Jews in Moslem Lands*. New York 1946.
Levi, Israel. Une mission en Orient. *Les Cahiers de l'AIU*. Dec. 1956, pp. 3–11.
Levy, Ḥabīb. Tārikh-i-Yahūd-i-Irān (in Persian). (History of the Jews of Iran). 3 vols. Teheran 1960.
Lewis, G. *Turkey*. New York 1955.
Libanaise, République. *Recueil de statistiques générales 1947/1948*. Beyrouth 1949.

Loewy, A. The Jews of Constantinople. *AJA*, 1889/90, pp. 58–69.

Longrigg, S.H. *Four Centuries of Modern Iraq*. Oxford 1925.

—. *Iraq, 1900–1950*. London 1953.

Loupo. Les Synagogues d'Adrianople. *Bulletin*, 1888, pp. 111–112.

Louria, Leon (1886). Écoles de garçons de Baghdad. *Bulletin*, 1886, 2e sem., pp. 56–59.

—. (1907). Israélites de Perse. *Bulletin*, 1907, pp. 66–86.

Lutzki, A. Ha-"Francos" be-Ḥalab ve-hashpa'at hacapitulaẓiot 'al tushaveha hayyehudiyim (The "Francos" and the effects of the capitulations on the Jews of Aleppo). *Zion*, 1940–1941, pp. 46–79.

Mahalal Ha'adani. *Bein 'Adan ve Teyman* (Between Aden and Yemen). Tel Aviv 1947.

Margoliouth, M. *A Pilgrimage to the Land of My Fathers*. London 1850.

Marmorstein, Emile. Two Iraqi Jewish Short Story Writers. *Jewish Journal of Sociology*. Dec. 1959, pp. 187–200.

Messeret, El. Weekly in Ladino, Izmir.

Miloslavsky, Yuri. *Les boucs emissaires*. Jerusalem 1969.

Miṣbāḥ, al-. Weekly in Arabic. Baghdad 1924–1929.

Mishlowaḥ manot el benei Yisrael me'ereẓ Paras me'et haḥivrah hanoda'at beshem Kol Yisrael Ḥaverim (Sending of (Purim) gifts to the Jews in Persia from the society known by the name of *Alliance Israélite Universelle*). Paris 1874.

Mizraḥi, Ḥanina. *Yehudeī Paras* (Jews of Iran). Tel Aviv 1959.

Moch, Maurice. La communauté juive d'Egypte en voie de disparition? *Les Cahiers de l'AIU*, Fev. 1957, pp. 14–18.

Morag, Shlomo. *Ha'ivrit she-be-fī Yehudei Teyman* (The Hebrew spoken by the Yemenite Jews). Jerusalem 1965.

Muradi, Shlomo. Happra'ot be-Mashhad be Pesaḥ 5706 (The pogroms in Meshed in Passover 1946). *Edot*, 1946/47, pp. 129–131.

Muṣawwar, al-. Weekly, Cairo.

Neumark, Ephraim. *Massa' be-ereẓ haqedem* (Journey in the countries of the East), with introduction and notes by A. Ya'ari. Jerusalem 1947.

Niego. Israélites de Turquie d'Asie. *Bulletin de l'AIU*, 1906, pp. 85–103.

Ort Yearbook 1957. New York 1958.

Paix et Droit. Monthly, Paris 1921–1940.

Pariente, S.T. (1879/80). Report of the educational institutions in Smyrne. *AJA*, 1879/80, pp. 87–92.

—. (1884). Anatolie. *Bulletin de l'AIU*, 1884, 1er sem., pp. 50–56.

—. (1893/94). Report by M.S.T. Pariente on the work accomplished by the *Alliance Israélite Universelle* and the Anglo Jewish Association . . . *AJA*, 1893/94, pp. 61–68.

Qubain, F. Social Classes and Tensions in Bahrain. *The Middle East Journal*. Summer 1955, pp. 269–280.

Rajab al-, Hāshim Muhammad, *al-Maqām al-'Irāqī* (The Iraqi Maqam). Baghdad 1961.

Rathjens, Carl. *Jewish Domestic Architecture in San'a, Yemen;* with an introduction and appendix by S. D. Goitein. Jerusalem 1957.

Ratzaby, J. *Yahadut Teyman* (Yemenite Jewry). Israel Defence Forces 1958.
—.Gallot Musa' (The Exile of Musa') in: *Sefunot*, V, Jerusalem 1961, pp. 397–414.
—.*Bo'ī Teman* (Come Thou South). Tel Aviv 1967.
Rihani, Ameen, *Arabian Peak and Desert*. New York 1930.
Rivlin, E. and J.J. Lekorot hayyehudim be-Dammesek bammeah harvi'it laelef hashshishi (History of the Jews in Damascus in 1541–1640), in *Reshomot* (Tel Aviv), 1926, pp. 77–119.
Rivlin, J.J. *Shirat Yehudei hatargoom* (Poetry of Jewish Kurds). Jerusalem 1959.
Rosanes, Shlomo. *Korot hayyehudim be-Turkya u-be-arẓot ha-kedem* (History of the Jews in Turkey and the Eastern Countries), vol. IV. Jerusalem 1935.
Rosen, Léon (1957). Notes en marge d'un séjour à Téhéran. *Les Cahiers de L'AIU*, Fev. 1957, pp. 7–13.
—. (1959). Les écoles de l'Alliance en Iran. *Les Cahiers de l'AIU*, Sept.-Oct. 1959, pp. 16–33.
Salām, al-. Weekly in Arabic. Beirut 1946–1948.
Samuel, S.M. *Jewish Life in Asia*. London 1881.
Sapir, Jacob. *Sefer massa' Teyman* (A book of a journey to Yemen) with an introduction and notes by A. Ya'ari. Jerusalem 1951.
Sassoon, David. S. *A History of the Jews in Baghdad*. Letchworth 1949.
—. *Massa' Bavel* (A journey to Babylon) with an introduction and notes by Meir Benayahu. Jerusalem 1955.
Schechtman, J.B. *On Wings of Eagles*. New York 1961.
Schur, Wolff. *Maḥazot heḥayyim* (Views of life). Wien 1884.
Sémach, Y. À travers les communautés israélites d'Orient. *Paix et Droit*, Mai 1930, pp. 7–12; Dec. 1930, pp. 10–12; Avril 1931, pp. 7–10.
—. Une mission de l'*Alliance* au Yemen. *Bulletin*, 1910, pp. 48–167.
Shinah, Salman. *Me-Bavel le-Ẓiyon* (From Babylon to Zion). Tel Aviv 1955.
Shoshkes, Henry-Ḥayyim. *Mehakremlin 'ad happeramidot* (From the Kremlin to the Pyramids). Jerusalem 1959.
Shumsky, A. *The Clash of Cultures in Israel*. New York 1955.
Sicron, Moshe. *The Immigration to Israel, 1948–1953*. 2 vols. Jerusalem 1957.
Sidi, M. Hayyehudim be-Mosul (The Jews in Mosul). *Mizraḥ u-Ma'arav* (Jerusalem), vol. I, 1919/20, pp. 247–258.
Silver. Les juifs de Kamechlie. *Paix et Droit*, Août 1934, pp. 10–14.
Somekh (1884). Alep. *Bulletin*, 1884, 1er sem., pp. 56–57.
—. (1889). Israélites de Turquie. *Bulletin*, 1889, pp. 37–48.
—. (1905). Israélites du Yemen. *Bulletin*, 1905, pp. 88–96.
—. (1907). Écoles primaires. *Bulletin*, 1907, pp. 100–103.
Spicehandler, E. *Contemporary Iranian Jewry* (Hebrew). Jerusalem 1970.
Statesman's Yearbook 1935. London 1936.
Stern, H.A. *Dawnings of Light in the East* . . . London 1854.
Tādrūs, Tādrūs Mīkhāīl. *Sharḥ al-aḥwāl al-shakhṣiya lil-Miṣriyin alghayr Muslimīn* (Explanation of the personal status of non-Muslim Egyptians). Alexandria 1956.
Taragan, B. *Les communautés israélites d'Alexandrie*, aperçu historique depuis les temps des Ptolémés jusqu'à nos jours. Alexandrie 1932.

—. *Lekorot haqehellah hayyehudit be-Alexandria be arba'im shanah ha'aḥaronot 5666–5706* (History of the Jewish Community in Alexandria in the last 40 years 1906–1946). Alexandrie 1947.

Thomas, Z.V. and R.M. Fray. *The United States and Turkey and Iran.* Cambridge 1951.

Turquie. *Annuaire Statistique. 1931/32.* Ankara 1933.

—. *Annuaire Statistique, 1959.* Ankara 1961.

Turkey. *Census of population, 23 Oct. 1955.* Istanbul 1961.

—. *Census of Population, Oct. 6, 1960.* Ankara.

—. *Census of Population, October 1965.* Ankara 1969.

Weingrod, A. *Israel: Group Relations in a New Society.* New York 1965.

Wellsted, J.R. *Travels to the City of the Caliphs.* 2 vols. London 1840.

Wilson, A. *Mesopotamia.* 2 vols. London 1936.

Wolff, J. *Researches and Missionary Labours Among the Jews, Mohammedans and Other Sects.* London 1835.

—. *Travels and Adventures.* London 1861.

Ya'ari, A. Massa'ot (Travels of) Rabbi David d'Beth Hillel. *Sinai,* IV, 1939, pp. 24–53.

—. *Hadfus ha'ivri bearẓot hakkedem* (Hebrew prints in Eastern countries). 2 vols. Jerusalem 1937–1940.

—. *Hadfus ha'ivri be-kushta* (Hebrew prints in Istanbul). Jerusalem 1967.

Yahudiya Masriya. *Les Juifs en Egypte.* Genève 1971.

Yalkuṭ Hammizraḥ Hattikhon. Monthly in Hebrew. Jerusalem 1935–1951.

Yavnieli, Shmuel. *Massa' teyman* (A journey to Yemen). Tel Aviv 1952.

Yellin, David. Kehellat Izmir (Jewish community in Izmir). *Hashshaḥar* (Odessa), Vol. III, 1898, pp. 460–467.

Yesha'yāhū, I. and Ẓadoq, A. (eds.). *Shvoot Teyman* (The repatriation of Yemen). Tel Aviv 1945.

Yeshurun. Weekly in Arabic and Hebrew. Baghdad 1920.

Yishai, Moshe. *Ẓir blo to'ar* (A minister without title). Tel Aviv 1950.

Ẓadok, Joseph. *Besa'arot Teyman* (In the storms of Yemen). Tel Aviv 1956.

Ẓadok, Moshe. *Yehudei Teyman* (Yemenite Jews). Tel Aviv 1965.

Zenner, Walter P. Syrian Jews in Three Social Settings. *Jewish Journal of Sociology,* June 1968: 101–120.

Ẓror igrot, mar'ot, ha'rakhot 'al hashoah be-'Aden ve-aḥareha (Collection of letters, views, estimates on the holocaust in Aden and after it). Tel Aviv 1948.

INDEX